Cure Your Cancer

Your Guide to the Internet

By

Bill Henderson

Get And Stay Well
http://www.GetAndStayWell.com

ISBN: 1-4107-3593-1 (e-book)
ISBN: 1-4107-3592-3 (Paperback)
ISBN: 1-4107-4269-5 (Dust Jacket)

This book is printed on acid free paper.

1stBooks - rev. 06/06/03

Table of Contents

PREFACE

Hi. My name is Bill Henderson. Just over 12 years ago, in November 1990, my former wife, Marjorie began her four-year bout with cancer. She died on November 1, 1994. Her many operations, chemotherapy treatments and intense pain made her wish often in her last two years for a quick death, or "transition," as she called it.

After watching that, it was hard for me to believe that millions of people each year had to endure that same torture. I have read widely in these ten years, searching for an alternative. I have found many.

This book is the result of my search. Not only have I found more humane and effective treatments for cancer, I have discovered that our medical system is dominated by big drug company money. Instead of pursuing the research into natural substances and therapies that seem to have great promise and which have, in fact, cured cancer for thousands of grateful patients, our system suppresses them.

With better information, I know cancer patients and their caregivers can work more effectively with the many competent physicians I will help you find to get control of their diseases permanently. Also, those of us who don't have cancer yet can avoid it and other degenerative diseases.

The major difference between now and 1990-1994, when I was searching for information to help Marjorie, is the Internet. Now cancer patients have a deluge of information available including testimonials from survivors, access to supplements, communication with doctors and clinics and a mountain of information on over a hundred gentle, non-toxic treatments.

With the overload of information available today on the Internet, there is only one major problem. You need a guide to help you sift through it. This book is designed to provide you with that.

The first edition of this book, published on the Internet as an e-book in November 2000 was quite popular. In the first two years, over 900 people in 40 countries bought it. I gave away another 300 plus copies to people who could not afford it and to family and friends. I have published 33 free newsletters over the last two years with information I discovered along the way. Over 3,200 readers have opted to receive this newsletter about twice a month. I have tried to incorporate all the useful information from these newsletters, including feedback from my readers, in this second edition of the book.

My goal in this book is to help you gain the confidence to co-doctor effectively. I want you and your loved ones to become "smarter than your oncologist." Above all, I want to make sure you are not victims of the cancer "system," as my wife, Marjorie, was.

You have received with this "Cure Your Cancer" book four additional "booklets" at the end of the book. Their titles are:

"Stop Your Aging With Diet"
"Stop Your Aging With Exercise"
"Beating Diabetes"
and "Cure Your Back Pain"

Before you read this book, I must give you the following warning and disclaimer:

The author of this book is a researcher and writer, not a physician. The facts presented in the following pages are offered as information only, not medical advice. Their purpose is to create the basis for informed consent. Although there is much that each of us can do in the area of prevention, self-treatment for clinical cancer, diabetes and back problems is not advised. The administration of therapy for these maladies, including nutritional therapy, should be under the supervision of health-care professionals who are specialists in their fields.

CHAPTER 1 – INTRODUCTION – WINNING THE CANCER WAR

"The natural healing force within each one of us is the greatest force in getting well."
Hippocrates (400 B.C.)

I am **thrilled** with the prospect of being able to help you cure your cancer or that of your loved ones.

The word cancer in your diagnosis **always** creates fear. You must accept this and vow to fight it. A cancer diagnosis is **not a death notice**.

An Instant Survivor Hot Line

Here's a Cancer Hot Line for you to call **right now**. It is (800) 433-0464.

Richard Bloch, a cancer survivor and co-founder of the tax-preparation firm, H & R BLOCK, INC, founded this Hot Line. In 1978, Bloch was diagnosed with terminal lung cancer and given three months to live. He is still alive and well 25 years later.

The above Hot Line connects you to a volunteer group of cancer patients who take phone calls from newly diagnosed cancer patients. Call them **now**.

Many cancer patients find support groups especially helpful. It certainly doesn't hurt to meet people who were given death sentences 10 years ago…and **are still alive**.

Now that you have a "lifeline" to another cancer patient, let's talk about **co-doctoring**, the main theme of this book

What is Co-doctoring?

Do you believe you have to co-doctor with your physician? So do I. Look at this as a **"How To" book** on co-doctoring.

First, you must understand the **causes** of cancer. Then, you can intelligently evaluate treatment options. Sensible cancer treatment involves treating the causes, **not just the symptoms**.

But you can't do this on your own. To treat cancer, you must be **tested often** to tell if the treatment is working. "Do it yourself" and you are almost certainly going to die of your cancer. Learn to co-doctor and you have a good chance to **regain complete health**.

In other words, if you think your oncologist (cancer doctor) has all the answers, then you are **wasting your time** reading this book.

Two Brief Examples

Let me tell you two brief anecdotes. A friend was hale and hearty for three full years, because she listened to me and **took the natural substance** (MGN-3) I bought for her. She was nearly dead after over two years of chemotherapy for her metastasized breast cancer. She started on the substance I gave her in October 1998 and **was well** (according to her oncologist) by December 1998. She was fine for the next three years and did not continue to take it. She danced flamenco every Friday and Saturday night at a local Spanish bistro in addition to working 50 hours a week. Unfortunately, she **continued to smoke**. Her cancer returned in November 2001. She is very sick now and is preparing to return to her home in ~~·--·~ ~· ·~ die. Details are in Chapter 2.

Another gentleman with **liver cancer** in Atlanta, Georgia began taking the MGN-3 I recommend and shared this book with his oncologist. His cancer went into remission in a **couple of months** and he is **cancer-free now**. He is continuing to take the MGN-3.

Either of these people could be you or your loved one. Cancer cures are **available**. They are **non-toxic**. They are made from **natural substances**. They **do not destroy** your quality of life. Instead, they rebuild your body's natural defenses. They work on almost **all kinds of cancer**. Of course, they will not work for long if you continue unhealthy lifestyle decisions like smoking and eating a "Standard American Diet" (SAD).

Why should you believe me? Well, first because I'm **not selling anything** (except this book). My newsletter service is free. Second because your only other choice is to **remain in "the system."** Very shortly, we will discuss the consequences of that. And finally, because I have proven over the last two years that **people who follow my advice get better**. We can't say "cured" of cancer in only two years, but many of them in 40 different countries are completely healthy again.

Don't Fire Your Doctor — Yet

As an informed consumer of medical service, you will be **empowered**. When the doctor's advice tracks with your knowledge, you'll **confidently accept** his/her treatment. When you need to, you will intelligently opt to **seek a second, third or fourth opinion**.

Unless your doctor is constantly studying microbiology, neurology, endocrinology, nutrition, immunology, alternative medicine and lots more disciplines, he/she is **not fully qualified** to advise you on beating your cancer. No human being can read and evaluate all the information currently available.

Put yourself in your doctor's shoes. She was trained in a medical school environment where **drug companies** provide most of the **research grants** and curriculum materials. Conventional (allopathic) medicine is taught to consist of treating "disease" and **symptoms** with **synthetic drugs**.

Once she is in practice, several drug company "representatives" every day **bombard** her, each leaving her free samples. A Health Maintenance Organization (HMO) is looking over her shoulder, **criticizing** every diagnosis, every test. **Attorneys** await her least slip or recommendation of "unusual" treatment, misdiagnosis or prescription of the wrong drug. She is more and more **narrowly specialized**. Even keeping up with the **explosion** of information in her own specialty is virtually impossible because of the demands of patient care on her time.

With insurance companies and Medicare/Medicaid paying **only a fraction** of what she bills, she is under **extreme economic pressure** to keep patient "face-to-face" time to the bare minimum. One study showed that the average patient spends **only two minutes** with the doctor during each visit.

Is it any wonder that 51% of doctors in a recent large survey said they **would not go into medicine again** and 65% said they would **not recommend it to their children** as a career.

Even if they weren't so busy, there are very few doctors who understand the relations between lifestyle, environment and disease. The average M.D. received **two hours** (clock hours, not credit hours) on **nutrition and preventive medicine** in his six to ten years in medical school and hospital internship. Nutrition is a science **at least as complex** as conventional medicine.

I'm not offering medical advice. I'm not qualified to do that. Nothing you read here should be accepted as **medical**

opinion. However, I think I am qualified to offer you **information you may be unaware of** — information which will help you locate a better medical professional and cooperate better with that doctor to **heal** your or your loved one's cancer.

Four Essentials

I have watched hundreds of people battle cancer in the last thirteen years. Those who have been successful share four essentials.

Essential #1: A Positive Attitude

Cancer is **curable**. It doesn't matter what "stage" or type of cancer. **All can be cured**. People who believe this with all their heart and soul **get well**. Those who doubt it **don't**. It's that simple. Really.

How do you get and keep a positive attitude? Simple, but not easy. **Gain knowledge** about the wide variety of cancer survivors and how they survived. This is **not** a search for the **"magic bullet"** that cures all cancers. There is no such thing.

There are, however, literally **hundreds** of substances that are non-toxic and natural. Each has cured **thousands** of cancer patients. There are **simple life style changes** (diet, supplements, exercise) that restore health. Many of them are quite **inexpensive.**

Believe the above paragraph and I can help you get well. Doubt it and I probably can't. At the same time I have been able to help **literally hundreds** of people around the world, several friends and family members have succumbed to cancer during this same three years. There is a saying that **"There is no prophet in his own home town."** When people I am close to do not follow my advice, it is painful and difficult for me to

5

accept. However, the joy of hearing from one cancer survivor who has profited from my information offsets that.

As long as I can, I will continue to offer this information. If I can save **even one person** from unnecessary death from cancer, it is worth it. At this moment, **my mission** is to help **you or your loved one.**

Essential #2: An Advocate

If you have been diagnosed with cancer, you need to find your closest friend or relative and ask them to **be your advocate**. Cancer evokes emotions in almost everyone that are **hard to deal with**. You naturally fear for your life. You fear disability possibly **even more**. You are quickly exposed to confusing terms and **advice of all types** from well-meaning sources.

By reading this book, you are preparing yourself to **do battle** with the cancer "system." This battle is sometimes **difficult and stressful.** The path you are choosing is controversial. You need help and "moral" support.

You are going to need to do **research** to find the information and resources (doctors, clinics, supplements, etc.) you need. This research **does not** require a **great deal of time**, using this book as a guide to the information available on the Internet. We're talking about the equivalent of **3 or 4 ten-hour days** to become "smarter than your oncologist." Most cancer patients do not have either the **energy or patience** to devote this much time to getting "up to speed."

If you don't believe my estimate of the time needed to "get smart," take a **half hour right now** and study this web site. You can e-mail or call Robert Harrison with questions about his information. All of it **tracks exactly with my research** of the last several years. As he says, **"Current cancer treatments seem to make no sense once you understand the basics of**

cancer." Here's the web site. Come back here when you're done:

http://www.gethealthyagain.com/cancer.html

If you looked at the order form for the supplements Robert Harrison is selling, you found they **were not cheap**. None of them are covered by any insurance. I will help you find the cheapest sources for the substances and services you need. But, inevitably, you must face the question **"How valuable is your recovery from cancer to you?"**

[Incidentally, none of the substances or other resources mentioned in this book result in one dime of income for me. I must keep it that way to maintain my own integrity and, more importantly, your confidence in my sincerity.]

Do not worry about the cost right now. I'm going to show you lots of substances and sources that are **quite inexpensive** and, more important, **that work**.

In summary, when your friend or loved one who is a cancer patient asks you to be their advocate, **accept gratefully**. There is no more spiritually fulfilling and uplifting role in this world. Your service will quite possibly **save your relative or loved one's life**. It most certainly will help him or her **avoid the drastic damage** done to their lifestyle and well being by the cancer "system."

Essential #3: The Right Medical Professional

This book will feature knowledge from **many M.D.s**. All of them have broken the mold of the doctor who is concerned only with **treating symptoms** and curing disease. They have done unique research resulting in **breakthrough knowledge** about understanding the **causes** of cancer and treatments that work to **reverse it at the cellular level.** They are also concerned about prevention.

To help you understand what I mean, I will give you two examples.

First, **Dr. Matthias Rath** is a German M.D. who has gained worldwide recognition for his unique documentation of the **cause of cancer metastasis** (spreading of cancer cells to other parts of the body). He discovered and published this in the mid-1980's jointly with Linus Pauling, Ph.D., the famous physicist and winner of two Nobel prizes. The result of their research is now readily available and is effective in **preventing metastasis**.

Dr. Rath treats cancer of all types and stages (as well as heart disease and AIDS) using **Vitamin C** and two specific amino acids **(L-lysine and L-proline)**. He and his research VP traveled all over the United States in 2002 giving seminars on this subject (and, yes, selling his supplements at exorbitant prices). You can read his books (in the language of your choice) and review his videos online at **no charge**. Just go to:

http://www.naturally-against-cancer.org

For the second example, here's a quote from one of my newsletter readers:

"Dr. Jon, a wealthy retired oncologist, has one of the top rated alternative health newsletters on the web. His site at http://cat007.com/ is well worth perusing. About a year and a half ago he started the Generic Vitamin Co-op, getting manufacturers to make vitamins to his specs, which are then sold just above cost (enough to maintain the small staff who ship the products, perhaps 5% markup). His beta sitosterol [a prostate health supplement] is 150mg standardized at 40% potency, and a 60 count bottle is only (drumroll please) $9.46! He also sells the Linus Pauling Anti-Cancer Formula (C, Lysine

and Proline) [see paragraph above on Dr. Rath] for a 90 count
at $9.45. You really ought to check out both the websites I'm
sending you!

These vitamins are at
http://www.ourhealthcoop.com/products.htm

Jeff (a new subscriber to your newsletter)"

The "Dr. Jon" who Jeff refers to is **Dr. Jon Brooks**. He is,
indeed, a 69 year-old "oncologist" who was practicing in
England when he retired in 1989. In his own words, he **"...got
tired of failing"** and decided **"...there's got to be another
way."** He made his millions in stock (mostly Microsoft), not
oncology. With plenty of money, he decided to devote his life to
bringing useful substances and truth to all of us.

A curmudgeon and iconoclast, he, nevertheless, has
spawned a source of supplements that you **must** examine. The
"OurHealthCoop" site above is the **cheapest and highest
quality source** of many supplements I have found. They are
literally sold at just **slightly (5%) over manufacturer's cost**.
For example, a 90 count bottle of Omega-3 Salmon Oil, a 30-
day supply of 1,000 mg capsules, sells for **$2.45**. A 2-ounce jar
of Progesterone Cream ($39.95 retail) is **$10.73**. They even
have a program for providing vitamin/mineral supplements **free**
to the poor. It is a non-profit endeavor run by a wealthy couple
in West Palm Beach, Florida who took it over from Dr. Brooks
after he got it up and running.

He is still involved in the quality control. In fact, he sends
one capsule from every batch received at Our Health Coop to
the lab for analysis. Recently, when a COQ10 supplier didn't
measure up to his standards, he **cut them off** for three months.
Quality control is a **major** problem with supplements. Dr.
Brooks claims that **at least half** of these products do not
contain what they claim. I have personal experience with
several which were not what they claimed. The only guarantee

you have is the integrity of the source, which is hard to determine except by trial and error.

You will find at Dr. Brooks' web site, the http://www.cat007.com which Jeff mentioned, a **wide variety** of information on alternative medicine. There is also a 2 ½ hour November, 2002 interview with Dr. Brooks available at that web site. If you have Windows Media Player or similar software, give it a listen. You'll find it amusing and informative.

How Do YOU Find One?

You would not have read this far unless you were interested in the help available from **alternative, complementary or integrative** medicine. So, how do you find a competent medical professional sympathetic to this approach to treat you in your area? Fortunately, it is **not difficult** any more. Even folks in remote areas can usually find someone within 100 miles or so of their home.

My Personal Experience

I recently decided to "walk the walk." I had been recommending to hundreds of cancer patients for two years that they find a qualified medical professional sympathetic to **Complementary & Alternative Medicine (CAM)**. I decided to find one that I could put my trust in for myself.

I called a unique "holistic" dentist here in San Antonio who had treated my wife for her problems with root canals. I asked his wife, whom we had gotten to know because she worked in his office **"Who would you go to in San Antonio if you were looking for a 'holistic healer?'"** She gave me four names. Two were osteopaths, one a naturopath and one a nutritionist. A friend of ours, who is also a nutritionist, had recommended **one of the same osteopaths** when I asked her the same question.

I interviewed all four of them — three by telephone and e-mail and one in person. Among the questions I asked them were:

"Do you treat prostate cancer?" Substitute your type of cancer. The answer you want is "Yes."

"I take a lot of supplements. How do you feel about that?" The answer you want is **"That is fine,"** not *"Don't waste your money. Just eat a balanced diet."*

*"I feel you should help me, but that **I am in charge of my own health**. Is that consistent with your approach?"* The answer you want is, of course, an **enthusiastic** "Yes."

"How long have you been in practice?" Listen closely for the type of experience he/she has. Try to go into detail about previous practice sites, etc. in your interview. The value of his/her experience is strictly a **judgment call** on your part.

*"Would you be willing to give me the **names of three of your patients** who would be willing to talk to me?"* The answer you want is something like *"If they agree after I call them, I'll be happy to give you their names."*

The one I interviewed in person, as you might have guessed, was the osteopath recommended by both friends. He accepts Medicare. The others did not. He **did not charge** me for this initial interview, which lasted 40 minutes. He gave me all the right answers and we found we had a lot in common (military service, belief in alternative medicine, etc.). It was the first time in my life that I had spent that long talking to **any** medical professional about health matters.

I have designated him as my Primary Care Physician. He treats cancer, along with all other medical problems, using both alternative and conventional means. In fact, he says he **"treats people, not disease."**

Your quest may not be as easy or rewarding as mine. But start with your **personal network** of friends and people in the healing profession – nurses, doctors, dentists, nutritionists, owners of health food stores, etc. Once you have exhausted that resource, go to one of the following sites and **search for people in your area.** It won't take you very long.

Using The Internet

Keep in mind, some alternative therapists may **not be allowed to treat cancer** depending upon the laws and politics of their country, region, state, province, etc.

To get an idea of the restrictions, and to get some excellent advice on choosing and working with a practitioner right for you, you may want to read the following article:

http://www.doctoryourself.com/news/v1n24.txt

www.acam.org. The American College for Advancement In Medicine. This fine organization deserves special attention. It provides information on cancer-related alternative and complementary therapies, and lists MDs and Osteopaths in your area open to them, at least to the extent allowed by the laws of their states. After using their searchable database to find alternative practitioners near you, call these people and discuss your situation. They may know other therapists near you offering a specific treatment you may want — detoxification, for example. Note: ACAM is a good place to start your search for an alternative care physician or therapist in your area. My osteopath is the only member of this organization in San Antonio.

The Alternative Medicine Yellow Pages. A printed publication. It is a spin-off from the website www.alternativemedicine.com. Phone (800) 435-1221 for more information.

www.lef.org/doctors/doctors.html. Here is a list of progressive doctors in many countries compiled by the Life Extension Foundation (LEF). As in the ACAM site above, these are generally open-minded individuals who understand and believe in alternative therapies.

www.whale.to/cancer/doctors.html. A site with a good list of alternative care doctors, clinics and hospitals in the USA and some other countries.

www.naturopathic.org/find_nd.htm This site locates naturopathic doctors (NDs) near you. This rapidly growing health care discipline seeks to discover the underlying cause of a disease and treat that rather than just eliminate symptoms, the approach used by the conventional medical establishment. Expect to hear a lot more about NDs as time goes by. These people actively seek out the best alternative therapies. Some states today, like Washington and Oregon, license them on a par with MDs.

www.cancure.org An excellent site with many alternative doctors, hospitals and clinics from around the world.

www.alternativemedicine.com One of the best. Has a search feature using your city and state information that allows you to locate an open-minded practitioner near you. Burton Goldberg, this organization's founder, is one of the world's leaders in advocating Freedom of Choice in health matters for doctors and patients alike.

http://www.CancerOption.com/services/clinic_directory/index.asp

A searchable database of clinics and hospitals that treat cancer claiming they have complementary and alternative practitioners and therapies. What to watch out for here and in other conventional treatment centers is the use of the word "alternative" in the description of their services. They know full well how much public interest there is today about alternatives. Not to criticize this particular organization, but many conventional clinics and hospitals may call a new pharmaceutical drug an "alternative". Or, they'll put a massage or physical therapist on staff and call him or her an alternative therapist. This dubious tactic is for advertising and marketing purposes, not health and healing. At least this site is very well organized. Decide for yourself about it.

www.geocities.com/ray_m_89119/clinics.html A good listing of alternative care clinics, including some in Mexico and Germany.

www.talkinternational.com/clinics1index.htm   Alternative doctor and clinic listings for Canada, USA, United Kingdom, Sweden and Denmark.

Third Opinion. This important and useful book by John M. Fink is a detailed International Directory of Alternative Therapy Centers for the Treatment and Prevention of Cancer and other degenerative diseases. A very popular publication, it is available from amazon.com.

www.homeopathic.org A searchable database listing naturopaths, MDs, and other practitioners who use homeopathy. Large directory. Again, they may or may not be able to treat cancer depending on the legalities in their state.

Homeopathy has been very popular in Europe for decades. England's Queen Elizabeth uses a homeopathic doctor.

American Holistic Medical Association. Provides information on alternative and complementary therapies and sells a referral directory of doctors by mail for $10. www.holisticmedicine.org

www.cancercure.ws/cancercure/references.htm   A   good website with a long list of alternative doctors and clinics in America and in foreign countries. The site is not organized alphabetically, so a lot of wandering around is required.

www.nfam.org National Foundation for Alternative Medicine. This is a new organization dedicated to information on the best alternative and conventional cancer treatments and facilities worldwide. A former American congressman named Berkeley Bedell, who was cured of prostate cancer by alternative means after his conventional doctors gave up on him, started it.

www.cancure.org Founded by G. Edward Griffin, author of "World Without Cancer". A lot of excellent information on finding alternative doctors and clinics in various countries.

Above all, **don't give up**. The truth is that there is a medical professional that will treat you and respect your wishes regarding alternative, complementary or integrative medicine. All you have to do is find him or her.

Essential #4 – Get Truckin'

Now for Essential #4. You **must start**. Don't wait until you find a great CAM professional. While you're searching for him or her, start taking supplements that are inexpensive, that help **any** cancer and that make it easier for you to regain your health. Change your diet using the guidelines in Chapter 4. Time is more important to you now than at any time in your life. Untreated cancer does not stop spreading. You must begin your battle **NOW.**

Beware! Many oncologists will insist that supplements **interfere** with the effects of chemotherapy. If you hear this, you know it is **time for a second opinion**. Many studies have shown that this is **just not true**. You must rebuild your immune system, preferably coincident with the chemotherapy.

In Chapter 4, I will show you a method using the same chemotherapy drugs your oncologist uses, but in a very **low-dose** form that causes none of the side effects of normal chemo. Called **IPT**, this is definitely one of the treatments about which you want to **"get smarter than your oncologist."**

In summary, you need to keep in mind the four "Essentials:"

➢ A Positive Attitude

➢ An Advocate

➢ A Competent CAM Medical Professional

➢ And Get Truckin'

In the Chapters 5 and 6, I will discuss most of the available CAM cancer treatments in some detail. For now, I would like to help you understand two essentials for you to win your battle: 1) The cancer "environment" you are in; and 2) The true cause of cancer.

CHAPTER 2 – THE CANCER ENVIRONMENT

"Most people would rather die than think. In fact they do."
Ralph Waldo Emerson

"Unproven Remedies"

In the past 70 years, at least **100 cures** for cancer have been discovered. You will find information on most of these in Chapters 5 and 6. Would it surprise you to know that **every one of these 100** is currently on the "Unproven Remedies" list maintained by the American Cancer Society (ACS)?

Doesn't it seem logical that **at least one** of these would have been thoroughly researched and investigated and found to have **some** use for at least **some** cancer sufferers? Isn't it mind-boggling that **every single one** is still labeled "unproven," in spite of the lapse of **decades** since their discovery?

But it's worse. Not only has our **cancer "system"** failed to prove and endorse these cures, the discoverers (most of them reputable MDs and researchers) have been **hounded** with lawsuits, license suspension and even jail sentences for treating cancer patients.

What do these cures have in common? **Only one thing**. None of them can be **patented** and sold through the "standard" distribution system monitored by our Food and Drug Administration (FDA).

And yet, the U.S. alone has spent **thousands** of man-years and over **one hundred billion dollars** on cancer research just since the "War on Cancer" began in 1971. Cancer deaths in the U.S. have risen every year since.

Drug Company $$$$

You can only understand the cancer treatment "system" in this country and, to a greater or lesser degree, in other countries, if you understand how much **power** the drug companies wield in our culture. Drugs used in cancer treatment are **all** produced and sold as **"chemotherapy."** What this means is that synthetic drugs must be compounded, and run through years (typically about **10 years**) of testing. This process costs between **$200 million and $500 million**.

Gene therapy and immune system vaccines are being researched now. They too must be tested through this **enormously expensive** system. There are lots of **natural** immune system boosters that are effective in fighting cancer. They cannot be patented because the substances in them are from nature, not synthesized by man; ergo they can't get FDA approval to treat anything.

Why not let "natural" remedies **co-exist** so people can make their own choices? That would seem logical, but there are Federal and State laws in the United States and other countries that **prohibit** this. Currently, under U. S. Federal law, **no natural substance** can be advertised as a cure for **any** condition – period.

Drug Cartel Takes Over Europe

On March 13th 2002 the European Parliament – a 626-member legislature representing the 15 European Union countries – passed the **"EU Directive on Dietary Supplements."** This is based on a United Nations Commission called "Codex Alimentarius Commission," formed in 1963.

This UN Commission had the innocuous goal of standardizing food production standards in all UN countries. In 1995, **Big Pharma** succeeded in getting the umbrella of this Commission expanded by the UN to cover food supplements. Now, with several drug company executives **in influential positions** in the EU Parliament, they have essentially **"passed a law against prevention."**

One German doctor, Dr. Matthias Rath, claims to have collected 604 million signatures on a petition to block this "Directive." It passed anyway.

The effect is to make **300 food supplements** — including chromium picolinate, yeast, lysine and selenium – **illegal for over-the-counter sale**. Other supplements that remain in stores will contain very low dosages. For example, the highest dose of Vitamin C available without a prescription will be **60 mg**. For me to take my 3 grams a day, I'd have to take **50 tablets** instead of the three I take now.

The EU Directive grants a **transition period** of three years for vitamin supplements already on the market. But in 2005, every EU country (all 15) will be **required** to implement this directive. One of my newsletter readers in Holland told me it has **already** been fully implemented in her country.

For an interesting article from London's Guardian, go to this web site:

http://www.cat007.com/guardian.htm

Is It Coming To The U.S.?

There are rumors that the FDA is attempting to implement the **same restrictions in the U.S.** This despite the Dietary Supplement and Health Education Act (DSHEA) passed by Congress in 1994 to head off the last attempted power grab of this nature by the FDA. The DSHEA classified supplements as food and allows manufacturers to inform the public about how supplements affect the "structure and function" of the body. The FDA, of course, has put many **restrictions** on this in the ensuing years.

Drug Marketing

The marketing of toxic drugs lies at the heart of the "war on cancer." For example, in one study, the **cost of drugs** was 55 percent of total treatment cost for small-cell lung cancer.

An article in the Journal of the American Medical Association (JAMA) recently stated that **oncologists** (cancer doctors) make an average of **$253,000 a year**, of which **75% is profit from chemotherapy drugs** administered in their offices.

If you have any doubts about the drug company omnipresence in our lives, all you have to do these days is **turn on your TV**. It seems like every other commercial is for some prescription drug. What's going on here?

In 1997, it became legal **for the first time** for drug companies to plug their wares **directly to the consumer** (you and me). In those 5 + years, the spending on TV and print advertising by Big Pharma has ballooned.

Would you believe that in 2001 alone, the drug companies spent **$15.7 billion** (with a "b") on **TV and print ads for prescription drugs?** This is more than any other industry

20

spends on advertising. More than the auto industry, the housing industry, retail giants like WalMart and so on.

Why? Well, it's pretty obvious. The **brainwashing** of the U.S. public continues. Got a problem? A prescription from your doctor is all you need to fix it. No need to worry about all those goody-two-shoes urging you to eat sensibly and exercise. Just jot down the latest name for a drug that just cost Bristol-Myers-Squibb or Merck $500 million to bring to market and go **bug your doctor** to write you a prescription for it.

Just as important as the hype it gives their products is the **incredible clout** this spending gives the drug companies with the media. Why else would the media conveniently **fail to note** the unpleasant or **even lethal** side effects of prescription pharmaceuticals? These side effects are the **fourth leading cause of death** in the United States – right behind heart disease, cancer and stroke.

The U.S. spent **1.5 TRILLION DOLLARS** for health care in 2002. You might think most of this money went for hospital care.

Wrong!

Americans have spent **more on prescription drugs** than hospital care for the last several years. About two-thirds of this is wasted on drugs that only **treat symptoms** and allow the person to deteriorate without addressing the **underlying cause** of his/her disease.

Insane Profits

Are the drug companies crazy to spend $500 million to develop a drug? **Crazy like a fox!** Here is just one example. **AstraZeneca** is a drug company you have probably never heard of. According to Forbes magazine (March 18, 2002), they are the world's fourth-largest pharmaceutical company.

21

IN 2001 ALONE, AstraZeneca made **$630 million** on the sale of **Nolvadex** (a.k.a. tamoxifen), a breast cancer drug. This drug has been on the market **since 1973**. They made **$728 million** on the sale of **Zoladex**, a prostate/breast cancer drug. It was **introduced in 1987**. They made another $569 million on Casodex, another prostate cancer drug introduced in 1995. Within two years, says Forbes, this company's sales of **cancer fighter drugs alone** will top **$2.5 billion** a year.

One company, Bristol-Myers-Squibb, spends more than **one billion dollars** per year on research and employs 4,000 scientists and support personnel. It holds patents on **more than a dozen drugs** approved by the FDA for the treatment of cancer; this accounts for **almost half** of the chemotherapy sales in the world.

Influence – Far And Wide

Bristol-Myers-Squibb also **creatively influences** cancer research. It gives out awards, lectures and grants of many kinds. It pays for updates to orthodox cancer textbooks, and **supports research** and **"data management"** of clinical studies on its patented agents. Other cancer drug companies do the same.

Memorial Sloan-Kettering Cancer Center (MSKCC) in New York City is at the forefront of cancer research and has been for **at least the last 30 years**. Drug companies, again with Bristol-Myers-Squibb leading the way, occupy a **very strong position** at Memorial Sloan-Kettering. At one time, in 1995, for example:

➢ James D. Robinson III, the **Chairman** of the MSKCC **Board of Overseers and Managers,** was a **director of Bristol-Myers Squibb**.

➤ Richard L. Gelb, **Vice-Chairman** of the MSKCC board, was **chairman of the board of Bristol-Myers Squibb**.

➤ Richard M. Furland, MSKCC **board member**, retired in 1994 as the **president of Bristol-Myers Squibb**. He has also been a director of the Pharmaceutical Manufacturers Association.

➤ Benno C. Schmidt, **Honorary co-chairman** of MSKCC, was the **founder and board member of Genetics Institute**, a Massachusetts-based company that manufactures drugs for the cancer marketplace. He was also a **director of Gilead Sciences (which makes cancer-related drugs); Matrix and Vertex Pharmaceuticals**. He received the Bristol-Myers Squibb Award for distinguished service to cancer research in 1979.

➤ Paul A. Marks, M.D., the **President and CEO** of MSKCC, was a **director of Pfizer**, which manufactures cancer-related drugs. He was also on the board of National Health Labs and of Life Technologies.

FDA – The Federal Watchdog?

Well, what about the federal government bureaucracy responsible for protecting you and me from such greed-oriented businesses, the Food and Drug Administration (FDA)? Sorry, folks. This agency is even more **corrupted by drug money** than the EU Parliament.

One study recently showed that **55% of FDA executives** go to work for pharmaceutical companies when they leave the FDA. 20% of the FDA employees who work on the drug approval process are **actually paid** by the drug companies. Would you think they would be completely objective? Hmmmm.

In May, 2001, the Los Angeles Times published an article by David Willman entitled **"New FDA Policy Resulted in Seven Deadly Drugs."** He described how easier FDA standards on drug approval were prescribed by Congress in 1993. After a two-year investigation, the L.A. Times reported that in "adverse event" reports filed with the FDA, the **seven drugs** were cited as suspects in **1,002 deaths**. Because these deaths are reported by doctors, hospitals and others on a **voluntary basis**, the true number of deaths **could be much higher**, according to epidemiologists.

The seven drugs – Lotronex, Rezulin, Posicor, Redux, Rotashield, Propulsid and Raxar – are among the **hundreds of new drugs** approved by the FDA since 1993. A telling statistic: these seven drugs alone generated **$5 billion** in U.S. sales **before they were pulled from the market** by the FDA. Another interesting statistic: In 1988, **only 4%** of the new drugs introduced into the world market were approved first by the FDA. In 1998, the FDA's first-in-the-world approvals had **spiked to 66%!**

Once the world's safety leader, the FDA was the **last to withdraw** several new drugs in the late 1990s that were banned by health authorities in Europe.

Doctors Comment On The FDA

"This track record is totally unacceptable," said Dr. Curt Furberg, a professor of public health sciences at Wake Forest University. "The patients are the ones paying the price. They're the ones developing **all the side effects**, fatal and non-fatal. Someone has to speak for them."

It's not that doctors didn't speak up against these drugs. *"They've lost their compass and they forget who it is that they are ultimately serving,"* said **Dr. Lemuel Moye,** a University of Texas School of Public Health physician who served from 1995 to 1999 on an **FDA advisory committee**. "Unfortunately, the public pays for this, because the public believes that the FDA is watching the door, that they are the sentry."

The FDA's shift is felt directly in the private practice of medicine, said Dr. William Isley, a Kansas City, Missouri diabetes specialist. He implored the agency to **reassess Rezulin four years ago** after a patient he treated suffered **liver failure** taking the pill.

"FDA used to serve a purpose," Isley said. "A doctor could feel sure that a drug he was prescribing was **as safe as possible**. Now you wonder what kind of evaluation has been done, and what's been **swept under the rug**."

The FDA Responds

The FDA's response: *"All drugs have risks; **most of them have serious risks**,"* said Dr. Janet Woodcock, director of the FDA's drug-review center. Once a drug is proven effective and safe *[in the case of chemotherapy drugs, half the test subjects survive it!]*, Woodcock says, the FDA depends on doctors "to take into account the risks, **to read the label**...We have to rely on the practitioner community to be the **learned intermediary**. That's why drugs are prescription drugs."

Dr. Woodcock alluded in a recent interview to the difficulty she feels in rejecting a proposed drug that might have cost a company **$150 million or more** to develop.

The "Bottom Line"

Dr. Woodcock, how many people have you heard of who have been killed by an overdose of Vitamin C or any other supplement?

Question All Medications

Do you see how important it is to "second guess" your doctor? **Question everything.** If you or your loved one are being prescribed a medication [especially chemotherapy], **ALWAYS** ask to see the statistical studies and warning labels which are **required to be read by physicians**. Obviously, they don't have the time to study them all. You **MUST take the time.** Your life or your loved one's life may be in danger.

Suppression of Competition

The logical question is "Why does the FDA and the EU go to such lengths to **suppress** non-toxic treatments for cancer and other diseases?" The only answer is that our medical system, in both the U.S. and Europe, has become dominated by **drug company money**.

Conspiracy?

The true nature of the Big Pharma influence on governmental and private agencies can only be appreciated with **a lot more detail** than I can provide you here. The best way to appreciate this problem I know of is to read a book called **"Politics in Healing – The suppression and manipulation of American Medicine" by Daniel Haley**. It was published in 2000 and is available in most bookstores and from amazon.com.

Haley has documented **10 case studies** of systematic suppression of **proven cures – mostly for cancer**. Substances like Glyoxilide, Krebiozen, DMSO, Colustrum, Hydrazine Sulfate, 714X, Aloe Vera and Cesium Chloride are covered in great detail along with names like Royal Rife, Harry Hoxsey, Dr. William Koch, Dr. Andrew Ivy, Gaston Naessens, Dr. Robert Becker and Dr. Stanislaw Burzynski.

Here's what Julian Whitaker, M.D., prominent leader in alternative medicine says about this book:

"Daniel Haley has written a very important book about the medical profession, detailing the struggles between good and evil as no one ever has before. Incredible as these stories are, they are true!"

The suppression Daniel Haley documents has been an **obvious conspiracy** among the American Medical Association (AMA), the American Cancer Society (ACS), the National Institutes of Health (NIH), the FDA and the Federal Trade Commission (FTC) to serve the **Big Pharma cartel**.

This is not an easy book to read. As I finished each chapter at night, I would grumble to my wife about the **evils of big money** corruption in our country and the millions of people dying needlessly because of it. Nevertheless, it should be **required reading,** at least for every American and European.

If you are in a hurry to discover the best ways to treat your or your loved ones cancer, I will forgive you if you put off reading this book. However, when you get the time, please **come back to it**. You will never look on our medical or political systems the same way again. In the meantime, if you must press on, please take my word for the need for you to exercise **great caution** in accepting anything you hear from our "conventional" (or "allopathic") medicine system without confirmation from several sources outside that system.

Should We Blame The Doctors?

Is your doctor a part of this conspiracy? **No.** Most doctors are dedicated, over-worked, even **heroic** champions of the restoration of their patients' health. Unfortunately for you, they are **products of a medical system** that is closed to innovation in very important ways. Most do not even consider treatments that do not fit the mold they have been **taught in medical school** and in all "continuing education" since. In fact, much of the "continuing education" of doctors is on junkets to exotic destinations **sponsored by the drug companies**.

What is the current **medical dogma** on cancer by which oncologists live? First, that cancer is a **foreign enemy** in the body that must be **attacked.** The only acceptable treatment is to cut it out, poison it or burn it. Second, that all **patented synthetic drugs** (chemotherapy, etc.) approved for them to prescribe are **superior to any natural, non-toxic substance** for cancer therapy. And finally, that food supplements are a **waste of money** for those who eat a "balanced diet." These three "wrong paradigms" almost insure that you will need to question their judgment.

Please don't just accept or reject my views on this. Check out some information from **real experts**. One example is the following article. The authors, Nicholas Regush, an experienced health reporter for ABC News and Dr. Joseph Mercola, one of the best-qualified medical professionals I have ever encountered, are certainly **not radical revolutionaries**. Their views are important to you, however, because you need to understand **what you are up against** in your use of our conventional medical system. Please read this article at this web site:

http://www.mercola.com/2002/feb/27/death_of_medicine.htm

The Cancer Industry

In his interesting book *World Without Cancer – The Story of Vitamin B17*, G. Edward Griffin puts it this way:

"With billions of dollars spent each year in research, with additional billions taken in from the cancer-related sale of drugs, and with vote-hungry politicians promising ever-increasing government programs, we find that, today, there are more people making a living from cancer than dying from it. If the riddle were to be solved by a simple vitamin, this gigantic commercial and political industry could be wiped out overnight. The result is that the <u>science</u> of cancer therapy is not nearly as complicated as the <u>politics</u> of cancer therapy."

Legislation claiming to protect the consumer of drugs is usually **written by** the drug industry. Politicians who are grateful for the financial support of the drug companies are eager to put their names on legislation and push for its enactment. Once it becomes law, it serves merely to **protect** the sponsoring drug companies against competition. Competition from natural cancer cures, for example. The consumer is **the victim** of this legislation.

In drug testing and marketing, unlike other industries that lobby Congress, there is the added necessity to pretend that everything is being done scientifically. Therefore, in addition to recruiting the aid of politicians, **scientists** must also be enlisted – a feat that is easily accomplished by the judicious allocation of funding for research.

Some History

This process is nothing new. Former FDA Commissioner James L. Goddard, in a **1966** speech before the Pharmaceutical Manufacturers Association, expressed concern about **dishonesty in testing** new drugs. He said:

"I have been shocked at the materials that come in. In addition to the problem of quality, there is the problem of dishonesty in the investigational new drug usage. I will admit there are gray areas in the IND [Investigation of New Drug] situation, but the conscious withholding of unfavorable animal clinical data is not a gray area. The deliberate choice of clinical investigators known to be more concerned about industry friendships than in developing good data is not a gray area."

Goddard's successor at the FDA was Dr. Herbert Ley. In 1969, he testified before the Senate committee and described several cases of **blatant dishonesty** in drug testing. One case involved an assistant professor of medicine who had tested **24 drugs for 9 different companies**. Dr. Ley said:

"Patients who died while on clinical trials were not reported to the sponsor... Dead people were listed as subjects of testing. People reported as subjects of testing were not in the hospital at the time of the tests. Patient consent forms bore dates indicating they were signed after the subjects died."

Another case involved a **commercial drug-testing firm** that had worked on 82 drugs from 28 companies. Dr. Ley continued:

"Patients who died, left the hospital, or dropped out of the study were replaced by other patients in the tests without notification in the records. Forty-one patients reported as participating in studies were dead or not in the hospital during

the studies… Record-keeping, supervision and observation of the patients in general were grossly inadequate."

Money corrupts. Really big money **corrupts completely**!!

The Lancet Nails Drug Company Research

For a view on this subject from an **impeccable source**, I suggest you read a recent article from *The Lancet*, the esteemed British medical journal. It covers research funded by drug companies and was posted by **Dr. Joseph Mercola** in his great newsletter. You can read the article and Dr. Mercola's comments on it at this web site:

http://www.mercola.com/2002/nov/20/drug_companies.htm

While you are there, sign up for Dr. Mercola's newsletter. It is a treasure trove of health information delivered weekly to your e-mail box. It's free.

A Personal Anecdote

About 6 years ago, my urologist prescribed **Hytrin**, a drug manufactured by **Abbott Laboratories**, for my enlarged prostate. It was quite effective in reducing my nocturnal ups and downs. It relaxes the prostate and bladder muscles. Hytrin is also used to treat high blood pressure, which I don't have.

For the first three and a half years, my co-payment for Hytrin was **$60**. I needed a refill about once a month. When I asked the pharmacist if there was a generic, he said no, that Abbott Labs had a **patent** on it and only the named drug could be sold.

Well, guess what? In the middle of 2000, I happily found that Abbott Labs patent had **expired**. I found out only because my pharmacist filled my prescription with the generic (terazosin hydrochloride) and my co-payment was **$5**, instead of $60.

The plot thickens. In September 2000, about two months later, I received a letter from my urologist's office. They were running a **clinical trial** on a "new" drug to treat enlarged prostates and they wanted **volunteers** for the test. I was curious, so I called them. It turned out that this office, the **largest urology clinic in San Antonio**, had a specialized staff for drug testing.

They asked me a few questions. Apparently, I qualified and they asked me to participate in the test — what's called a **Random Clinical Trial**. It requires the participants to take no medication (stop the terazosin) for one month and then try the "new" medication for three months — unless, of course, you got the **placebo** (sugar pill), which neither you nor the docs would know about. One half of the people would get the "new" drug and **one half the placebo**.

Guess what the "new" drug was? Not hard, was it. It was **Hytrin II**. A "new", and, of course, **newly patented** form of the drug. It was supposed to "improve the quality of the treatment" of BPH (Benign Prostatic Hypertrophy), which is what I, and most males my age, have, an enlarged prostate gland. I politely declined to participate in the clinical trial.

What's **wrong** with this picture? Well, several things:

1. Do you think it is **coincidental** that Abbott Labs just finished developing Hytrin II **a few months** after their patent for Hytrin I ran out?

2. Do you think it is **ethical** for a large urology clinic to act as the agent for a drug manufacturer in a clinical trial? Isn't this something of a **conflict of interest**? The rumor is that they get $8,000 per recruit from the drug company.

3. Do you think either Abbott Labs or my doctor thought about the **financial impact** of a "new", drug on me or other seniors?

4. Do you think either the doctor or Abbott Labs were concerned about the **withdrawal symptoms** for people like me, which I found out about recently when I tried to stop taking this drug?

5. Why do you think the presidential race in 2000 made a BIG DEAL out of a **"prescription drug benefit"** for seniors? Why is this still a big issue in Congress in 2003? Could it have something to do with the **political contributions** from the drug companies? Remember, that prescription drug benefit comes right out of **taxpayers' pockets**.

6. Why aren't we debating about how to keep the drug companies from **gouging** Americans while they sell the same drug at **one-tenth the cost** in Europe and Canada?

Relief From Canada

In September 2000, William Raspberry, wrote a column in the Washington Post about *"One Long-Term Cure for High Drug Prices."* Here are a few paragraphs from that article:

"There are at least two pieces of the problem of high cost of prescription drugs, Rep. Bernie Sanders, an independent from Vermont, has been saying for some time now.

But most of the political and journalistic focus has been on only one piece: The 'outrageously high price' of medications. He'd like to call attention to the other half of the problem: The fact that Americans 'are paying by far the highest prices in the world for the same exact drug – not a generic, but the same exact drug.'

The solution, he says is simplicity itself. Allow registered pharmacies and drug distributors to purchase FDA-approved drugs anywhere in the world for resale here. Reimportation, he calls it in the bill he hopes will pass Congress before the campaign recess."

[NOTE: The bill passed and was signed into law by President Clinton. Two years later the Bureau of Health and Human Services has yet to write regulations to implement it because they are concerned for the "safety" of consumers....Hmmmm]

"'This is important stuff,' Sanders said in a telephone interview from his Burlington office. 'I traveled to Canada with a group of women with breast cancer, and we looked at the price of tamoxifen, a drug that is widely prescribed for the treatment of breast cancer. You could get it in Canada for a 10th of the U.S. price.

If this bill were to go into effect tomorrow, U.S. pharmacies would be purchasing tamoxifen in Canada and retailing it here at 30 to 50 percent less than they now charge.'

Sanders says the same thing applies to any number of drugs – all approved by the FDA and originally manufactured in or exported from the United States.

'Pharmacies should be able to purchase these drugs the same way other companies purchase shoes, slacks or washing machines,' he says.

...The biggest obstacle to passage this term is the pharmaceutical industry, Sanders says. 'They are the most powerful lobbying force on Capitol Hill,' he said. 'They've spent tens of millions in opposition of this bill.'"

So What?

Where does all this leave you, the cancer patient or caregiver? Well, hopefully, it leaves you **somewhat skeptical** about claims by the cancer "industry" that all therapies not sold by Bristol-Myers-Squibb or Merck or Abbott Labs or whoever are **"unproven" and therefore pure "quackery."**

As a bare minimum, to avoid what happened to Marjorie, my former wife, and me, you **must** educate yourself. You must be prepared to get more than one opinion. Then, when you've found the doctor (or homeopath or naturopath) that you trust, you **must be prepared to co-doctor** with him or her throughout your treatment.

This book is designed to end your **blind** faith and trust in our system of cancer "therapy" and arm you with the power to search beyond it. Faith is fine, if it derives from the **power of knowledge** and trust in your physician.

You Have The Power — Use It

I'm going to arm you with information — from books, the Internet, newsletters, magazines and any other source. You will be able to **take charge** of your health. I am hoping you will not be satisfied with **treating symptoms**. You will want to **treat causes**.

But before you can treat causes, you need to understand them.

Several years ago, one of my wife's doctors told me, "80% of it is still mystery to us." At the time, I didn't know what he meant. Now, I think I do.

What he meant was that what happens in your body **at the cellular level** is indeed mystery to almost all doctors.

> ➤ Interactions between your **brain** and your **immune system**.
> ➤ How **certain supplements** affect your cells' health.
> ➤ What **stress** does to your immune system.
> ➤ Exactly what **chemotherapy** does to your immune system.
> ➤ What other gentle, non-toxic treatments are available to **treat cancer**.
> ➤ How **non-toxic substances** can boost your immune system.
> ➤ What organs are affected by **nutritional** deficiencies (or excesses).
> ➤ How exercise and nutrition affect diseases like **diabetes**.
> ➤ What **"free radicals"** do to your cells and your health.
> ➤ Which **antioxidants** are the most effective against free radicals.
> ➤ What **natural substances** provide your body with antioxidants.
> ➤ **...and many, many more.**

Do You (Still) Trust Your Doctor?

As those of you know who have read this far, I advocate **"co-doctoring."** In my humble opinion, it's the only way to get and stay well. From my personal experience, doctors' knowledge is **quite limited.** Those of you who have researched cancer treatments for any length of time certainly know more than your doctor about **natural treatments, diet and the true causes of and cures for cancer.**

While you must co-doctor, you must also find a **trusted medical professional** to monitor and oversee your cancer treatment. This is not a "do-it-yourself" project. If you haven't found that wonderful medical person who is sympathetic to your use of "alternative" (I hate that word!) treatments, keep looking. They are out there. Their numbers are **growing daily**. Chapter 1 in this book has several resources you can use to locate one.

You **must not trust** everything you are told by a person with M.D. after their name. You must **monitor** everything that is done to your loved one in a hospital. That means spending the night in their hospital room with him/her. I have found that it is very hard to convince many people of those **two simple facts**. If you have had that same frustrating experience, here are a few statistics that might help you next time.

Doctors are the third leading cause of death in the United States. In causing the death of their patients, they trail only heart disease and cancer. There are currently more than 250,000 deaths per year from **iatrogenic** causes. That long word means **"induced in a patient by a physician's words or actions."** Here's the breakdown:

12,000	Unnecessary surgery
7,000	Medication errors in hospitals
20,000	Other errors in hospitals
80,000	Infections in hospitals
106,000	Non-error, negative effects of drugs

This information is from an article by Dr. Barbara Starfield of the John Hopkins School of Hygiene and Public Health in the *Journal of the American Medical Association* (JAMA Vol 284, July 26, 2000). The above statistics come from the review process that happens after every death in a hospital to determine the true cause of each death for insurance purposes and to get **smarter about treatment**.

Unfortunately, the hospitals seem to be **losing the latter battle**. If you think those numbers have gotten smaller in the last 30 months, you're much more of an optimist than I am.

Do you really think hospitals accurately report that it was the chemotherapy **treatment** itself that **killed the patient**? I personally know several cases where this was the true cause. A good estimate is that **at least half** of the 550,000 deaths each year attributed to "cancer" in the U.S. were actually **caused by the cancer "therapy."**

In Canada, where they have "socialized" medicine, it seems that doctors can be somewhat more frank than they can in the U.S. The **McGill Cancer Center** in Montreal, Quebec, one of the largest and most prestigious cancer treatment centers in the world, did a study of oncologists to determine how they would respond to a diagnosis of cancer. On the confidential questionnaire, 58 out of 64 oncologists said that **ALL chemotherapy programs were unacceptable to them and their family members.** The overriding reasons they gave for this decision were that the drugs are **ineffective** and have an **unacceptable degree of toxicity**. These are the same doctors who will tell you that their chemotherapy treatments will shrink your tumor and prolong your life!

Are you sufficiently skeptical about medical advice? Good! Let's get down to the business of making you "smarter than your oncologist." Let's first take a look at what cancer is and what causes it.

CHAPTER 3 – WHAT IS CANCER?

"The Philosophies of one age have become the Absurdities of the next and the Foolishness of yesterday has become the Wisdom of tomorrow."
Sir William Osler (1902)

Cancer is Simply...

A cancer diagnosis scares **all of us**. I have **no more vivid memory** than seeing my former wife's body after it had been wracked by **four years of cancer**, chemotherapy, operations and painkilling drugs when **she died** on November 1st, 1994.

Her bout with cancer started me on my search for answers. How can we cure it **gently**? How can we **prevent** it? To do either, we must first **understand** it.

Some Cancer Numbers

First, let me give you a few numbers. Cancer is the second leading cause of death in the United States. About 22% of all deaths each year are blamed on cancer.

Notice the word "about". As I mentioned above, my former wife, Marjorie, died on November 1, 1994 after a **four-year bout** with cancer. On her death certificate, her doctor wrote **"heart failure"** as the cause of death. Obviously, any statistics on death rates need to be taken with a grain of salt. My doctor friends tell me that the law requires them to enter the **final** cause of death, not the **precursor,** whatever that means.

More than a **million** Americans are diagnosed with cancer **each year** and more than half a million death certificates cite cancer as the cause of death.

Another 800,000 develop **small, "non-invading" cancers** and various mild kinds of skin cancer. Both types generally do not spread and can be easily removed. These "non-invasive" cancers are **not counted** in the annual cancer statistics.

For **women 35 to 74**, cancer is the leading cause of death. For **men** of the same age range, cancer is **second** only to cardiovascular disease as the leading cause of death.

Despite the high incidence of cancer and our federal government's **"War on Cancer",** begun in 1971 and supported by over $100 billion dollars of research, virtually **no progress** has been made in curing the most common forms of cancer.

According to the World Health Organization, there were **10 million new cases** of cancer in 1996, and in 2001 they predicted a yearly total of **14.7 million**. These numbers are so huge that the suffering they imply is incomprehensible.

In the United States, the death rate from cancer had **risen 6%** by 1994 from 1970, just before the "War on Cancer" was launched. Despite the large number of people who have **stopped smoking** in recent years, according to the National Cancer Institute, the incidences for some of the most deadly cancers are **sharply increasing.**

To put it another way, **every other man** and **every third woman** in the United States will get cancer — unless we understand it better and make the lifestyle changes I will show you.

If a tumor is found early and can be removed, it will not **regrow or appear elsewhere about 50%** of the time. Once a cancer has **metastasized** (spread to other sites in the body), chemotherapy and/or radiation will stop it only about **10% of the time**.

40

Where Does It Come From?

Most cancers arise from our interaction with the world around us. Almost **one-third** of all cancers diagnosed in Europe and in the United States can be linked to **tobacco** use. These account for more than 150,000 deaths in the United States each year.

Food choices contribute to another one-third of the cancers, especially stomach and colon cancers.

Thinner people are at **lower risk** of breast, prostate and uterine cancer. This is probably because these cancers are linked to high exposure to the sex hormones, estrogen and testosterone. These hormones are **stored in fat**.

People who drink **alcohol** excessively have higher levels of **mouth and liver** cancer.

People who have spent too much time in the **sun**, particularly before the age of 30, are more likely to develop **skin** cancer.

Occupational hazards, such as **asbestos and formaldehyde**, account for about **5%** of all cancers.

The key words in cancer treatment today are **"avoidance"** and **"early detection."** Without a doubt, the best way to fight cancer is to avoid getting it in the first place.

What Exactly Is Cancer?

What follows is information available in more detail in a book called *REAL AGE by* Michael F. Roizen, M.D. Dr. Roizen's book and the related website and daily "tips" are one of the **many resources** I will recommend to you (see Appendix A).

Cancer means the **growth of tumors**. It's a category that includes a broad range of diseases.

About 5 to 10% of all cancers stem from inherited genes. The other 90 to 95% are caused by **genetic "mistakes"** which develop **over your lifetime**. Mutations in your DNA after you are born are these mistakes. We accumulate them.

Cancer is a **temporary malfunction in our DNA.** This is the substance that regulates the growth of the body. It is contained in every cell we have. It is the **"instruction book"** for your body. It determines the color of our eyes, how tall we are, that we have an arm instead of a wing…

If you have a computer and I give you two manuals, each **three inches** thick, you'll **never** learn to use your computer. But if I tell you to read pages 10 through 15 and you will learn how to use your computer, you will do that.

When your body needs a cell, at the last minute it decides if it needs a kidney, eye or fingernail cell. The body then tells that cell **which pages** of the DNA to read. When it takes the place of a dying cell, it begins to function in that capacity.

This DNA is **duplicated with every cell division**. Average adults have 75 trillion cells in their body. Once again – **75,000,000,000,000 cells**. 99% of the cells in our bodies are called "somatic" cells. All of them except brain and nerve cells get replaced thousands or hundreds of thousands of times during our lifetime. In **seven years** this process of cell division and death replaces virtually **every cell** in our bodies.

Another way to look at this is that **every day** about **30 billion cells** get replaced in our body. Why is this important? Because cancer is caused by mutations that occur during this process. We all produce **thousands of cancer cells** every day.

Division Problems

When a cell divides, the DNA in that cell is copied and passed on to the new cell. But the DNA in any one cell can become damaged. Pieces of the instructions on the genes can get **knocked out or changed** – mutated.

If this mutation occurs in the wrong place – in an active gene, for instance – it can **disrupt the function of the cell**, causing it to die.

Your beautiful body includes a **regulatory system** that is mind-boggling. For example, when you get a simple cut on your hand, your cells go to work to repair the damage. When enough cells have gathered around the cut to heal it, the cells **stop dividing**. Ever wonder why? Because there is a **"suicide gene"** in the DNA which says "Enough, already."

Not only is the total number of cells kept in check, but also **"proofreader"** genes in the DNA look for mutations. When they find one, they either fix it or kill the cell. They are on duty 24/7. Isn't this stuff **amazing**?

Your **immune system** also kills off these damaged cells by the millions every day. It is your **second line of defense** against mutated cells.

If the mutation happens, however, in a portion of the cell's DNA that **controls cell growth**, i.e. an "oncogene," the result is a rapidly growing and dividing cell – **out of control** – or what we call "cancer."

The cell has **lost its "suicide"** function. The **"proofreader"** gene missed the mistake. Your immune system **is too weak** to provide its normal second line of defense. Result: **The Big C.**

The mutated cells usually travel to the **weakest and most highly stressed organ** in your body and you have a tumor. The cancer tumor grows because the **"daughter"** cells inherit the same mutation.

How do these mutations occur? Two ways:

> ➢ One is a **random mistake** in the DNA duplication process. Not much chance for you to control this. But not much reason for concern, either. The cell cycle controllers (proofreaders and suicide genes) and your immune system kill these "mistakes" as soon as they happen.

> ➢ The second way is damage to the DNA caused by **"free radicals"** or other irritants like radiation.

What Are Free Radicals?

Free radicals, the most common cause of cancerous DNA damage, **are** under your control. What are free radicals? Every day, we produce or take in millions of them. They are compounds that have **one unpaired electron** in their atomic makeup.

Try as you might, you **cannot avoid** free radicals. They are in your body and in the atmosphere. They result from the process your body uses to break down food, among **many other causes**. But they are also caused, and can be controlled, by the lifestyle decisions we make every day. What lifestyle decisions? Want a few examples?

> ➤ **Cigarette smoking** causes the largest number of free radicals of any lifestyle activity. Eventually, the number of free radicals it produces overcomes your body's elaborate defenses and you, the smoker, get lung cancer, emphysema, heart disease, and many more maladies.

> ➤ The **more fat** you take in, the **more free radicals** you produce. Particularly damaging are trans-fatty acids found in abundance in the "Standard American Diet" (SAD). McDonald's French fries, for example, have one of the highest concentrations of trans-fatty acids of any food.

> ➤ Food and vitamins and other supplements provide **"anti-oxidants"** which can kill off the free radicals by the **millions**.

> ➤ All of these lifestyle choices are **cumulative** – for better or worse.

In addition to cancer, free radical damage also causes senility, arthritis, hardening of the arteries, and the declining function of your immune system as you age.

Helping Your Immune System

A multitude of studies in recent months confirm the immune system's function in both preventing and **curing** cancer. Almost every day a new study is published in the search for drugs and vaccines that boost the immune system's ability to fight off cancer.

As we will see in Chapter 5, these drugs are **not necessary**. At least five substances that are **non-toxic and**

harmless to take have been proven to boost your immune system's ability to "mop up" mutated cancerous cells.

Here's a quote from Dr. Roizen's book:

"As you age, your second line of defense, your immune system, tends to be less vigilant and does not as readily detect and destroy these abnormalities. The weaker your immune system, the more likely that it will not provide the necessary backup. The longer you live, the more likely that you will get improper cell divisions, the more likely that the DNA in a specific cell will contain a mutation, and the more likely that your immune system won't be there to catch a mistake.

The most important thing to remember is this: ***You can slow, and even reverse, the rate of aging of your immune system.***" [Emphasis added].

Dr. Roizen goes on to explain causes and prevention measures for various types of cancer. If you would like to read more of his work, his book is called *REAL AGE —Are You as Young as You Can Be?* copyright 1999 by Michael F. Roizen, M.D. Also, check out his web site: http://www.realage.com/

My wife Terry and I took Dr. Roizen's quiz to determine our "Real Age". The quiz covers a wide variety of **lifestyle questions**, each of which either adds to or subtracts from your chronological age. Mine came out to **minus 16** (making my "Real Age" 52). My wife's came out to **minus 14** (making her "Real Age" 32). To take this quiz, just go to his website by clicking on the link above.

Dr. Roizen has an extended discussion on antioxidants (Vitamin C, E, etc.) and their role in controlling the **"free radicals"** which damage the genes in your cells.

It is pretty clear from all the research I have done that most cancers can be prevented by proper **diet, supplements and exercise**. Each of these three can be visualized as a leg on a

three-legged stool. If any one is neglected, the stool collapses – your body degenerates and you get sick. We will cover supplements and diet guidelines in this chapter. Diet and exercise are the subjects of "booklets" which accompany this book.

[NOTE: Many people have pointed out to me their view that this "stool" actually has a fourth leg. They say it is our **spiritual nature** and its positive effect on our health. I will not try to influence you one way or another on this subject. Consider it and make personal judgement.]

Treating Your Cancer

In summary, **CANCER IS NOT A "DISEASE."** It is simply your body's own cells which have assumed an **abnormal function** as a result of damage to their normal functioning. Stem cells multiply much more rapidly than cancer cells...so cancer cells are **not** even the most **rapidly dividing** cells in your body. They're just abnormal cells that need to be brought under control.

Your body produces cancer cells **every day**, by the thousands. Your normal cell policing mechanism takes care of them – until it can't any more. Then you are diagnosed with cancer.

Your cancer probably **took years to develop** to the point where it can be detected. If you need a cause, blame it on your lifestyle. With that understanding, you also know that treating cancer is a **lifelong process**. Once you have the cancer under control, or in "remission," you must continue to battle it with good lifestyle choices and support for your immune system for the **rest of your life.**

You can look on cancer as a **chronic condition,** something like hypertension (high blood pressure), heart trouble or diabetes. You must keep your body in top-notch cancer fighting shape. You **cannot** just revert to your old lifestyle and expect the cancer to stay away.

Actually, the title of this book is misleading. Instead of a **futile search** for a "cure," you should be looking for a way to get your cancer cells back **under control**. This is exactly what I am trying to show you how to do in this book.

It's Baaaaack!

Unfortunately, **when cancer recurs**, because it was not kept under control, it tends to metastasize (spread) **more aggressively.** But, don't worry. In Chapters 4 and 5 and the bonus booklets on Diet and Exercise, I'm going to show you exactly how to avoid this.

Conventional cancer treatment (surgery, chemotherapy and radiation) **destroys your immune system**. Oncologists pay little attention to rebuilding it or changing your lifestyle. This is why cancer patients treated with conventional treatment seem to get better, only to have the cancer **recur** in a few months or years in a more aggressive form.

The succeeding chapters in this book will deal **in detail** with specific options available to every cancer patient. Many of these are supported by major research efforts. Many of them have spawned **groups of survivors** that have formed to get the information to other cancer sufferers.

In **Appendix A, Resources Summary**, is a complete list of the resources you can use to find more detail than I can include in this book. Also, the web sites will allow you to keep up-to-date on new developments as they occur, as will my newsletter.

Cancer Prevention

Many of the anti-oxidants our body needs to gobble up the free radicals and prevent cancer **must come** from supplements. If you've talked to your doctor lately about this subject, you were probably not encouraged by his response. Most physicians feel that supplements are **unnecessary**. A "proper" diet will provide all the vitamins, minerals, enzymes you need, they say. Just eat a "balanced" diet.

One prolific author on cancer – its treatment and prevention — is **Ralph W. Moss, PhD**. Dr. Moss has written **10 books** on cancer therapy, causes, cures, prevention, etc., including *Questioning Chemotherapy, Herbs Against Cancer* and *The Cancer Industry*. This excerpt [along with my comments in the boxes] is from one of his latest books, published in 2000, called **Antioxidants Against Cancer.**

"Attitudes of Doctors

Thousands of scientific articles *point to the power of antioxidants, yet many doctors are not taught about this in medical school. Others may know about this exciting development but **shy away from it** because they fear peer pressure or stigmatization. And all too often, doctors respond to positive reports with a **warning** that patients **should not** take food supplements.*

*The conventional line is that research is promising, but there just **isn't enough data** on which to base firm conclusions..."*

> Are you beginning to see the importance of "co-doctoring" with your physician?

*"Certainly, few medical interventions can have **less risk** than eating a diet **high in antioxidants**. We are not talking about taking arsenic here, but about **brightly colored fruits***

49

and vegetables, *as well as concentrated extracts. Yet many physicians draw the line when you discuss antioxidants and say, '**Much too risky. Not enough known.'"***

"*No wonder laypeople are turning to books, magazines, and Websites for information on antioxidants, and that many patients **hesitate to even discuss** questions of nutrition with their doctor. Patients are becoming more educated **(sometimes more educated than their doctors!)** and more empowered.*"

I certainly hope that **you** will feel "more educated than your doctor" and definitely **empowered** when you finish reading **this book**. Right now, that is my whole **reason for being!**

If you would like to read more of Dr. Moss's work, these excerpts are from his book *"Antioxidants Against Cancer"*, copyright 2000, by Ralph W. Moss, Ph.D. You may also want to visit his web site: http://www.CancerDecisions.com.

Effective Antioxidant Supplements

We've been talking about **antioxidants** in relation to cancer prevention. They are also important in the prevention of heart attacks, strokes, macular degeneration of the eye, and about **one hundred other illnesses** associated with aging.

The reasons for including antioxidant-rich foods and supplements in your daily routine go **far beyond cancer**.

Let me give you here the best source for a **supplement** that covers all the bases. If you know of a better one, I'd like to hear about it. Please send me an e-mail at: bhenderson@GetAndStayWell.com

For just **over 17 years**, I have been receiving a newsletter called **"Alternatives"** written by **Dr. David G. Williams.** His writings about everything having to do with healthy living have been **immensely helpful** to my family and me.

[By the way, **nothing** I recommend in this book **results in even one dime of income** for me. I am truly writing this for your benefit, not for mine.]

You are very fortunate. About three years ago, **Dr. Williams** completed his **website.** It now contains archive copies of his monthly newsletters, all the way back to 1985. This is a Mother Lode of health information. You can purchase for four or five dollars any of the back issues that interest you. Check it out at http://www.drdavidwilliams.com/.

About the antioxidants…Dr. Williams, about 6 years ago, put together something he called **"Daily Advantage".** It is a little transparent plastic package containing 8 capsules. My wife and I each take one package with breakfast and another with lunch, as Dr. Williams advises.

Here's how he describes the "Daily Advantage" nutrient package:

*"I've carefully chosen the **65** vitamins, minerals, antioxidants, herbs, superfoods, amino acids and digestive enzymes that are in Daily Advantage, based on all my **years of research** into nutritional supplementation.*

*...these hard-to-find nutrients work together to **supercharge the antioxidants** in the vitamin complex, making the overall formula more powerful and better able to destroy the **free radicals** attacking your cells."*

Here are the ingredients in each Daily Advantage set of capsules:

Essential Vitamins and Minerals:

Vitamin A	5,000 IU
Vitamin C	2,000 mg
Vitamin D	800 IU
Vitamin K	60 mcg
Thiamine (Vitamin B1)	50 mg
Riboflavin (Vitamin B2)	50 mg
Niacin	126 mg
Vitamin B6	110 mg
Folic Acid	400 mcg
Vitamin B12	100 mcg
Biotin	300 mcg
Pantothenic Acid	150 mg
Calcium	1,000 mg
Iodine	100 mcg
Magnesium	500 mg
Zinc	20 mg
Selenium	200 mcg
Copper	2 mg
Manganese	10 mg
Chromium	200 mcg

- Molybdenum — 100 mcg
- Potassium — 100 mg
- Vanadium — 150 mcg
- Choline — 100 mg
- Quercitin — 50 mg
- N-acetyl cysteine — 50 mg
- Trace Minerals Complex — 50 mg
- Lemon Bioflavonoids — 40 mg
- Para-aminobenzoic acid (PABA) — 30 mg
- Inositol — 100 mg
- Silica — 26 mg
- Rutin (from buckwheat) — 10 mg
- Hesperidin (from citrus peel) — 10 mg
- Boron — 1,000 mcg

Advanced Antioxidant Shield

- Vitamin A (as beta carotene) — 15,000 IU
- Vitamin E — 400 IU
- Tocotrienols (from rice) — 20 mg
- Coenzyme Q10 — 10 mg
- Alpha-Lipoic Acid — 10 mg
- Lutein (from marigolds) — 6 mg
- Lycopene (from tomatoes) — 6 mg

Herbal Superfood Booster

- Spirulina (from algae) — 750 mg
- Turmeric (from root) — 200 mg
- L-Taurine — 200 mg
- Siberian Ginseng Root — 180 mg
- Bee Pollen — 100 mg
- L-Carnitine — 100 mg
- Royal Jelly — 50 mg
- Astragalus (from leaf) — 50 mg
- Ginger Root — 50 mg
- Gymnema Sylvestre — 50 mg
- Pancreatin — 50 mg

- Ox bile   50 mg
- Green Tea Extract   50 mg
- Siberian Ginseng Extract   50 mg
- Panax Ginseng Extract   40 mg
- Betaine Hydrochoride (HCL)   20 mg
- Ginkgo Biloba   10 mg
- Lipase   10 mg
- Cellulase   10 mg
- Maltase   10 mg
- Protease   10 mg
- Amylase   10 mg

In July 2002, Dr. Williams added an 8th brown capsule to the package at no extra charge. He calls it "EFA Advantage." It consists of several fish oil (mercury-free) extracts rich in Omega-3 fatty acids. Here is the composition:

- EPA (Eicosapertaenoic Acid)   100 mg
- DHA (Docosahexaenoic Acid)   150 mg
- Other Omega-3 fatty acids   50 mg
- Gamma Linolenic Acid   50 mg

You can get more information at his website or by calling **Mountain Home Nutritionals** in Ranson, West Virginia, the people who distribute **Daily Advantage** for Dr. Williams. They can be reached at (800) 888-1415.

We pay about **$45 monthly apiece** for Daily Advantage, including shipping by Priority Mail. I cannot even imagine how much it would cost us to buy these ingredients at the local health food store. We attribute our glowing health largely to this product, a **sensible diet** and **regular exercise**. We don't smoke. We drink very moderately (less than one glass of wine or equivalent per day).

Vitamin B or Not to B

I can't tell you how many lists I have read of vitamins, minerals, amino acids, etc. like the one above and **what each does for my body**. Have you done that? Doesn't each one make your **eyes glaze over**? They sure do mine.

To this day, I have **no idea** why it is good for me to eat some choline, querectin, astralagus or ginger root each day. If a gun were held to my head, I **could not** tell you what all of Dr. Williams' **65 ingredients** do for me…or what dire results would threaten my body if one were eliminated.

The **exceptions** are the **antioxidants** — which include Beta-carotene, Vitamin E, tocotrienols, coenzyme Q10, alpha lipoic acid, lutein and lycopene. These I have studied enough to **know why** they are good. They are the best thing you can take to **prevent cancer** and lots of other **degenerative diseases**. Also, I know that **Vitamin C** is great for your production of **collagen** that supports your joints, soft tissues, proper bone formation and prevents metastasis of cancer (see below). It also helps maintain **strong blood vessels**, your **immune system** and your body's own repair capabilities.

All I can tell you is that since beginning his **Daily Advantage** supplement program in 1996, my wife and I have had **no recurrence** of the many colds, flu and other maladies that we suffered through before we started on it. This includes many years when I took "drugstore" supplements every day.

We have **lots of energy**, we **sleep well** and we enjoy **exercise**. We also enjoy **sex**. She enjoys her **gardening and cooking**, as well as **Yoga**. I walk 18 holes of **golf** twice a week, **sing** in a men's a cappella chorus and quartet and **play bridge** on the computer with people from all over the world.

After Antioxidants, What?

So, you've bought Dr. Williams **Daily Advantage** or whatever you think is better and you're **taking it every day.** Is that all? Not quite.

Ultra-Fit

The doctor most directly responsible for my gaining control over my health is **Dr. Joe Davis.** I met him at one of his Ultra-Fit "wellness" centers here in San Antonio in 1992. I was 60 years old and in pretty sad shape.

Dr. Davis is an **internal medicine** specialist. He also is a **human being** who has fought through **obesity** and **alcoholism** to become a competitive weight lifter and founder of multiple Ultra-Fit centers around the country.

His book "Ultra-Fit" and the wellness centers were the result of his working with **thousands of patients** over a span of **15 years**, most of whom were obese and out-of-shape. Let me quote from Dr. Davis's book "Ultra-Fit" along with my comments.

*"It is my personal belief, as a physician of internal medicine, that **dietary factors** serve as the principal cause of our **most common killers** in the United States. The consequences of eating **too much fat** result in huge, staggering, burdensome **problems.** It costs society **billions and billions** of dollars each year to stem fat-related diseases."*
[Which diseases is he talking about? All degenerative diseases. Specifically: cancer of the colon; cancer of the breast; cancer of the uterus; cancer of the prostate gland; cancer of the lung; gouty arthritis; degenerative arthritis; heart attacks; high blood pressure; strokes; diabetes; and suicide, to name a few.]

*"I am not over-dramatizing fat-related illnesses. Sure, **other factors** figure into the equation that triggers **any one** of these illnesses.*

*However, simply because you carry **excess fat** on your body you **increase your chances** of developing one of these illnesses in your lifetime. The **longer** you carry excess fat, the **greater** your chances."*

Dr. Davis is not trying to make you feel guilty. In fact, he says the blame for all the obesity in our society belongs to evolution.

*"The human animal has **evolved genetic machinery** for conserving and **storing calories as fat** during intermittent periods when food is lacking. Only since the twentieth century have we developed the technology for food production, storage, and distribution so that, for practical purposes, we **no longer suffer from a lack of food** — or at least not in the affluent parts of the world.*

*Think about that. For millions of years, man constantly **searched for food**, suffered famines. Suddenly, in the last **fifty years**, the United States suffers from **excess** food production.*

*It takes **work not to become fat** in America!"*

Where To From Here?

Free radicals are **bad**. Fat causes **more**. What do we do about it? Dr. Davis prescribed **changes in lifestyle** – diet, exercise and even mental images. He cited hundreds of examples of how his patients applied these ideas.

Will it work for you? Probably. Several "booklets" come with this book. In the first two, **"Stop Your Aging With Diet;"** and

"Stop Your Aging With Exercise;" I will cover in detail how I have applied the ideas of Dr. Davis and other physicians and therapists.

Now, we will turn to your most immediate concern — "How do I put this knowledge to work to **cure** my (or my loved one's) cancer?" Please read on.

CHAPTER 4 – CURING YOUR CANCER

"As a chemist trained to interpret data, it is incomprehensible to me that physicians can ignore the clear evidence that **chemotherapy** *does much, much* **more harm than good.***"*
Alan C. Nixon, Ph.D., Past President, American Chemical Society

The Basics

Cancer patients regularly **endure** treatments that are every bit as **barbaric** as the "bleeding" treatment used by doctors in the 15th century. Why? The answer lies in the **"politics" of cancer**.

If chemotherapy or radiation of any kind has been suggested for you or anyone you know or love, you **MUST** do some reading on your own and form your own opinion. I saw my former wife's body slowly **tortured and destroyed** by "chemo cocktails" over **four long years**. It reduced her to a **scrawny, pain-wracked invalid** without, in my judgment, extending her life by **even one day**.

Let's take a closer look at the **"conventional"** cancer treatments — surgery, chemotherapy and radiation, also called "debulking" therapies..

Surgery

If you have one of the most common forms of cancer — breast, prostate, colon, lung, spleen, etc. — a **"hard" tumor** is usually found. This is a characteristic of about **90% of the cancers** reported every year. At some point, your oncologist or surgeon is going to suggest **removing it**. Marge had it done several times.

The reading I have done suggests that frequently the **surgical removal** of the tumor often **causes metastasis** that may not have occurred. You will be worse off for having the surgery, even if you recover fully from the surgery.

The surgeon will say, as he did to me, **"We got it all."** He will be **wrong**, most of the time.

A cancer tumor the size of your thumb contains **billions** of cancer cells. If only a few of these individual rascals escape the surgeon's knife, **as they always do**, your cancer is very likely to recur, unless you carefully rebuild your immune system.

The statistics say that if a tumor is found **"early,"** it will only reappear 50% of the time. With what we know about cancer statistics, I would expect this one to be **optimistic**. But, let's accept it. You have a **50/50 chance** that you will be just as bad off **after the removal**. Plus, you have **some chance** that you will be **much worse off**, because metastasis will occur.

As we will see shortly, there are at least a hundred treatments with natural substances which all have **evidence** that they cure some **terminal** cancer patients. Please **explore** some of them before you turn your care over to a surgeon, oncologist or radiologist.

Each of these treatments shows **positive results within weeks**, results that can be detected with conventional methods — MRI, CT scan, PET scan and blood tests. Depending on the stage of your cancer, you may want to try them before, during, after **or instead of** your "conventional" treatment. If your cancer doctor won't discuss this intelligently with you, **please** find another cancer doctor.

Chemotherapy

For the purposes of this discussion, we will refer to chemotherapy as the **poisoning** of dividing cells using **cytotoxic drugs**. That's what chemotherapy is.

There are lots of other drugs used in cancer treatment to manage adverse reactions to the poison; alter hormonal balance; modify biological responses; or boost the immune system (interferon, etc.). For simplicity, we will not discuss those.

Chemotherapy uses various combinations of **toxic drugs** to poison cells as they divide. Remember the number **75 trillion**? That's the number of cells in the average person's body. **Each day, 29 billion or so** of these replace themselves by division. The cancer cells are dividing to form new malignant cancer cells. **Billions** of healthy cells are also **dividing every day** to replace themselves.

The chemotherapy "cocktails" **cannot distinguish** between cancer cells and healthy cells. They **bombard** them all with the same napalm. Ever wonder why almost all chemotherapy patients **lose their hair**? Guess where some of the **fastest dividing cells** in your body are? You guessed it. They're in your hair. **Not cancer cells**, just healthy cells replacing themselves. But there are lots more in your intestines and other vital organs and in your bone marrow. **Blast them all!** That's why all chemotherapy patients **feel like hell** and most **wish they were dead**! Marge sure did.

Does this strike you as **barbaric treatment**? Wouldn't you be looking for **anything but** this way to "treat" your patients if you were an oncologist? Most of them are well meaning but **caught up in the system**. The **drug money** (much of it involved in chemotherapy) drives the system. Most of the people doing the **alternative research**, at least in the U.S., are **not practicing cancer doctors** (oncologists). The research the

61

cancer doctors do is **almost totally** under the spell of the **money** provided by the **drug industry**. It is actually funded by drug companies.

There are **a few malignancies** that are **highly responsive** to chemotherapy. In October 1971, Dr. Gordon Zubrod, a leader of the National Cancer Institute, presented a list of these. All of these are **rare in adults**. But, most important, the list **has not changed** since 1971. Here it is:

Burkitt's lymphoma; Choriocarcinoma; Acute Lymphocytic Leukemia; Hodgkin's Disease; Lymphosarcoma; Embryonal Testicular Cancer; Wilms' Tumor; Ewing's Sarcoma; Rhabdomyosarcoma; Retinoblastoma.

That's it. In the 32 years since that list was published, there is **no solid evidence** that chemotherapy for the other, more common, cancers results in **significant increased survival**.

I would not rule out using chemotherapy, particularly if I had one of the rare types of cancer listed above. One of **my daughters** had Wilms' Tumor when she was **three**. Removal of the affected kidney and chemotherapy **saved her life** and she had no recurrence. She died (was murdered) at **age 34**, but that's another story.

You, too, may know someone who has had their cancer go into "remission" after treatment with chemotherapy drugs. They are among the lucky ones. But, please **consider IPT** (discussed below) and other gentler alternatives before you accept "high dose" chemotherapy.

Sometimes chemotherapy and/or radiation can be used effectively to **"debulk"** the tumor before using one or more of the non-toxic therapies we will discuss.

Approach chemotherapy with a very skeptical attitude. Most of the time you don't have to subject yourself or your loved one to this **medieval form of "treatment."**

Consider that since 1971 when the "War On Cancer" started, about **$2 trillion** (with a "t") has been spent on conventional cancer treatment and research. Yet, despite the government and private sector's work to put a positive face on cancer survival rates, they **have not improved**. The latest statistics show more Americans dying from common cancers than ever before. For example, the January 10, 2002 issue of the *New England Journal of Medicine* stated that 20 years of clinical trials using chemotherapy on advanced lung cancer have yielded survival improvement of **only two months**.

According to an article in the January, 2003 issue of *Life Extension*, *"the institutions we have counted on to find a cure (National Cancer Institute, American Cancer Society, drug companies, etc.) have failed. This is not an allegation, but an admission made by the National Cancer Institute itself."*

Knowledge is power. If your doctor won't cooperate with you in experimenting with some of the treatments we will discuss, you should **get another doctor**. (See the list of resources for finding one in Chapter 1 above.)

Radiation

The third "approved" method of treating cancer is **radiation therapy.** If you have cancer, the subject **will come up.** For certain cancerous tumors, radiation is effective in **reducing the size** of the tumor. Most of the time the side effects are significant and very harmful. Once again, radiation **does not distinguish** between **cancer cells** and **normal cells**.

All cancerous tumors are made up of about 90% non-cancerous cells and 10% cancer cells. **Reducing the tumor**

size does not equate to **curing the cancer** (or getting it under control).

If you are considering either chemotherapy or radiation, you should definitely read a book called *Antioxidants Against Cancer,* by Ralph W. Moss, Ph.D., copyright 2000, published by Equinox Press, Inc. and available at most bookstores and amazon.com.

Dr. Moss is familiar to you if you've read everything in this book. His **ten previous books** cover the waterfront of cancer therapy. This one, however, gives a very up-to-date look at the **importance of antioxidants.** They are vital for both fending off cancer and other disease and for **tolerating** better both **chemotherapy and radiation**.

More importantly, he points out that patients who have had chemo or radiation **never recover** the antioxidant levels in their bodies without appropriate supplements. These antioxidants are **vital to life**. He discusses each supplement in depth and how various chemo drugs and radiation affect it.

Insulin Potentiation Therapy (IPT) – One Great Alternative

There are many options available to you. Here is some detail on one I think **every** cancer patient considering chemotherapy or radiation should look at.

Caring Medical – Dr. Hauser

Here's how two of the most experienced people in the U.S., Ross Hauser, M.D. and Marion Hauser, M.S., R.D. of Caring Medical Clinic in Rock Park, Illinois describe the procedure:

"During Insulin Potentiation Therapy a small dose of insulin is given to the patient that induces a state of low blood sugar (hypoglycemia). When the patient begins to have symptoms such as a feeling of lightheadedness and weakness (hypoglycemia symptoms) [this happens in about 30 minutes], low doses of traditional chemotherapy are given by intravenous push. When insulin is given, the cancer cells are fooled into thinking they are going to be fed food, when in reality they are going to be destroyed by chemotherapy. Thereby, smaller, safer, more effective doses of chemotherapy can be administered in place of high dose chemotherapy."

What is a Potentiator?

A potentiating agent is one that **increases the effectiveness** of another agent. In regard to chemotherapy, a potentiator (insulin, in this case) **increases the kill power** of the drug toward cancer cells. Because of this ability, a **lower dose** of the medication is needed to get the same pharmacological effect.

Dr. Ross Hauser says *"Various substances can be used to optimize the cancer-killing effects of chemotherapy, in addition to insulin, dimethyl sulfoxide (DMSO), oxygen therapies, and hyperthermia.*

Scientific studies have shown that vitamin E, vitamin C, coenzyme Q10, beta carotene, glutathione, N-acetylcysteine, glutamine, selenium, genistein, diadzein, quercetin, melatonin, green tea, vitamin A, milk thistle, Coriolus versicolor, vitamin K, bupleurum, and rabdosia have been shown in studies to potentiate the killing effects of chemotherapy.

When one reviews the literature, there is resounding evidence that nutrients and herbal remedies enhance the killing effects of chemotherapy and subsequently reduce its side effects. It is more than overdue that modern oncologists realize this fact and start prescribing some of these nutriceuticals for their patients."

But Does It Work?

This procedure increases the effectiveness of the chemotherapy agents by **10,000 times**, which allows **very small amounts** of chemo to be used, thus virtually **eliminating** the side effects of conventional doses. The results, as confirmed by several of my readers, can be dramatic.

Why doesn't your doctor know about this effective, less expensive, less damaging protocol? The FDA hasn't approved it, except as an "experimental procedure." Thus, insurance companies and Medicare generally will not pay for it.

The National Cancer Institute (NCI) has had a researcher assigned to study it and do clinical trials since September 2000, but he has been given **no funding yet.** Don't hold your breath until he gets this money. You don't have to wait for the bureaucracy to get around to approving this procedure. IPT has been used very successfully to fight cancer for **over 70 years** and **it is legal**.

Currently there are about **80 doctors worldwide** trained on this procedure in the U.S., Canada, Mexico, Argentina, Brazil, France and Ecuador. There is also one trained veterinarian in Arizona. One of the MDs who has received the IPT training is Dr. Douglas Brodie of Reno, Nevada, a prominent CAM practitioner. I'll tell you how to find all the trained doctors in a minute.

The Doctors Garcia – True Pioneers

Dr. Donato Perez Garcia, Sr. discovered IPT and began using it in Tijuana in 1930. Here are some **interesting statistics**. At the IPT course in Las Vegas, Nevada in February 2001, **Dr. Donato Perez Garcia** showed a slide of the morbidity (adverse effects) that his family (three generations of physicians) has had administering IPT.

Donato Perez Garcia, Sr., M.D. (ORIGINATOR OF IPT) (1896-1971) YEARS OF DOING IPT 1930-1971: **41 YEARS MORBIDITY 0%**

Donato Perez Garcia Bellon, M.D. (1930-2000) YEARS OF DOING IPT 1956-2000: **44 YEARS MORBIDITY 0%**

Donato Perez Garcia, Jr., M.D. (Still living) YEARS OF DOING IPT 1983-2000: **17 YEARS MORBIDITY 0%**

The family of three physicians who founded IPT and have over 100 years of experience with it (there is some overlap in their careers), have never had any adverse reaction **because of IPT**. By contrast, **hundreds of thousands** of cancer patients die of high-dose chemotherapy **in the U. S. alone** every year.

Because the doses of chemotherapy medications used during IPT are **10-25%** of the amounts given during traditional cancer care, the side effect risk is **diminished greatly**. The only side effect from IPT is fatigue during the day of treatment.

One of the main reasons that people get IPT is because it is a great alternative to high dose chemotherapy with all of its side effects that can include suppression of the immune system, hair loss, nerve, heart, kidney, liver injury and, of course, death.

Why doesn't your oncologist know about this if it has been around for 75 years? It's not because it hasn't been documented to the cancer "system." In fact, IPT physicians have **briefed the National Institutes of Health** several times. There are **numerous published studies** in professional journals.

One obvious reason why it is not popular is the potential **loss of money** to the cancer industry. It is estimated that every cancer patient will produce **$500,000** for the industry by the time he/she is given his or her last treatment. Such a simple, effective, and dramatic treatment that uses much less of the chemotherapy drugs would severely **cut into the industry's profits**. You do not have to be a victim of this evil greed.

To get smart quickly about this treatment, go to this web site:

http://www.iptq.com/

Among much other information there, you will find a long interview with **Donna McDermott**. She is a breast cancer patient cured using IPT. In the interview, she describes her entire case — before, during and after the IPT. Dr. Donato Perez Garcia (see above) treated her in Tijuana.

At that same site, you will also find a listing of **all the qualified doctors**, arranged by experience or location.

To complete your investigation, check out this other site. It is Dr. Hauser and his wife's clinic site (the people I quoted at the beginning of this section). You will find many **convincing testimonials** there from their patients. They have written a book on this subject and they publish an interesting weekly newsletter. Their site is:

http://www.iptcancer.com/

The Cost

Several of my readers who have used this treatment in various parts of the country confirm that the cost is about **$13,000** for the initial three weeks of treatment. It is done on an out-patient basis, but you need to stay in the vicinity of the clinic because **treatments are done daily**. The regimen includes other treatments such as intravenous Vitamin C, immune system boosters, oxygen therapy, hyperthermia, etc.

Selecting A Treatment – Some General Guidelines

> ➢ If you can afford it, go **wherever** you need to. Mexico, Canada, France – wherever. The perfect doctor for you may not be in your country or state.

> ➢ Insist on a proven **track record** with your type of cancer. If the doctor or clinic will not give you **references** willing to talk to you, continue your search.

> ➢ If you can't afford travel to a clinic, **don't worry**. Just select one of the treatments I describe in this book, **find a doctor in your area to help you** and keep trying additional treatments until you find a combination that works.

> ➢ Don't accept **"response rate"** statistics. If the tumor "responds" to a particular treatment, that is counted as a plus by most oncologists. This is **irrelevant** to you, however. What you are interested in is **5-year survival rates** plus the **quality of life** during and at the end of the 5 years.

> ➤ Use **Internet** searches. Discuss on the many **forums** available the treatment options available to you with **real people** who also have your type of cancer and have recovered (or have not). Several of these forums are covered in Appendix A to this book.

> ➤ Avoid **"mainstream"** clinics and doctors – M. D. Anderson, Mayo Clinic, Sloan-Kettering Cancer Center, etc. The treatments you will receive there are never going to include the options you will read about shortly. Remember the American Cancer Society's "unproven remedies" list. None of the most prominent mainstream doctors and hospitals can stray from conventional treatments – surgery, chemotherapy and radiation. You need your doctor to **supervise** your exploration of **other non-toxic cures**, many of which are listed in this book.

> ➤ Don't balk when your health insurance or Medicare **does not cover** the treatment you are considering. You are dealing with **your life** here. Nothing is more important than finding the cure for your cancer. If you cannot afford it, find a friend or family member willing to lend you the money to do it right. You will **live to repay them** – believe me.

> ➤ Get **appropriate tests**. I will cover these in the next section.

Tests That You Must Have

In recent years, effective tests using modern technology have been developed which help to treat your cancer. Here are several you will definitely need:

"Standard" Blood Tests

You've been having blood tests all your life. But did you realize that they are full of **vital information** for you about disease prevention?

Did you realize that your doctor probably has not given you any of that information — probably because he/she **doesn't know what it is**?

Rather than bore you with my recent experience, I'll just give you some of the lessons I learned and a resource to help you learn them too.

I recently had a complete blood test performed at **"Lab One"** in San Antonio. It was unique in two ways. First, I ordered and paid for it myself by calling the people at this web site:

http://www.directlabs.com

Second, it was **complete**. 33 elements of blood chemistry tested. Most of the blood tests ordered by your doctor are quite limited. HMOs are very picky about what they will pay for. So, unless some diagnosis calls for it, **many elem**ents in the blood test are omitted because they add to the expense.

Once I had my blood test results, I sent them to my friend **Cy Bursuk**, a consulting nutritionist and lifelong expert on the subject of blood test interpretation. The same day I faxed the blood test results to Cy, he faxed me back an eight-page form called a **"Bionutritional Blood Test Profile."** Each one of 33 elements of the blood chemistry is described. Both the "Optimum value" and "Optimum range" are shown, along with a description **in plain English** of what it means if that element is high or low.

It was very interesting that for all 33 "Elements," the "Optimum Range" was **much tighter** than the "Limits" shown on the lab's printout of the blood test. For example, item #1 is Calcium. The standard blood test limits were 8.5 to 10.6. My 9.2 reading was well within limits. On Cy's profile, however, the "Optimum value" was **9.9** and the "Optimum range" was **9.7 to 10.2.**

The explanation for "Decreased Calcium" in Cy's profile said: *"May indicate poor enzymation (chemical changes) of fatty acids and improper protein digestion in the liver."*

Cy says that the normal blood test limits indicate that when you are outside them, you have a **"clinical" condition** — i.e. something which needs to be "treated" by the doctor, no doubt with some type of **synthetic drug**. What Cy tries to do, with the 15,000 people he has worked with to date, is to catch **sub-clinical conditions** which can be treated and corrected with changes in diet and supplementation. A very different approach.

Several other items (iron, LDH) in Cy's profile confirmed that I have weak liver, pancreas and spleen function. All three **need support**. Interestingly, according to Cy, I do **not** need to "detox" the liver. In fact, he said that would just aggravate the condition. The liver, pancreas and spleen need "support."

Moral of this story:

1. Taking charge of your own health includes understanding your blood tests.

2. Normal blood tests give you no clue about sub-clinical problems which can be dealt with before they become disease. Even if they did, your doctor is unlikely to know how to treat them — except to treat the symptoms with some kind of prescription drug.

3. The "normal" blood test your doctor gives you is limited. Almost all doctors work under the "eagle eye" of an HMO. The

more complete blood tests are more expensive. Draw your own conclusions.

4. Most degenerative disease (like cancer, diabetes, arthritis, etc) has given clues in the blood chemistry long before it is diagnosed by medical doctors. In most cases, it can be headed off by changes in diet and supplementation.

To learn more about Cy Bursuk and his approach to blood chemistry analysis and nutrition, go to his web site:

http://www.cybur.com/

Live Blood Cell Analysis

This test may also be called a **"phase contrast lens"** study. A simple blood drop sample is taken and placed under a high-powered microscope. On a TV monitor, you will **see** the formations and activity of all your cells – red, white and platelets – floating around "live and in living color."

You and the doctor or nutritionist will be able to see whether they are functioning properly or if they are deficient or malformed and **what the cause is**. You will also see if you have a lack of enzymes, liver congestion, kidney congestion, fungal formations and **much, much more**.

This is one test that you will be able to **see for yourself** and not just get a result from your doctor's lab. The doctor will prescribe supplements, vitamins, herbs or minerals that are specific for the condition that this test shows. There is no magic to this test. It is very logical. It costs only **about $40.** Subsequent tests can be put on the same video tape, so you can easily compare them.

The **cost** of this test and treatment is in the **supplements**. But instead of the "hit and miss" approach most of us take to vitamins, herbs, enzymes and other supplements, you will be taking **those you specifically need** for your condition.

Any M.D., N.D. (naturopathic doctor) or nutritionist who has the equipment can do this test. Ask about it before you select your doctor or clinic.

Thyroid Panel T3, T4 and TSh

Your health insurance and Medicare cover this test. A **hyperactive or hypoactive thyroid gland** is one of the contributory factors to many major diseases or conditions such as heart disease, cancer, parasites, blood clotting and others. It is a simple blood test. There are homeopathic and naturopathic remedies for low functioning or over-functioning thyroids.

Trace Mineral Test

This test costs about $150 and **may be paid for** by your health insurance or Medicare. Your blood sample is sent to a lab such as Metatrix in Norcross, Georgia. There are others that can do it. It takes about a week to get the results. The **profound importance** of this test is that it reads and outlines every mineral in your body. Heavy metals such as zinc, aluminum and iron where an excess can cause a problem are shown. Mercury leaching from **fillings in your teeth** will show up. Deficiencies in needed minerals such as manganese, selenium, magnesium, etc. are shown. Your naturopath or Medical Doctor can then recommend specific supplements, vitamins or herbs for your condition.

Natural Killer Cell Activity Test

This test (sometimes called a "four-hour radioactive-chromium release assay") determines the degree of strength of your Natural Killer (NK) cells. As we will see in the next section, **NK cell activity** is an indicator of the ability of your immune system to "mop up" cancer cells. Unfortunately, there are no guarantees. Some cancer patients have strong immune systems.

As Dr. Ross Hauser of Caring Medical Clinic (see below) says:

"Checking immune function is important in cancer, because if a person has a strong immune system even though the cancer is getting out of control, it probably means that his or her immune system is not recognizing the cancer as something abnormal that needs to be killed. Some people's cancers have a tremendously strong ability to hide from the immune system. In such a situation, where a person has good immune function via blood tests and a lack of infections and colds, but yet there is evidence that the cancer is progressing, then aggressive therapy like IPT (see above) is needed."

Anti-Malignin Antibody in Serum (AMAS) Test

This is advertised as the "most accurate cancer test in the world." It can detect cancer nearly **two years before** any other method now in use with accuracy **above 99%.** Even more important, it can accurately detect the **recurrence** of cancer – any form of cancer – long before other cancer "marker" tests, with far fewer false positives.

Most **doctors are unaware** of this test. It is not marketed like other, much more expensive, tests such as PET scans, CT scans, etc. It is performed only at the lab owned by the couple that discovered the antibody in **1974**. They have patented the

75

test. Any doctor can order it from Dr. Bogoch's Oncolab, 36 The Fenway, Boston, MA 02215, (800) 922-8378. The cost: $135.

No one test is perfect. In the case of the AMAS test, it doesn't work for advanced cancer cases. The antibody it tests for is not there. Also, there have been cases of false negatives reported, **particularly for breast cancer**. However, I would strongly recommend that you discuss this test with your doctor. If your doctor is not interested, you can order the test kit and information yourself and **find another doctor** to prescribe it for you. One of my readers in Montreal did just that for his wife. Just call (800) 9CATest.

How Often To Test

Even a healthy person should have these tests done once a year. Whatever they cost can easily be made up by **targeting your supplements** to your specific condition instead of guessing at dosages. If you have cancer, the live blood cell analysis should be done **monthly** and the Natural Killer Cell Activity Test done **quarterly**. This is because your supplements have to be regulated as you become healthier. The AMAS test kit has guidelines for how often to test.

Don't Panic

Above all, **don't panic** at your cancer diagnosis. A cancer diagnosis, no matter how severe, is **not a death notice**. Many thousands of people who have had severe, Stage IV metastasized cancer are **completely well today**. You can be, too. The treatment methods and tests in this book will give you your health back.

Whether you are the patient or caregiver, when your experience with cancer is over, you will have **learned many valuable lessons** about lifestyle that will help you live a long and happy life. Count your blessings!

Your Rights As A Patient

Sometimes I think the word patient was applied to us innocent users of the medical "system" because we are so.....patient. As a cancer "patient," it will pay you to be **IM**patient. As a cancer **advocate** for a friend or loved one, it will serve you well to be **even more impatient** than the patient.

Nothing will be more important in the initial days after your diagnosis than **knowing your rights** as a patient. Here is an excerpt from another book by Dr. Ralph W. Moss. Published in 1995, the book is called **"Questioning Chemotherapy."**

"The patient's rights

*This book offers people with cancer some of the information they need to take a **more active role** in their choice of treatments. But patients are sometimes **confused** about what rights they have regarding their choices*

*Dr. Martin Shapiro of UCLA has told the informative story of a patient of his, a man in his thirties with advanced lung cancer, which had already failed to respond to **three different chemotherapeutic regimens**.*

*When he came in to start a **fourth one**, Shapiro asked him if this was what he really wanted to do.*

'Do I have any other choice?' the patient asked. The man was ready to do whatever he thought the doctor wanted, spurred on by stories of the wonders of chemotherapy. 'Unduly optimistic publicity helps to create a climate in which patients resign themselves to chemotherapy for conditions in which it does not work,' Shapiro concluded.

So let me state this clearly: **If you are a sane and sentient adult you have an absolute right to take or refuse any treatment**. *You are certainly within your rights to continue chemotherapy, if that is your wish, even if you or your doctor thinks the odds are slim that it will help you. You can also* **walk away** *from any cancer therapy situation and* **nobody can stop you**. *Here are some other possible choices:*

> ➢ *You may choose the* **alternative** *approach. For instance, you may go to a domestic or foreign clinic; work with an alternative doctor or health care practitioner; or procure* **unconventional** *treatments that are* **not** *necessarily* **approved of by the government** *or medical authorities.*

[We'll discuss several of these alternative options in the next chapter.]

> ➢ *You may choose to enter an* **experimental protocol** *sponsored by the NCI [National Cancer Institute], or another such institution. Lists and descriptions of such treatments are available via the* **computerized PDQ system,** *or, in the U.S., by calling the NCI's Cancer Information Service at 1-800-4-CANCER.*

> ➢ *Or, you may decide to work with your loved ones and health-care providers to '***maximize comfort and function***, to sort through the maze of emotional and social problems evoked by the illness, and even to* **grieve together** *over the impending death.'*

You have a **right** *to a* **copy of your medical records**. *You can always ask for a* **second, third, or fourth opinion**. *You can* **demand answers** *to all your questions in a language you can understand. Especially, you can always ask to* **see proof** *of the effectiveness of the treatment being offered in terms of* **actual...survival** *and/or improved quality of life.*

You always have the right to ***'informed consent,'*** *to be told and* ***understand*** *exactly what is going to be done to you.*

And just because it is called **informed consent does not mean that you have to consent**, after you are allegedly informed. At any point, **you can refuse**. You do not have to be 'reasonable' or to live up to anyone else's standards, **including your doctor's.**

The worst that will happen is that the **doctor will get angry**. But the doctor should know that if he or she **refuses to treat a patient** on capricious or unreasonable grounds, this may be **actionable** behavior." [translation: you can sue him/her for malpractice].

Well, dear friends, if my late wife and I had **known what I know now**, we would have approached her cancer treatment **much differently** than we did. Please learn from our **expensive mistake**.

I **urge** you to read Dr. Moss' book, and any others you can lay your hands on. You will soon have enough **information** (far more than I can give you here) on which to make a **rational choice of treatment**. Again, this book is "Questioning Chemotherapy", by Ralph W. Moss, Ph. D., copyright 1995 and published by Equinox Press. And don't forget Dr. Moss' web site. It's at:

http://www.cancerdecisions.com/

Let me conclude this section by quoting again from Dr. Moss:

"Consider this sage advice from a cancer patient's widow, who wrote to ***The Cancer Chronicles*** *(11/93):*

79

*'**Question** your doctor. Question him **every step of the way**. The more serious the condition, the more serious the treatment, the **more stringent the questioning** must be. If you don't have the energy, enlist the help of someone who does.... **Don't be afraid to fight**. Question your doctor, the same way you would a politician, for the two are not dissimilar. If your doctor won't answer the questions, **find one that will**.... There is a **party line** within the medical system. Question your doctor. **Always.'***

*And indeed, **some doctors** welcome intelligent dialogue, and **appreciate** the chance to share the **complexities of their science** with inquisitive patients. Others don't. If a doctor gets angry, condescending, or evasive, it may be **time to look for another doctor**. Never allow yourself to be hustled. Most likely you pride yourself on being a **knowledgeable consumer** in the general marketplace. Be an **informed medical consumer**, as well.*

*You now have a yardstick by which to **measure the effectiveness** of cancer treatments. If a drug or regimen has not been **proven to cure**, significantly **prolong actual survival**, or improve the **quality of life** — if it only temporarily shrinks tumors, with a probable loss in well being — then it is at most entirely **experimental and unproven**, and should not be represented as anything else. At worst, it could be not just ineffective, but **painful, destructive — even fatal**.*

*It may be time to look into other **alternative, nutritional, or nontoxic** treatments. It is my personal opinion that the **best of these treatments** are based on more plausible theories and **offer more compelling evidence** than most chemotherapy; they certainly do **far less harm**.*

*Patients and their loved ones are often understandably **devastated** when they learn that they have cancer. It is an **additional blow** to learn that chemotherapy is **not likely to*** *help*, much less cure. But cancer is **not a death sentence**. It can be a **turning point**.

The **loss of illusions** may be the **beginning of wisdom**."

Need More On This Subject?

If you'd like to read one of the best summaries of why "alternative treatments" are necessary and which ones to pursue, go to this web site and read the views of Dr. Ralph Moss and Dr. Julian Whitaker:

http://www.cat007.com/ifihadcancer.htm

Now, for some specific self-treatments that I recommend you begin **immediately,** please read on.

CHAPTER 5 – CANCER SELF-TREATMENTS THAT I RECOMMEND

"All of my knowledge is learned by standing on the shoulders of geniuses." Albert Schweitzer

In this section of the book, I will describe cancer treatments that you need to **discuss with your doctor**, no matter who he/she is. However, if your current doctor is **not sympathetic** to these treatments, **start them anyway** while you look for one who is. They are treatments for which a **vast library** of information is available. They have been proven over many years to work on all types of cancer.

I will discuss in detail the ones I would adopt **if I had cancer**. What type of cancer? It wouldn't matter. Whatever type and stage of cancer I was diagnosed with, I would do the same things described here. Many of these are not expensive. Guaranteed to work? Sorry. **No guarantees**.

You must research these beyond the information in this book. Do so **before** you discuss them with your doctor. In that way, you will be in a position to judge his/her reaction when you bring up the subject. **Don't just "ask your doctor"** about them. As I mentioned above, very few doctors are as knowledgeable about these cancer cures as you will be in a few minutes. Before you bring these up, you must be **thoroughly** convinced of their efficacy.

MGN-3

Here is a letter from my file. I wrote it to Dr. Tim Nealon, a golf buddy. Dr. Nealon is currently an Associate Professor of Microbiology at a local university. In six years of golf together, he and I had discussed the microbiology of everything from **AIDS** to **root canals**.

Dr. Nealon was a **pioneer** in the mid-1980s in isolating the **AIDS virus**. For 13 years, he has been one of **5 permanent members** from the United States on the **International AIDS Commission**, which meets quarterly in Europe.

I wrote him the following letter to get his opinion on **MGN-3**.

"May 12, 1999

Dear Tim,

Here is some info on MGN-3. I think we discussed this before. I'm curious about your opinion, particularly since it says in the research summary (see paper clip) that it was presented to the International Conference on AIDS.

To briefly recap, after I read the enclosed 'Alternatives' newsletter in September '98, I bought about 6 bottles of the MGN-3. I gave them to a friend of ours. She had been treated for cancer for 2 1/2 years. After her breast was removed, it came back and metastasized to her pleural cavity and her spine. This despite extensive chemotherapy. She could barely walk, had lost 25 pounds or so and was in terrible pain.

She took the MGN-3 starting in mid-October, '98. She seemed to get better pretty much immediately. By mid-December, she had gained back 20 pounds, gone back to work and felt much better. About that time, she had another MRI done and asked Terry and me to accompany her to her appointment with her oncologist. Her English is not perfect and she wanted to be sure she understood everything. I said nothing to him about the MGN-3. He said the latest MRI showed not only that the cancer had stopped spreading, but that a remission seemed to be underway and he was stopping all further treatment until he saw some sign that it was needed.

She has continued to improve and just returned last week from a month long trip to Spain. I did not continue to buy any more MGN-3 for her after that first dose (she is quite poor), because before I got her the first dose, I got her to promise to quit smoking as a condition of the gift. She promised. She didn't quit. In spite of that, at least to date, the 'cure' seems to be working.

Granted, the above is an anecdote. But it is quite dramatic and convincing for me, because we had watched her throughout the deterioration and the recovery. I have just bought another set for Terry and me. We are taking the 'maintenance' dose of 1 gram a day.

I'm really interested in your opinion. Is the science valid? If so, what other positive effects should one expect? For example, should it help my chronic sinusitis? Should it help Terry avoid routine things like bladder infections? Should it prevent virus infections (colds & flu, for example)? Should it help PREVENT tumors if taken regularly?

I hope this is of some interest to you. If not, don't worry. It's just hard to find a medical person with whom you can discuss this kind of thing rationally.

Thanks.

Bill

Enclosures:
1. Alternatives newsletter, September '98
2. MGN-3 info from supplier"

To bring this story up to date, for about 35 months after the date of this letter, our friend was hale and hearty. She worked 50 hours a week. She had an active social life. In fact, she danced flamenco on Friday and Saturday nights at a local Spanish bistro. She had taken no more MGN-3... and she still smoked.

Then, about April 2002, her cancer returned, with a vengeance. We have tried to give her other things like pau d'arco tea, but she has continued to deteriorate. As I write this, her doctors have given up and she is selling her furniture and preparing to return to Spain to die.

As for Dr. Nealon's reaction, he called me after reading the letter and enclosures. He said, "The science is correct." In response to my other questions, he said it makes sense that this type of immune system booster would help in the treatment of many viral or degenerative diseases, but he couldn't comment on it more specifically without a lot more study.

Remember **Dr. David Williams**? In Chapter 3, we talked about his "Daily Advantage" supplements with the **65 ingredients**. Well, since reading his September, 1998 newsletter on MGN-3, I have read numerous other research reports, including several by the discoverer, Dr. Mamdooh Ghoneum.

After all the research I've done, I went back and **reread** Dr. Williams' newsletter dated September 1998. I felt a strong sensation that here was the logic that linked together **everything** I had read — from Dr. Roizen to Dr. Clark to Dr. Davis to G. Edward Griffin and all the rest.

First, some background. I've been receiving Dr. Williams' newsletter "Alternatives" for **17 years** — ever since he began publishing it. **I trust him**. He has helped me understand and treat my toenail fungus and my general well-being and everything in between.

The September 1998 issue of his eight-page newsletter was **devoted to one topic**. It was the first time before or since. Usually he covers 2, 3 or 4 topics in each monthly newsletter. As I mentioned above, this issue (and all the rest) is **available now** on his web site: http://drdavidwilliams.com/

Your Body's Anti-Cancer System

MGN-3 is an overall immune system stimulant. It is particularly effective in strengthening the **Natural Killer (NK) cells**. The NK cells are the body's first line of defense (after the "suicide" and "proofreader" genes) against cancer as well as viral and bacterial infections.

Significantly, it is the level of **activity** of the NK cells, not their numbers, which determines the **odds of survival**. Much research has confirmed that people with low NK cell activity are much more likely to experience diseases like cancer.

MGN-3 has also been shown to increase **activity levels** of other immune system cells. Some of these are **T cells and B cells**. It also increases production of several cytokines, such as interferon gamma, tumor necrotic factor-alpha (TNF-A), Interleukin-2 and Interleukin-12. But let's try to explain what it does in plain English.

Obviously, the immune system is **very complex**, with about 130 different kinds of cells. Suffice to say that MGN-3 has been proven to perform **all** the functions being searched for by drug research centers studying vaccines and other ways to **stimulate the immune system to cure cancer**.

Who is Dr. Ghoneum

The primary researcher and discoverer of MGN-3 is Dr. Mamdooh Ghoneum. He is a research immunologist. He earned his **Ph.D. at the University of Tokyo**, Japan, in radioimmunology. He did post-doctoral work at the UCLA School of Medicine in **cellular and molecular immunology**. Currently, Dr. Ghoneum is Chief of Research, Department of Otolaryngology, Charles Drew University of Medicine and Science in Los Angeles.

Dr. Ghoneum is internationally recognized as an **expert** in the emerging field of **cancer immune therapy**, a field of therapy that uses **biological response modifiers** (BRMs) to activate NK cells to kill cancer cells in the body. Dr. Ghoneum has been studying BRMs made from **natural compounds** – compounds derived from mushrooms, herbs, fungi and bacteria – as well as synthetic BRMs, drugs like **Interleukin-2 and Interferon** (both of which may be mentioned by your cancer doctor, so you need to be familiar with them).

For about **thirty years**, the field of cancer immune therapy has suffered great setbacks due to the **toxicity** associated with many of these BRMs, both natural and synthetic. Dr. Ghoneum believed that somewhere there must exist a natural compound

– a BRM – that would **stimulate the immune system** without producing **toxic side effects**. About eight years ago, **he found it**.

"I came across a natural substance that was so promising, so profoundly superior to anything else I had ever evaluated," he said, *"that I abandoned all other projects, including NIH [National Institutes of Health]-funded research, in order to focus entirely on this substance."* Today this substance is known as **MGN-3**. [Note: The initials stand for the last names of the three principal scientists who discovered it – i. e. the "G" is for "Ghoneum."]

Dr. Ghoneum says that MGN-3 proved to be superior, not only because of its **lack of toxicity**, but also because it maintains the boost to the immune system over time. In contrast, he found that the effectiveness of **other BRMs** diminished as time passed, even when the patient continued to take it.

"In long-term follow-up of our patients (up to 5 years), we have observed that the enhancing effect of MGN-3 on NK cell activity is maintained indefinitely with continued administration."

What is The Supporting Evidence?

Dr. Ghoneum offers 7 published studies in scientific and medical journals to support his belief that MGN-3 is the most effective BRM immune system enhancer available today. His studies include data from **72 human patients**, as well as test tube and animal data.

Dr. Ghoneum's earliest studies (in about 1995) involved **32 cancer patients** with different types of advanced malignancies. *"These patients had received and completed conventional therapy such as surgery, chemotherapy, radiation or hormonal therapy prior to participation in the study. The baseline NK cell activity was found to be low in all patients (10.8%-49%)."*

"Oral ingestion of MGN-3 at 45/mg/kg/day led to a significant increase in NK cell activity after only 1-2 weeks. The increase in baseline NK cell activity after two weeks of administration ranged from 145%-332% in breast cancer patients, 174%-385% in prostate cancer patients, 100%-240% in leukemia patients and 100%-537% in multiple myeloma patients."

"The increase in NK cell activity was maintained for five years with continuation of MGN-3 therapy," commented Dr. Ghoneum.

Dr. Ghoneum's research also indicates that, in **combined use** with chemotherapy and hormone therapy, administering 3 grams of MGN-3 per day (that's the $9 a day level — not cheap!) **alleviates the side effects** of the drugs and improves the quality of life:

> ➤ It often **prevents** the reduction in the number of white blood cells usually caused by chemotherapy and radiation.
>
> ➤ It increases **interferon gamma** production.
>
> ➤ It is effective with **many** kinds of cancer.
>
> ➤ When it is used with Interleukin-2, the dose level of Interleukin-2 can be reduced to a tiny level that doesn't trigger the **usual hazardous side effects.**
>
> ➤ MGN-3 and Interleukin-2 act **synergistically**. Together they are often much more effective at activating the immune system than either used alone.

Cancer and The Immune System

You probably have no trouble accepting that the immune system has to be **strong to deal with viruses and bacteria**. But what about cancer? What does a strong immune system have to do with cancer? **Everything!**

Dr. Ghoneum believes that cancer develops when the immune system is **weak, malfunctioning or absent**. He says, *"I think of it like, when the cat's away, the mice will play."*

As I mentioned above, the NK cell function test tells your cancer doctor how active your NK cells are. In a healthy person, the expected level is **60-75%**. In cancer patients, NK cell activity ranges from **0% to 30%**.

Dr. Ghoneum's research on MGN-3 includes about 225 cancer patients from many parts of the world – many of them in Japan. As each patient enters the research study, his or her **baseline NK cell activity** is established.

Then the NK cell activity is monitored as the MGN-3 (at 3 grams per day) is administered. Dr. Ghoneum says that once they are activated, *"the NK cells become **quite rapacious** in their search-and-destroy activities. Upon encountering a tumor cell, the activated NK cell **attaches to the membrane** of the cell and **injects cytoplasmic granules** that quickly dissolve the target cell [his research papers include pictures of an NK cell firing these granules into a cancer cell]. In **less than five minutes**, the cancer cell is **dead** and the NK moves on to its **next victim**. A single NK cell can destroy up to **27 cancer cells** before it dies. A single NK cell, once activated by MGN-3, can often bind to **two or more cancer cells at once**, and destroy them."*

Here's Dr. Williams' in his newsletter Alternatives discussing Dr. Ghoneum and MGN-3:

"Simply knowing about this gentleman's discovery and how to use it could one day save your life. I'm not exaggerating here — there's really nothing else quite like it. And within a few years, I have a feeling you'll be hearing a lot more about it in the popular press...provided of course that it doesn't get suppressed by the pharmaceutical giants or some federal agency (and that's a big 'if'). This one compound has the potential to change the way conventional medicine has approached health problems for the last 100 years."

When and How to Use It

Dr. Ghoneum says that the best time for a cancer patient to begin using MGN-3 is either while he or she is **in the process of "debulking"** (surgery, chemotherapy or radiation) or **immediately** thereafter. Participants in his ongoing research take 3 grams a day until there is no sign of cancer remaining. Then, after **2-3 additional months** of taking 3 grams per day, their dosage is reduced to 1 gram a day.

When used during debulking, Dr. Ghoneum says, MGN-3 has often **reduced the unpleasant side effects**; but immediately after debulking is probably the most important time to use MGN-3, because the **number of cancer cells** are, in all likelihood, at their lowest. This gives MGN-3 its best chance to **get rid** of these cancer cells that escaped the debulking therapy, and **keep them from coming back.**

Dr. Ghoneum says, *"Conventional medicine has excellent anti-tumor therapies that can **significantly reduce** the number of cancer cells. Unfortunately, we have seen that it is difficult to achieve a 100% kill rate without killing the patient in the process. At best, we can hope to **kill 95-98%** of the cancer cells with these therapies. At this point, a patient may be considered to be 'in remission.' Therapy is discontinued and the patient is closely monitored. However, as most oncologists are painfully aware, these remissions **are frequently short-lived**."*

91

Most chemotherapy "cocktails" **suppress the immune system**, lowering the activity of anti-cancer cells. Following chemotherapy or radiation, the few hardy cancer cells that survive are **left to multiply unchallenged** by your damaged immune system. When the cancer resurfaces, it does so with **increased ferocity** and drug resistance.

The practice of **"watchful waiting"** practiced by most oncologists **wastes a golden opportunity** to administer the *coup de grace* to the cancer. Boosting the immune system with MGN-3 allows the body to **eliminate the remaining cancer cells** that escaped the chemotherapy, radiation or surgery.

Dr. Ghoneum says that sometimes cancer patients want to try MGN-3 before agreeing to their oncologist's recommendation for a debulking therapy. He cautions you **not to postpone** debulking therapy. If the number of cancer cells outnumber the NK cells by too great a margin when you begin using MGN-3, then the NK cells – **even if highly activated by MGN-3** – cannot win.

Listen to Dr. Ghoneum again. *"MGN-3 cannot and should not replace debulking therapy, especially in cases of advanced malignancies. In these cases, even an extremely active immune response is easily overwhelmed by the huge numbers of cancer cells present. Instead, I recommend that cancer patients with solid tumors begin MGN-3 immuno-therapy **concurrent with, or immediately following** debulking therapies. With this strategy we have the best chance of winning what essentially becomes **a war of numbers**."*

Testimonials

In the last 18 months, I have gotten several convincing testimonials from readers who have used MGN-3 for some months.

Jan says *"I'm still taking MGN-3...**not one cold** this winter season...a first for many years! It's been a year since my surgery to remove **uterine sarcoma** and so far so good on all follow-up tests."*

Dr. Randy says *"After two months on the **MGN-3** and ellagic acid, his oncologist stated, 'I don't know why you're not sick. You should be in the hospital. You should be filling up with fluid still and this doesn't make sense.'*

*We finally found an oncologist who would support us in our decision to **NOT take chemotherapy**, but he still thought that we would be entering hospice in the next few weeks."*

Blanca says *"Just wanted to share some good news with you. If you remember, I told you my daughter had to start chemo again because she relapsed. Well, I started her on the MGN-3 in addition to the chemo. While on the chemo, I gave her the MGN-3 and she **did not get sick once**. In addition to this, she is completely off chemo and the doctor says there's **no cancer found**! I attribute this to the **MGN-3** and, of course, many, many prayers. Thank you so much for this valuable information. I will continue to give her the MGN-3. Please keep up the good work and MAY GOD BLESS YOU."*

And finally, an inspiring story involving MGN-3 and other supplements which you'll read about later:

"Hi Bill:

*Thanks much for your guidance and advice, you are doing a great deed for humanity. By way of recognition I must report to you the **great results** we had through your recommendations.*

*My wife age 55 was diagnosed with a malignant tumor in the left breast in Dec. of 2000 about 5 cm inoperable. We used hormonal therapy + vitamins. It did shrink to about 1/2 the size, but then the hormonal therapy **stopped working** and it grew back to about 6 cm with metastases to lymph and manubrium.*

*At that point the oncologist who is open minded decided we have to be **more aggressive** and use chemo. Based on your advice, we started using Dr. Budwig's diet fo/cc + red raspberries, **MGN-3**, co-Q10, Wobenzyme. She had 4 treatments with chemo all the time complementing it with the above regimen.*

*Today I'm happy to report that we did a full body pet/ct scan. The results came back: a **complete resolution** in the left breast, **no lymphatic involvement**, an **80% reduction** in the manubrium uptake. Quite dramatic to the amazement of my oncologist, who told me he did **recommend this regimen to other patients, even some of his family members.***

*It also helped her to **minimize the side effects** of chemo. Throughout the whole time, she never missed a day of work except the day of the treatment.*

I'm sure reports like this will make you happy and give you more spirit and determination to go on with your great work in helping mankind. Let God be on your side in all your endeavors and let him give you health and happiness forever. Thanks a Million,

Simon"

Where to Get MGN-3 Capsules

If you want to buy MGN-3 tablets, you can order them online. The source for all MGN-3 capsules is the same, Lane Labs. Ask about prices on both the 250 mg and 500 mg size. The **three gram per day** dosage recommended by Dr. Ghoneum is six of the 500 mg capsules or 12 of the 250 mg capsules per day for 3-4 months. Then the dosage is reduced to **1 gram per day**, or one-third of the above. This he recommends continuing indefinitely, if you have been diagnosed with cancer.

The absolutely cheapest source I have found is http://www.vitaglo.com. A bottle of 50 MGN-3 capsules (250mg each) sells for **$39.95** with free shipping in the U.S. At the web site above, enter a search for MGN-3. If you don't mind on-line ordering with your credit card, the savings are **significant.**

If you live in another country, a good source is http://www.austinnatural.com. They ship to any country where customs allows import of these supplements. Shipping cost to Canada is under $5 and to other countries under $15.

MGN-3 and beta glucan are also available, at **substantially higher prices**, at most health food stores.

Enhance the Effect With Beta Glucan

Both before and after Dr. Ghoneum's discovery of MGN-3, there have been numerous studies of another natural substance called **beta glucan**. Hundreds of tests on animals and humans have shown that beta glucan is very effective in activating one of the key cell types in the immune system – the **macrophage**. This word derives from the Greek words meaning "big eater."

The macrophage cells have been called the **"control centers"** for the immune system. In addition to gobbling up foreign matter in your blood, they **send out signals** to the NK, T, B and other immune system cells telling them to attack certain "invaders." Anything that helps your macrophage cells work better is **definitely a part of your cancer treatment**.

If you can afford it, you should take about **500-1,500 mg** of beta glucan daily along with the MGN-3. A bottle of 60 beta glucan tablets (500 mg strength) sells for about $56 at almost any health food store. It has been given a GRAS (Generally Recognized As Safe) designation by the FDA. That just means it has **no known adverse effects** nor does it interfere with any other substances or drugs.

Beta glucan is a common substance **marketed by many sources** (unlike MGN-3, which comes only from Lane Labs in New Jersey). These sources **vary widely** in the quality and strength of the beta glucan they provide. The best source I have found for ordering beta glucan is at the web site:

http://www.stopgettingsick.com/templates/news_template.cf m?id=1453

The source is in Norway with a distributor in the U.S. They call their product **Immutol**. It appears to be high quality. In short, this is where I would order it from if I were diagnosed with cancer.

In Summary

MGN-3 is a natural, **non-toxic** substance. It helps relieve the **side effects** of conventional cancer treatment – chemotherapy, radiation, surgery or hormone therapy. Most importantly, it is available **now** to boost your NK (and other) immune system "soldiers" to complete the "mopping up" operation after your conventional treatment is completed.

Taking MGN-3 (with beta glucan) will almost certainly **insure** that your cancer **will not recur**. Without it, your cancer will **almost certainly recur** months or years after completion of your "debulking" therapy. No instruments or tests today can detect the relatively small number of cancer cells that **always remain** after conventional treatment. Those cells are, by definition, the **hardiest**. With your immune system **destroyed by the chemotherapy**, radiation or surgery, they continue to divide in a **"cancer friendly"** environment.

If you or a loved one has cancer, MGN-3 (and beta glucan) will literally save your or your loved one's life. Best of all, MGN-3 and beta glucan are **"adjunctive"** therapies. This means their use does not require you to challenge your cancer doctor to approve an "alternative" treatment. With enough study of the available research, almost any respectable doctor should cheer you on in your use of MGN-3 and beta glucan. If he or she does not, **take them anyway**, using Dr. Ghoneum's guidelines, and consider finding another doctor.

I cover MGN-3 and beta glucan first in this book for a good reason. You can obtain them readily now **(by tomorrow using Next Day Air, if you wish)**, and you need not worry about seeking another cancer doctor before you begin taking it. Their only downside is the **cost of the capsules** themselves. But almost every other option I will cover in this book costs at least as much, and none of them, including MGN-3 and beta glucan, are currently covered by your health insurance.

Where To Get More Information

Copies of **complete research papers** and data on MGN-3 can be obtained from Lane Labs at (201) 236-9090. These include a lengthy article by Dr. Ghoneum on his work, including **six years of research on humans**. Case studies of the use of MGN-3 on patients can be found at the web site:

http://www.jafra.gr.jp/biokaizen-e.html

Dozens of research papers on beta glucan are available on the Internet. If you are interested, go to:
http://www.ncbi.nlm.nih.gov/PubMed/

Search for "glucan and macrophage." **Warning:** You will find the typical dense prose of research scientists in these papers, such as: "Surface expression of phosphatidylserine on macrophages is required for phagocytosis of apoptotic thymocytes." Maybe you'd just as soon take my word for it. [Chuckle!]

What About AHCC?

I have been asked several times to compare MGN-3 to AHCC (Active HemiCellulose Compound). You may hear claims that AHCC is "superior to MGN-3" or "the same as MGN-3." All I can tell you is that they are two very different products and that prior to his discovery of MGN-3 in 1996, Dr. Ghoneum **had been researching AHCC**. After he had determined the superiority of MGN-3, he **stopped all research** on AHCC to focus on MGN-3.

Other Great Immune System Boosters

I'm not exclusively hung up on MGN-3/beta glucan as the only way to boost your immune system. In fact, here are a couple of alternatives.

Oncolyn

When I discussed this subject with a friend who owns a health food store recently, she recommended I take a look at Oncolyn. She said it was **"better than MGN-3."** As with most supplements, there are indeed alternatives. I respect her opinion, so I did some research.

Like MGN-3, Oncolyn **destroys cancer cells** and neutralizes the toxicity of most chemotherapy drugs. It also, however, acts as a **powerful anti-oxidant**, inhibits angiogenesis (which both delays tumor growth and suppresses tumor metastasis), and "induces differentiation of cancer cells back to normal cells."

Powerful stuff. It was formulated by Arthur H.K. DJang, M.D., Ph.D., M.P.H. He is a U.S. licensed physician and certified specialist by the American Boards of Pathology and the American Board of Nuclear Medicine with expertise in Infectious Diseases, Biochemistry and Immunology (Ph.D), Preventive Medicine (M.P.H.) and Cytopathology. Impressed? Me, too.

Oncolyn is totally **herbal and non-toxic**. You need to consult with your medical professional, but at the doses I have seen recommended for cancer patients, it may be a **little less expensive** than MGN-3.

One of the things that is important to keep in mind, is that MGN-3 has proven effective in human trials. Oncolyn is new to me and I would investigate its history with human testing before

99

I would unconditionally recommend it over MGN-3. Oncolyn is available at most health food stores and on the Internet. To learn more about it, go to:

http://www.bellayre.com

If you would like to order it online, the best source is the manufacturer. Go to:

http://www.santeintl.com

BCI-26

Jim Roberts, a gentleman for whom I have enormous respect, sent me this e-mail on **BCI-26, an immune system booster**. Since it includes information on the product and his web sites, Roberts Review and My Cancer News, I'll just quote it:

"Dear Bill:

I think you should look into this product in conjunction with your book.

We have done extensive research on it here and it is now the only product we actually 'recommend' to all our visitors - healthy or ill - precisely for the reasons mentioned in your book in re: human auto-immune response. We are VERY careful about endorsing any medicine, herb, or product - but given the fact that this one is now listed in the 2002 PDR (Physician's Desk Reference) and has the FDA's coveted GRAS [Generally Recognized As Safe] rating - we feel it would be irresponsible not to inform the public about its merit.

BCI-26, an all-natural product has been bio-engineered into an immune system triggering, balancing, and fortifying agent. It is available over the counter and, surprisingly, was researched and partially developed by ConAgra and Dupont at a cost of

$50 million in conjunction with one of the world's leading immunologists, who has since joined the company that is now making and marketing it.

*We **DAILY** receive letters of thanks from individuals who have tried it, including **cancer patients**, Crohn's disease patients, HIV/AIDS patients, chronic fatigue syndrome sufferers, and others.*

You can find out more about it here:

http://distributor.mylegacyforlife.net/?site=/BioChoiceRx

*Be sure to click on the 'range of illnesses' link to see various patient and doctor **(including NAMES)** comments.*

*We find it heartening that the approaches listed in your book…as well as these new scientific - but over the counter - **CAUSE RELATED** therapies are finally being slowly brought to public attention.*

Jim

James J. Roberts
Executive Editor & Director
www.MyCancerNews.com
www.RobertsReview.com
c/o: Roberts, Prescott & Browne Int'l.
151 Duck Cove Road - Suite #2
Wickford, RI (USA) 02852-6219
Telephone: (401) 295-0007 (USA)
Email: JR@RobertsReview.com

Cancer Treatment Breakthroughs - Daily
From 2500+ medical journals, news outlets, gov't sources.
Latest treatments, diagnostics, research, survivor news.
Cancer pictures, prevention, alternative care options.
Patient financial & insurance guides.
(http://www.RobertsReview.com)"

Flaxseed Oil & Cottage Cheese – The Budwig Diet

Following is a reprint of an article that appeared in my "Cure Your Cancer" newsletter on July 16th 2002. For the first time in 20 months of publishing this newsletter twice a month, I **devoted the entire newsletter** to this subject. See if you agree with me on its pertinence to you or your loved one as an **effective and inexpensive** treatment.

In my research, I have run across Dr. Johanna Budwig's name several times. I always glossed over it when I heard her "formula" — a little flaxseed oil mixed with cottage cheese.

Bad decision!!

Thanks to one of you, my faithful readers, I was introduced to the **FlaxseedOil2** chat group. More about them in a minute. Here is a quote that I hope will rivet your attention on this topic.

An Oncologist Speaks

Dr. Dan C. Roehm, M.D., FACP, an **oncologist and former cardiologist** wrote an article in 1990 in the "Townsend Letter For Doctors." He said:

*"This diet is far and away the **most successful anti-cancer diet in the world**. What she (Dr. Johanna Budwig) has demonstrated to my initial disbelief but lately, to my **complete satisfaction** in my practice is: **CANCER IS EASILY CURABLE**. The treatment is dietary/lifestyle, the response is immediate; the cancer cell is weak and vulnerable; the precise biochemical breakdown point was identified by her in **1951** and*

*is specifically correctable, in vitro (test tube) as well as **in vivo (real)**.*

*I only wish that all my patients had a PhD in Biochemistry and Quantum Physics to enable them to see how with such **consummate skill** this diet was put together. It is a wonder. The champagne vehicle IS easier to assimilate and get someone almost on their death-bed going again. A retention enema of 250 ml (8.5 oz) of oil is another route to get this precious life-furthering, ELECTRON-RICH oil into the body. It can also be applied to the skin for transdermal absorption.*

*You will have to remain on this diet for a good **5 years**, at which time your tumor may have disappeared. Persons who break the rules of this diet, Dr. Budwig reports, (i.e. eating preserved meats, candy, etc.) will sometimes **grow rapidly worse** and cannot be saved after they come back from their spree **(bon-bons mean bye-bye)**.*

In 1967, Dr. Budwig broadcast the following sentence during an interview over the South German Radio Network, describing her incoming patients with failed operations and x-ray (radiation) therapy:

*'Even in these cases it is possible to restore health **in a few months** at most, I would truly say **90% of the time**.'*

*This has never been contradicted, but this knowledge has been a long time reaching this side of the ocean, hasn't it? Cancer treatment can be **very simple** and **very successful** once you know how. The cancer interests don't want you to know this.*

May those of you who have suffered from this disease (and I include your family and friends) forgive the miscreants who have kept this simple information from reaching you so long."

[signed] Dan C. Roehm, M.D. FACP

Did you see that Dr. Roehm is an oncologist and cardiologist? His views are based on his own observations of patients in his practice. Also note that Dr. Budwig's 90% figure does **not include chemotherapy recipients**! Don't lower your odds by taking chemotherapy.

Here's another quote from a noted doctor:

*"A top European cancer research scientist, Dr Johanna Budwig, has discovered a **totally natural formula** that not only protects against the development of cancer but people all over the world who have been diagnosed with incurable cancer and **sent home to die** have actually been **cured** and now lead normal healthy lives."*

Robert Willner, M.D., Ph.D.

The Magic Bullet?

Have I abandoned my position that there is **no single cure** for all cancers? No. However, would I sit up and take notice of this particular treatment if I were you? Darn right! I hope you trust me enough by now to know that I would not emphasize anything to this extent unless I was **thoroughly convinced** that you should try it. My wife and I are eating it every day.

What Is It?

It's so simple that it seems ridiculous. After 30 years of research, Dr. Budwig came up with **cottage cheese and flaxseed oil** as an effective preventative **AND CURE** for cancer and many other ailments.

Flaxseed oil/cottage cheese, or **FO/CC** as it is referred to on the chat group, is very simple to prepare. You simply mix one cup of organic cottage cheese **(no preservatives)**, low fat, with

2-5 tablespoons of flaxseed oil. Both ingredients are readily available at any health food store.

My wife and I use yogurt (live cultures, not the kind in the supermarket) in place of the cottage cheese. This is a suitable substitution, according to Dr. Budwig. It mixes much easier and we like the taste better. She says that using yogurt, you should **triple the amount**. In other words, about 3/4 cup yogurt to every tablespoon of flaxseed oil [you have to eat a lot more of it].

We add a package or two of Stevia as a sweetener and some almonds. Dr. Budwig says you can use a blender (pouring the FO/CC in **AFTER** it is well blended by hand) and then add any fresh fruits you like for flavor — bananas, strawberries, red raspberries (see below) — and even nuts, but **not peanuts**.

Why Does It Work?

The theory behind this odd combination? Dr. Budwig says the absence of **linoleic acids** in the average Western diet is responsible for the production of oxydase, which induces cancer growth and is the cause of many other chronic disorders. The use of oxygen in the body (one of the best ways to "erase" cancer cells) can be stimulated by **protein compounds of sulphuric content**, which make oils water-soluble and which are present in cheese, nuts, onion and leek vegetables such as leek, chives, onions and garlic, and **ESPECIALLY COTTAGE CHEESE.**

The flaxseed oil and the cottage cheese (or yogurt) must be **blended and eaten together** to be effective. They are synergistic. In other words, one triggers the healthful properties of the other. It is important to keep the oil in the refrigerator in the dark bottle it comes in. Light and heat quickly make it rancid. It will keep for **four months** in the refrigerator but only three weeks at room temperature. A word to the wise: Do not

105

buy it if it has been stored on a shelf at the store at room temperature.

So, you just eat the FO/CC mixture and wash it down with a Whataburger, french fries and a chocolate shake...NOT! As you might expect, the FO/CC is part of a lifestyle change that emphasizes food that is **not processed** and contains no **"hydrogenated" anything**. In addition, absolutely forbidden are:

Sugar
All animal fats
All salad oils (including commercial mayonnaise)
All meats (chemicals and hormones)
Butter
Margarine
Preserved meats (the preservatives block metabolism even of flaxseed oil)

Dr. Budwig's formula includes a **complete diet plan**, including a flax oil "spread," which can be used with fruits, vegetables, potatoes or grains such as rice, buckwheat or millet. It can also be added to sweet sauces and soups. There is also a flax oil "mayo" which can be used for salads or healthy sandwiches.

To get all the details on Dr. Budwig's diet and the "spread" and "mayo" recipes, just go to this web site:

http://www.positivehealth.com/permit/Articles/Nutrition/turner60.htm

More Science

In a book called "Oxygen Therapies" published in 1991, Ed McCabe offers this point of view on fatty acids:

*"The red blood cells in the lungs give up carbon dioxide and take on oxygen. They are then transported to the cell site via the blood vessels, where, they release their oxygen into the plasma. This released oxygen is 'attracted' to the cells by the 'resonance' of the 'pi-electron' oxidation-enhancing fatty acids. Otherwise, **oxygen cannot work its way into the cell**. 'Electron rich fatty acids' play a **decisive role** in respiratory enzymes, which are the basis of cell oxidation...*

*Don't eat anything hydrogenated **(like margarine or fried foods)** as it defeats oxygenation. Avoid products that say 'hydrogenated.'*

*We should eat essential polyunsaturated fatty acids to enhance oxygenation. They can be found naturally in carotene, saffron, and **FLAXSEED OIL**."* [Emphasis added.]

Dr. David Williams, my favorite health guru, has recently added four essential fatty acids (EFAs) to his Daily Advantage formula (see Chapter 3 above). An article in his newsletter urges us to **drastically increase** our intake of **Omega-3** fatty acids, the exact formula of flaxseed oil.

Here's a quote from a "promo" I received recently on it:

"In case you haven't heard the great news, Dr. Williams just added a powerful, new Essential Fatty Acids (EFAs) complex to Daily Advantage. These EFAs, particularly the omega-3s, are critical for your cardiovascular system, cholesterol, blood pressure, brain function, immune system, joints, and just about every other system in your body."

Don't concern yourself with the difference between Omega-3, Omega-6 and Omega-9 fatty acids. Just realize that Omega-3's should be about **four to one** to Omega-6's in your diet for your body to work properly. The ratio of our "normal" diet today is **just the opposite**...lots of Omega-6's and not nearly enough Omega-3's. Dr. Budwig's work has confirmed that this imbalance, caused by the "hydrogenated" fat in processed food, is the cause of most infirmities we suffer from. Several studies have shown that our typical Omega-3 level in our bodies is **80% below normal**. The flaxseed oil, when mixed with cottage cheese or yogurt, restores that balance...period. End of scientific story.

...But Does It Really Work?

Being **skeptical** of any new idea that makes bold claims is **healthy**. When you have cancer, it is **essential**. I was quite skeptical of this treatment at first. I joined the chat group and pawed my way through the 20-25 e-mails a day. You may, of course, do the same, if you are so inclined. All you have to do is send a blank e-mail to:

FlaxseedOil2-subscribe@yahoogroups.com

Maybe I can save you a lot of trouble. After reading the messages of this group for about three weeks, I became thoroughly convinced that they are onto something significant for **ALL** cancer patients.

First, almost all of the participants are **recovering from cancer** and other diseases (strokes, diabetes, etc.). Second, all of them, without exception, are thoroughly convinced that their recovery is the result of the Dr. Budwig protocol. The founder of the chat group, **Clifford Beckwith**, was cured of **Stage IV prostate cancer** in the early 90's by Dr. Budwig's protocol. He has been a **missionary** for this treatment ever since.

Meet Cliff Beckwith – The FO/CC Guru

Here are a few [unedited] words from the transcript of an audio tape made by Cliff Beckwith in July, 2001:

"Shortly after I found out I had trouble, we learned that a friend of ours had been having trouble since 1987. He'd been to the doctors; they had done various operations and tried different treatments but he didn't seem to be getting any better.

One day my wife and I visited him and talked about the oil. He decided to use it and began taking 2 tbsps a day [Now we know that probably was not quite enough]. The doctor said his bladder had crystallized and lost its elasticity. He couldn't stay out of the bathroom for 15 minutes. He couldn't go to church or carry on other normal activities. The doctor said it was a condition he'd just have to live with.

One day he went to the doctors for a physical and he told his wife that if he didn't get a good report he was going to quit using the oil. The doctor examined him and said, 'Mr. C, you've had cancer in your bladder but it's gone. The bladder is elastic again and everything is back to normal.'

In December 1993 we were having a tree cut and the contractor and I were discussing the oil. His assistant said, 'I've heard of that. I knew a man out west who found out he had colon cancer. He didn't let the oncologist do anything. He just used Flax oil and cottage cheese and the tumors disappeared.'

I have a cousin in California who lost his wife to cancer a number of years ago. He is militantly trying to get American doctors to look at this approach. He's talked to a group in Spain using an Omega-3 approach that is getting a 95% cure rate. Nothing in American medicine approaches that degree of success.

In 1994, I talked to Dr. Budwig. She said 'I have the answer to cancer, but American doctors won't listen. They come here and observe my methods and are impressed. Then they want to make a special deal so they can take it home and make a lot of money. I won't do it, so I'm blackballed in every country.'

Dr. Budwig has been nominated for a Nobel prize 7 times, but her methods have incurred the wrath of the establishment and she is passed over. Especially upsetting to the conventional cancer establishment is her refusal to use radiation or chemotherapy.

In the vast majority of the cases we have known about, there has been apparent recovery. Where it has not been successful, those with cancer have not used enough in the first place, or switched to Flax flakes or capsules.

Capsules scare me. In the first place, it takes a number of capsules to make a tbsp. and the sulphur-based proteins are still needed. Also, bottles of capsules are likely to sit around on shelves at room temperature. I know of one man who was quite badly off and began using the liquid oil and began making dramatic improvement. About a year later, I learned that he had died. I later learned that he had switched to capsules.

In a Christmas letter in December 1993, we heard that a friend of ours in Wooster, Ohio, was having a bout with ovarian cancer. The blood test for that condition is CA 125 and the normal is 35 or below. Her count was 75. Later I learned she'd visited my sister in September and was very apprehensive. She'd had about four rounds of chemo and couldn't take that. We sent information about Flaxseed oil in our Christmas letter.

Joanie is an RN and she and her husband had been missionaries in Sri Lanka. They bought the books and started using Flax oil. In February she was feeling fine. On May 12, 1994, she had a checkup and the count was 2 and she was praising the Lord. In October 1994, she had another physical and now the count was 1. Since then there's been no further indication of cancer."

If you would like to read more of Cliff Beckwith's account, including dozens of other examples of **proper and improper** use of this treatment, just go to:

http://www.beckwithfamily.com/Flax1.html

If you want a free copy of the audio tape, send Cliff an e-mail. His e-mail address: spinner@usit.net

What Does It Treat?

Dr. Budwig's formula has been used therapeutically in Europe for prevention and treatment of: Cancer; Arteriosclerosis; Strokes; Cardiac Infarction; Irregular Heartbeat; Liver (fatty degeneration); Lungs (reduces bronchial spasms); Intestines (regulates activity); Stomach Ulcers (normalizes gastric juices); Prostate (hypertropic); Arthritis (exerts a favorable influence); Eczema (assists all skin diseases); Old Age (improves many common afflictions); Brain (strengthens activity); Immune Deficiency Syndromes (multiple sclerosis, autoimmune diseases such as lupus).

Some Testimonials

Here are some more testimonials.

Siegfried Ernst, M.D.

Seventeen years ago Dr. Ernst had developed cancer for which he had major surgery requiring removal of his stomach. Two years later he had a recurrence of the cancer and was offered chemotherapy as the only available remedy. There was little hope for survival as virtually all individuals with recurrence of this type of cancer rarely last a year.

Dr. Ernst knew that chemotherapy was not only ineffective for his type of cancer but completely destructive of the quality of life, so he refused. He turned to Dr. Budwig and her formula for help. He religiously followed Dr. Budwig's formula and fifteen years later has not had any recurrence of cancer. He is in perfect health and is tireless for a man in his late seventies.

Maria W.

Maria W. tells her story in her own words: *"I was told by the most expert of doctors that I would have to be operated on to cut out the cancerous tumor that was causing a swelling under my eye. They explained that the size of the tumor was much greater inside and that there was very serious bone involvement. The malignancy was too far advanced to respond to radiation treatment. The doctors planned to remove considerable facial tissue and bone. I was afraid for my life, but being a young woman, couldn't bear the thought of such disfigurement.*

When I heard about Dr. Budwig's natural formula, I was skeptical but desperate for help. After four months on this regimen, the swelling under my left eye completely disappeared. The doctors at the University hospital gave me many exhausting tests. One told me, 'If I didn't have your previous x-rays and medical history in front of me, I wouldn't believe that you ever had cancer. There is hardly any indication of a tumor remaining.' I never thought using Dr, Budwig's formula would be so successful. My whole family and I are very grateful."

Sandy A.

An examination of Sandy A. revealed arachnoidal bleeding due to an inoperable brain tumor. The doctors informed Sandy that he was beyond medical help. At his expressed wish, Sandy was discharged from the hospital and sent home to die in peace.

A friend brought Dr. Budwig's formula to Sandy's attention. Sandy writes:

"Since I went on the Budwig regimen, the paralysis of my eyes, arms, and legs has receded daily. After only a short period of time, I was able to urinate normally. My health improved so rapidly that I was soon able to return to my work part-time. Shortly after that, I was again examined at the Research Center and my reflexes were completely normal. The Budwig diet saved my life! Ten years later, I was given a thorough examination at the Center as a follow-up.

My incredible recovery has been written up in many medical journals and I have become what they call a 'textbook case,' and all because of Dr. Johanna Budwig's simple diet."

Timmy G.

Seven years ago Timmy G. was diagnosed as having Hodgkins disease. The child was operated on and underwent 24 radiation treatments, plus additional experimental therapies that the experts hoped would be of some small help.

When Timmy failed to respond favorably to these heroic measures, he was discharged as incurable, and given six months to live and sent home to die.

The desperate parents contacted specialists all over the world. A famous newspaper took up Timmy's cause and ran editorials pleading for someone to come forth who could offer hope for the life of a child. All the specialists who replied confirmed the cruel prognosis: There was no hope or help for Timmy.

At this dark hour the miracle the family had prayed for happened!

Timmy's mother told her story to the press: *"A friend sent me a printed piece about one of Dr. Budwig's speeches. This material gave us hope and I contacted Dr. Budwig.*

In just **five days**, *(on the Budwig regimen) Timmy's breathing became normal for the first time in almost two years."*

From this day on, Timmy began to feel good again. He **went back to school**, *started swimming and by winter he was doing craftwork. Everyone who knows him says how well he looks."*

At age 18 Timmy is showing great promise in his university work. He knows he owes his life to Dr. Budwig and thanks her daily in his prayers.

What Ever Happened to Dr. Budwig?

Well into her 90's, Dr. Budwig has been active. She lectures on this subject all over Europe. Just recently, I have heard she is ill. God Bless her!

In Summary

Don't quibble. Don't put this off. Don't "wait to tell your doctor." In short, **just do it!!**

It's food. It's fairly inexpensive. It can't hurt you, unless the oil is rancid, which is pretty obvious. It'll smell. If it smells or tastes awful, don't use it. Take it back and get some fresh oil.

Lots of trivia on the chat board…high lignan oil vs. plain oil; ground flax seeds in addition to the oil or not; mix it by hand or in blender; flavor it with….well, you get the idea. **None of the people above worried about this stuff.** They just ate the mixture and got well.

Here's How

It's simple: Just buy **1% organic cottage cheese** or **"plain" yogurt (with live cultures).** Both should be without preservatives of any kind, so we're talking health food store, not supermarket. Buy the flaxseed oil (it's also called "linseed oil"), high lignan or not. Be sure the oil is fresh and cold, says "cold pressed" and is in a dark bottle. You can buy it at a great price online at:

http://www.swansonvitamins.com

Mix 5 or 6 tablespoons of the oil (shake it first if it is "high lignan") with 1 1/2 cups of the cottage cheese or 4 1/2 cups of the yogurt. Once it is thoroughly mixed by hand (or with an electric beater - **not in blender**), add whatever fruit or nuts (**no peanuts**) you like for flavor and put the whole thing in the blender to make a smoothie. Refrigerate it and eat it throughout the day. This is a **one-day dose** for a cancer patient (any stage, any type of cancer).

Next, take a look at Dr. Budwig's diet. See Chris Turner's article "Budwig Flax Oil Diet" at:

http://www.positivehealth.com/permit/Articles/Nutrition/turner60.htm

Don't continue on your "normal" diet and expect to get well. This is a **lifetime commitment**. If you drop it after the 3-12 weeks it takes to cure you, you will be **very sorry**. Don't do that!

For a lot more information, try this web site:

http://www.shirleys-wellness-cafe.com/flaxoil.htm

Want to read some books? Here are several for you:

"Flax Oil As a True Aid Against Arthritis, Heart Infarction, Cancer and Other Diseases," by Dr. Johanna Budwig. Amazon price: $6.95. Also available at the web site above for $5.56, but their shipping charge is about $6.50!

"The Breuss Cancer Cure: Advice for the Prevention and Natural Treatment of Cancer, Leukemia and Other Seemingly Incurable Diseases," by Rudolf Breuss. Amazon price: $11.00.

"How To Fight Cancer and Win," by William L. Fischer. Amazon price: $19.95. Includes three chapters on Dr. Budwig's protocol.

"The Oil Protein Diet Cookbook," by Dr. Johanna Budwig. Amazon price: $10.36. Dr. Budwig gives you lots of great recipes to make her protocol "user-friendly."

Dr. Matthias Rath – Vitamin C & Lysine/Proline

I mentioned Dr. Rath and his web site above, but I want to reemphasize his treatment to you as the **next thing** you should take after MGN-3/beta glucan and the Dr. Budwig's FO/CC.

The reason is that, like the first two treatments, this one is **gentle, non-toxic, and readily available**. Like the FO/CC, this one is also **inexpensive**. Not from Dr. Rath, but from Our Health Coop.

I suggest you go to Dr. Rath's web site and get **thoroughly familiar** with the volume of information available **free** there. You need to convince yourself of the value of this treatment. It literally **stops metastasis**, which is an essential step in treating any cancer. Here again is Dr. Rath's web site:

http://www.naturally-against-cancer.org

When you have explored the information there on his Vitamin C and the two amino acids (L-Lysine and L-Proline) come back here and I'll show you where to get it – cheap! [And I don't mean inexpensive – I mean **CHEAP**!]

To buy virtually the same formula Dr. Rath sells at about **one-fifth** of his price, go to:

http://www.ourhealthcoop.com

What you want to buy from them is the **"Heart Plus."** At this writing, the price for a 90 count bottle is **$9.45**. Yes, it works equally well for both heart disease and cancer. Read more about it at:

http://www.ourhealthcoop.com/ourhealth_he.htm

117

Notice that I devote much less space to Dr. Rath's compounds than to the FO/CC and MGN-3/beta glucan writeups above. Please **don't** interpret this as meaning they are **less important**. The only reason I can shorten the discourse is because Dr. Rath has such a **wonderful web site**, complete with **free** PDF e-books and video tapes in four different languages.

A Cancer-Fighting Diet

Next in order of importance for you, the cancer patient, is a **radically different diet**. It is almost certain that if your diet had been perfect, you wouldn't have cancer. None of us eat the perfect diet. **But now, you must!** No kidding.

Patrick Quillin – A True Expert

You don't have to take my word for it. Just read the **best book** on the subject I have found. It is *"Beating Cancer With Nutrition"* by Patrick Quillin. It is available from bookstores and amazon.com for about $24.95. You will not find any better bargain anywhere.

Nutritionists

Obviously, if you can afford it, the advice of a nutritionist is ideal. There are many of them and they use different tools (live blood cell analysis, infra-red scans, hair analysis, Ph testing, etc.). They are **not cheap**. Patrick Quillin is cheap.

Let me mention one thing you need to know about nutritionist advice. It will be **paid for by Medicare** if you have been diagnosed with:

1. Diabetes
2. Kidney disease

3. or you are on organ transplant follow-up

This is the result of a **law passed by Congress** effective January 1st 2002. If your doctor is not aware of this, have him/her check with Medicare. You may be able to get nutrition advice (and even some of the products and treatments) paid for by Medicare. Why they did not include cancer on the above list is anybody's guess.

DoctorYourself.com

Another interesting article on nutrition and cancer, especially the importance of vitamins, is at:

http://www.DoctorYourself.com/cancer_2.html

Dr. Dana Flavin-Koenig

One of the most interesting members of my **vibrant network** of cancer fighters is Dr. Dana Flavin-Koenig. She is an American living in Germany. She describes herself as a "physician, toxicologist, pharmacologist and nutrient biochemist." She has doctorates in three of those fields. She was chief toxicologist for the FDA for two years in the late 1970s.

What is important to us is that she has been researching the molecular biology of cancer **since 1979**. She has found that many nutritional substances can **inhibit specific functions** in cancer cells. We'll look at some examples of her discoveries in a minute.

A Delicious Irony

Dr. Flavin was married to the Director of Molecular Biology at Roche Group, the European conglomerate that includes Hoffman-La Roche, Inc., one of the largest pharmaceutical companies in the world. She says her divorce was at least partially caused by her **success at treating cancer with nutrition** and **her husband's jealousy** about that. Doesn't God work in mysterious and wonderful ways his wonders to perform?

An Advisor to the NCI

Dr. Flavin-Koenig is an **advisor to the National Cancer Institute** (NCI) in the U.S. She is working on a data bank for the NCI that will catalog the molecular biology of each cancer type along with a central information source for new treatments.

She treats **numerous cancer patients** successfully in Europe. One of them was one of my readers in Ireland, who gave her my e-mail address. Dr. Flavin-Koenig called me on the phone in August 2002. We talked for over an hour. Since then, she has sent me several long e-mails describing her successful treatments.

Dr. Flavin-Koenig's Treatments

Before I tell you her methods, I need to define a couple of two-bit words for you that are essential to understand them:

APOPTOSIS: Cell death programmed by a particular set of genes. In an earlier chapter, I "popularized" this concept by describing these genes as the "suicide" and "proofreader" genes. Another gene, called "bcl-2," inhibits this process. Cancer patients want apoptosis to happen to their cancer cells **pronto.**

ANGIOGENESIS: The development of a vascular network providing blood and nourishment to a new cancer colony. Obviously, cancer patients want to **disrupt** this process by whatever means. Two substances you may have heard of, and which I'll cover later, which purport to do this are shark cartilage and pau d'arco tea.

Dr. Flavin-Koenig recommends, based on her own observations of cancer cell activity in the biological lab and **23 years** of treatment of cancer patients:

BETA CAROTENE, which is Vitamin A in plant form. Dosage: 200 mg per day. She calls this the most important treatment (after stopping smoking) that she uses. It inhibits the "bcl-2" gene (see above) and makes cells **more sensitive to immune therapy**, as well as chemo and hyperthermia. Yes, Dr. Flavin-Koenig uses low-dose chemo, but **only to treat lung and colon cancer** but says *"it is not enough alone."*

VITAMIN A in cod liver oil, which also has Vitamin D. Dosage: one gram a day. This "limits the rate of DNA synthesis and **causes apoptosis** (see above) in most tumors — colon, prostate, sarcoma, lung, breast, etc."

[Note: Synthetic Vitamin A and that found in fish oils, like cod liver oil, can be **toxic if taken in excess**. Beta carotene is not toxic.]

SOY PRODUCTS (a controversial subject) "inhibit the receptors for hormones" and are therefore **effective in treatment of prostate cancer**.

FISH OIL. Dosage: 4 grams a day. It **inhibits angiogenesis** and the "ras" gene that feeds tumor growth. [Dr. Flavin-Koenig had not heard of Dr. Johanna Budwig until I mentioned her. She was interested and will research Dr. Budwig's flaxseed oil/cottage cheese protocol.]

N-ACETYLCYSTEINE. Dosage: 600 mg, 3 times a day. It inhibits angiogenesis, transforms "bcl-2" into "bax" [another gene], which **"makes it pro-apoptosis**. It also increases T-killer cells and binds with [gets rid of] nitric oxide which suppresses the immune system and stimulates tumor growth."

SODIUM SELENITE. Dosage: 400 micrograms a day. It inhibits the protein Kinase C. It should not be taken at the same time as Vitamin C.

VITAMIN C. Dosage: 3-5 grams a day spread through the day or 3 grams a day combined with 5-7 grams by IV twice a week. It increases hydrogen peroxide in the tumor cells [which **kills them**].

LACTOFERRIN. Dosage: 1 gram dissolved slowly in mouth at bedtime. It **inhibits angiogenesis** and binds with iron to decrease tumor growth. It also has anti-viral activity.

BROMELAIN - Dosage: 1 capsule 4 times a day. It also **inhibits angiogenesis**. It is an enzyme extracted from pineapples.

WOBE MUGOS (called "Wobenzymes" in the U.S.) - An enzyme mixture that **enhances the immune system** and helps block tumor growth, especially in colon cancer.

INDOMETHACIN - May require a prescription. It blocks the Prostaglandin E2 (PGE2) and ornithine decarboxylase. Both of these play a major role in angiogenesis and **tumor growth plus metastasis**.

DEVIL'S CLAW - A somewhat less effective substitute for above. Take 3 times a day.

THUJA - For cervical cancer. It is an anti-viral plant that comes in tincture form.

Some General Guidelines

For Prostate Cancer: Green tea and lots of soy products to reduce hormone receptors. Use melatonin - 9 mg - at night.

No Vitamin E except "succinate." Other types of Vitamin E protect tumors.

No iron, no B complex, no zinc.

Eat lots of fish (no shellfish — too much cholesterol), limited eggs, chicken, turkey. Eat all vegetable dishes, with olive oil.

No red meat and no unsaturated fatty acids. Instead olive oil and butter. Butter has butyric acid that **prevents DNA synthesis** (which is good). This is also found in wheat bran and figs.

Dr. Flavin-Koenig is constantly searching internationally for treatments including chemo, plants, teas, vitamins, hyperthermia, etc. Because of her encyclopedic knowledge she often consults with colleagues in hospitals **all over Europe** and with **MD Anderson and others in the U.S**. She is currently testing a tea from Turkey that cured liver metastases from kidney cancer. She is writing a cookbook for cancer patients.

My admiration for this lady is on two levels. First, of course, we share a common view about the proper treatment for cancer and a **zeal** to get this message to others. Second, though, is her **extreme integrity**. She lives a very modest life style, drives an old car and uses what money she has to support the treatment of her cancer patients who cannot afford it.

She has recently told me that she is so busy, it may be some time before she gets her cancer cookbook completed. My readers had been bugging her for information, so she sent me her list of "Foods to Avoid" and "Foods to Eat" for the cancer patient. Here are her two lists:

Foods To Avoid For Cancer Patients

SUGAR!!!!
- All drinks with sugar or phosphorus (e.g. soda pop, colas, soft drinks)
- Candies, cakes, cookies, etc.
- Ice cream
- Chocolate
White flour
Beef
Pork
All organ meats (brain, stomach, testicles, heart, etc.)
Sausages, bacon, cold cuts (except those from chicken or turkey WITHOUT nitrites)
Unsaturated fatty acids (corn oil, sunflower oil, etc.)
Margarine
Fried foods
All fast foods
Potato chips, corn chips, tortilla chips, etc.
Coffee
Cigarettes (duh!)
Nitrates/Nitrites (in lots of processed food)
Iron supplements
Zinc supplements
Vitamin B supplements (except B-12 twice a week)
Amino acid tablets like ornithine, arginine, glutamine, tryptophan, histidine...

That's it! Think that leaves you starving? **No way!**

Foods To Eat For Fighting Cancer

Organic chicken and some turkey
Fish (especially salt water types)

Natural rice
Hard cheeses
Seeds and nuts
Almonds
Bitter almonds
Oranges and lemons (and fruit juices without sugar, fresh is best)
Figs
Apples
Grapes
Pineapple (very, very good)
Carrots and carrot juices
Parsley
Tomatoes
Broccoli
Cauliflower
Peppers (red and yellow)
Sprouts (especially wheat)
Onions
Chives
Garlic
All salads, leeks, potatoes
Root plants in general
Shiitake mushrooms
Maitake mushrooms
Vegetables of all sorts
Soy products (all are excellent-they block hormone receptors and growth receptors)
Whole grains
Wheat bran
Yogurt (without sugar)
Lentils (all types of beans - mung, garbanzo, etc. They contain metastasis inhibitors)
Olive oil
Butter
Mineral water with high sulphur level
All herbs (curcumin is excellent)
Sesame

Green tea, black tea, nettle tea
Black kummel
Honey with honeycomb

That's all she mentioned. However, remember this lady has not met Dr. Johanna Budwig, the other wonderful German doctor of cottage cheese/flaxseed oil fame [see above]. So, keep taking your FO/CC, by all means. Also, Stevia is a fine natural sweetener for anything.

The "Stockholm Protocol"

Before we go any further, I need to tell you about a nutritional **prevention and treatment regimen** called "The Stockholm Protocol."

In April, 1998 a study by researchers at the Wayne Hughes Institute in St. Paul, Minnesota reported their results with a new treatment they call **"EGF-Genistein."**

According to their study published in *Clincal Cancer Research*, Genistein actually **reversed human breast cancer** in mice and was found to be safe in small animals and monkeys.

What is Genistein? It's found in soy (soybean products) - tofu, soymilk, soy flour etc. (but not soy sauce). Could this be why breast cancer is **rare in Oriental women** (unless they live in the U.S. and eat our diet)?

Genistein is an isofalvone with steroid-like properties. Another study by Dr. Walter Troll at the NY University Medical Center showed breast cancer incidence in mice was **reduced by 50%** using Genistein. A study by Dr. Coral A. Lamartiniere of the University of Alabama found the incidence of mammary tumors in mice were reduced by 40%. He told an NCI symposium, *"This study is the first to show in vivo that Genistein can protect against chemically induced cancer."*

The same mechanism found in breast cancer cells is also seen in **prostate, ovarian, bladder, liver, lung and melanoma** cancers. Thus, the researchers believe that Genistein will also be effective against those cancers as well. In fact, Memorial Sloan Kettering researcher William Fair, M.D., is now studying Genistein and other nutrients in a clinical trial on prostate cancer at the normally **conservative and conventional** NYC institution. Remember how many drug company executives are on the Sloan Kettering Board of Directors?

Further, Dr. Karl Folkers of the University of Texas and a team of researchers in Europe reported that **changes in diet** and a specific list of nutrients **eliminated breast cancer** and prevented its recurrence. They called it the **"Stockholm Protocol."**

If you are interested in information about diet, nutrition and the Stockholm Protocol, you need to join **People Against Cancer**. Check out their very interesting website at:

http://www.PeopleAgainstCancer.com

Incidentally, these diets are not just for prevention. They are also for **treatment** of active cancers.

Diana Dyer

If you'd like another slant on this subject, take a look at **Diana Dyer's** website. It's at:

http://www.DianaDyerMSRD.com

Diana self-published her 54-page cancer and nutrition booklet in 1997. It's called *"A Dietician's Cancer Story."* It is now the best-selling cancer and nutrition book on amazon.com.

The former hospital dietician decided to learn everything she could about cancer and nutrition after a 1995 breast cancer diagnosis. Then she began testing recipes to see how realistic they were. She developed dozens of healthful, easy-
to-fix meals. Particularly popular are her **"SuperSoy"** and **"PhytoChemical"** shakes.

Dyer, a mother of two, credits the diet and daily exercise with keeping her free of cancer for the past **five years**. She has set up an endowment with proceeds from the booklet to help underwrite research about how good nutrition can prevent the recurrence of cancer. For the full story of this remarkable lady, check out the web site above

Summary

The more I read, the more convinced I become that what we put in our mouths, more than any other one thing, is the **cause** of any original cancer episode and of **recurrence**. We've talked a lot in these pages about supplements and we'll soon discuss enzyme therapy. Certainly, many of these substances can contribute to your recovery. However, the **best and cheapest** way to restore your body's metabolism to its natural balanced state and regain your health is to **eat right.**

Do you realize?

- o The average American consumes **152 pounds of sugar per year!** Don't believe it? Just take a look at your pantry. All that sucrose, corn syrup, caramel color and fructose is just sugar in disguise.

- o **Acrylamide**, a proven carcinogen (cancer causing agent), is only allowed in your drinking water at a level of **0.12 micrograms per serving** by the Environmental Protection Agency (EPA). McDonald's French Fries, large, 6 oz. serving, contain **72 micrograms or 600 times the EPA limit**. Burger King, Wendy's, KFC, etc. are just slightly lower. Still want that "super size?"

- o The **processed food** we eat has had virtually all the good nutrients, plus all the digestive enzymes, processed out of it. Our bodies **can't produce the enzymes** needed to digest this stuff [see below].

- o The Standard American Diet (SAD) is **highly acidic**. In a 300-page book called *"The pH Miracle,"* Dr. Robert Young, a microbiologist and nutritionist argues convincingly that the **most**

important marker of good health is the pH level. We'll discuss this in detail later.

.....and there's lots more evidence that we **eat** ourselves into degenerative disease.

Greens and Enzymes

Bob Davis Whips Cancer

In November 2001, I discovered Bob Davis and his story. He has inspired me. But he has also furnished me with a ton of information about Complementary and Alternative Medicine (CAM) treatments for cancer. He will share them with you, too. You can find them at his web site:

http://www.cancer-success.com

Here, in his own words, is his story:

"I'm 80 years old, and I've overcome cancer twice!

In April 1996, I went to the hospital as an outpatient for an x-ray. They found that I had massive cancer. I had a mass in my abdomen a foot wide and several inches thick. Further, I had several masses in my chest, some of them 'the size of soft balls.' It was also determined that I had cancer in my bone marrow. I was immediately converted into an 'in' patient and started on a very heavy chemotherapy program. I had chemo in April, May, and June, with no effect on the cancer. It seemed to thrive on the stuff.

It was the middle of June when my doctor told me that the chemo wasn't working. He later told me that another treatment would kill me. I knew that this was true because my body was ravaged by the chemo. I was curled up in a fetal position unable to sleep or eat. I was emaciated and had excruciating pain all through my body.

I asked my doctor what we were going to do. He said, 'Try..........something else.'

The previous February I had called a college chum who had devastating arthritis. He couldn't climb stairs or drive his car. I asked him how he was doing and he said 'Fantastic!' He told me that he was taking an herbal product and it had eliminated his arthritis in three weeks. I asked him what it was and he said 'Dried green barley leaves.' He gave me the 800 number and I ordered a bottle for my wife who has arthritis.

It was the middle of June as I mention above, that I received a phone call from the owner of the company that provides the dried green barley pills. She asked me how I was doing on the pills. I told her that I wasn't using them. I had gotten them for my wife and they helped her when she remembered to take them.

I then said the most fortunate thing I have said in my life. I said, 'I'm fighting another battle.' She asked me what it was and I told her that it was cancer. She said, 'Oh, Mr. Davis, You don't know do you?' I asked her what was it that I didn't know and she said, 'Don't you know that cancer and arthritis can't grow in an alkaline body?' I told her that I had never heard that before. To make a long story short, I started taking the pills and in ten days my cancer was 95% gone! My next CT scan showed no cancer in my body and I have been cancer free ever since.

I was checked last month and I am still cancer free. I still take 20 200 mg. tablets of dried green barley every day. It costs me a whopping 95 cents or so.

Since then I have adopted a 95% (I do have birthday cake with a grandchild now and then) vegan diet which I really like. I feel better than I have in 40 years. People say I look younger. I have 'lotsa' energy.

I am eager to share information on cancer treatment and general health issues. I do occasionally speak at meetings on several related subjects. My favorite subject is ENZYMES!!!!

Bob Davis
Alternative Cancer Treatment Support"

Bob means it. If you want more information from him, he has it and is **sharing it with you on his web site.** He calls himself a reporter, not an adviser, as I do.

He has been communicating with other cancer patients for five years. He sent me copies of **40 e-mail messages** on a wide variety of CAM topics. Much of it was news to me. He has said I can share any of it I like with you. I am doing just that in this edition of my e-book. Much of it is now at his new web site above.

Like another 80-year-old cancer survivor in my network, George Freaner, Bob is a **"nut" about enzymes.** Their enthusiasm has convinced this young buck (hey, I'm just barely 71!) to get up to speed on enzymes. I've read most of a telephone book-sized reference book called *"The Complete Book of Enzyme Therapy,"* by Dr. Anthony J. Cichoke. It is very interesting. Almost every malady you can think of can be traced to **one or another enzyme deficiency**.

There are over 3,000 different types of enzymes in our bodies. Interestingly enough, the stuff that cured Bob Davis' cancer, green barley, contains all 3,000 of them, according to the discoverer, Dr. Yoshihide Hagiwara. Even before finishing the first few chapters of the Enzyme "encyclopedia," I had my whole family, including me, on the same thing Bob took. If you want to try it, it is called "Barley Power" and is put out by a company called Green Supreme. It comes in a **200 tablet**

bottle for $14.99. Larger sizes are less. Order it by calling (800) 358-0777 (they're in Pennsylvania). You'll be very glad you did.

Another Source

If you would like to try a different source, go to:

http://www.ourhealthcoop.com

Look for their product called **"Greens Plus."** Their 90 veggie capsules with a variety of "greens" and other ingredients sell for $8.74.

Take Enough

Bob's experience points up one other very significant point. When you start on a therapy, **be sure you take enough** of it to have the effect you want. Bob takes 20 barley green tablets every day. No "half measures" for this lad (hey, he feels like a young stud of 40!).

By the way, neither Bob Davis nor I have any financial connection with Green Supreme (or any other products). I charge for my book (because I've found more people read it when they pay for it), but Bob's services are free.

Enzyme Therapy In Plain English

Want to read a fine article on the importance of enzyme therapy in the treatment of cancer? I have posted this article, in plain text, on my web site. Just go to:

http://www.getandstaywell.com/WhyEnzymes.htm

The Importance of pH

Remember the Green Supreme company owner's statement in Bob Davis' account of his treatment *"Don't you know that cancer and arthritis **cannot grow in an alkaline body?"*** What exactly did she mean by that?

Your body fluids vary somewhat throughout your day in the degree to which they are alkaline or acid [except your blood, which your body keeps within a narrow range by whatever means necessary]. The easiest way to determine whether your body is in an alkaline or acid state is to **test your saliva**.

At the same "800" number above I gave you for the "Barley Power," you can order a roll or two of **pH test strips**. An 8-foot roll costs about $5. Every morning and evening, you can put a **one-inch strip** under your tongue for a couple of seconds and it will show you where you are on the alkaline to acid scale. Ideal is around 7.2, which is a slightly alkaline state.

With our typical acid diet, most of you will find that your pH is 6.4 or less. If the Barley Power or similar enzyme booster products are working correctly, this should **correct quickly to an alkaline state** (above 7.0) and stay there as long as you continue to take the "Greens" tablets, capsules or powder.

If you'd like a lot more background and detail on this subject, you will find it in the book *"The pH Miracle: Balance Your Diet, Reclaim Your Health"* by Robert O. Young. It is available from amazon.com for $10.47 for the paperback version or $17.47 for the hardback. As one reviewer says: *"I feel Dr. Young is going after the underlying 'cause' of disease and not just traditionally treating an ill with a pill!"*

Dave Perkins on pH

Here is an inspiring story. I'm not plugging any of the water products offered at this site, but I think you will enjoy reading Dave Perkins account of his recovery from **"terminal"** cancer. Just go to:

http://www.betterwayhealth.com/cancer-survivor.asp

Dave Perkins' sentence *"Cancer doesn't thrive in an oxygenated body!!!!"* is a good segue into our next subject.

Exercise With Oxygen Therapy (EWOT)

A message from another prominent member of my great network of cancer researchers and crusaders, **Art Brown**, introduced me to a new therapy. Here's Art's message.

*"The [EWOT] acronym stands for **Exercise With Oxygen Therapy**. A person simply spends about **15 minutes a day** on a treadmill while **breathing pure oxygen**. The oxygen under pressure is what does the trick, being forced into the body while the exercise circulates it around. There is a certain O2 pressure [6 liters per minute] required, certain vitamins to take 1/2 hour ahead of time etc. People seem to be claiming all kinds of wonderful rejuvenating effects for this treatment, especially among the elderly. **Robert J. Rowen MD** of California is one of its strongest proponents. In his former state of Alaska, he was primarily responsible for getting the USA's first state-wide laws enacted that **protect alternative practitioners from relentless attack** by the conventional medical crowd.*

I can't help but think this type of therapy might be highly beneficial to cancer patients. It is well established that oxygen is one of cancer's worst enemies."

Here's more on it from the web site:

http://www.alkalizeforhealth.net/freshjuices.htm

"EWOT

William Campbell Douglass, M.D. highly recommends EWOT. Exercise With Oxygen Therapy (EWOT) is doing light exercise, such as on a treadmill or stationary bicycle, while breathing pure oxygen. EWOT produces the benefits of hydrogen peroxide therapy and you can do it at home. Set the O2 flow at 6 liters per minute, hook the little tube to your nose, and exercise at a moderate pace for 15 minutes while breathing pure oxygen. As part of your cancer prevention and health maintenance program, do this at least once a month. If you are ill with any disease, do EWOT more frequently. In particular, do EWOT after operations, chemotherapy, radiation treatment, x-rays, and burns. Every spa, clinic and health club in the country should offer EWOT."

Find a doctor in your area interested in oxygen therapy at

http://www.oxytherapy.com

You will find a ton of information about oxygen and ozone therapies at the above web site.

.....And here's another web site with lots of information on this topic:

http://www.geocities.com/SoHo/Gallery/6412/EWOT.htm

Don't miss Art Brown's own web site. He is a **cancer crusader** who has written a book on the subject and has a very informative web site. Just go to:

http://www.alternative-cancer.net

Protocel/Cancell/Entelev & Graviola

In this section, I'll introduce you to two wonderful cancer survivors. They are both a part of my cancer "network." Both of them have indicated that they are happy to talk to you by e-mail if you have questions.

Tony Preston, Pancreatic Cancer Survivor

Tony Preston is a Senior Principal Engineer/Scientist with Atlantic Sciences and Technology as a contractor at Lockheed Martin Corporation. Read carefully what Tony says. He is a survivor of Stage IV pancreatic cancer (usually incurable at any stage). He feels so strongly about getting this information to other people that he has put up a web site with lots of links and Frequently Asked Questions (FAQs). Here's most of his January, 2002 letter to me:

"I wanted to send you this e-mail to tell you a little about my experience. I was supposed to be dead by last December.

I have pancreatic cancer. It spread to a lymph node just as I started chemo. I received Gemcitabine and Cisplatin, but that is not what has worked for me. I don't know if you have heard of Protocel (it was called Entleve, then the FDA got involved with an injunction, then Cancell, then another injunction, then with the Food Supplement Act around 1994, it is now legally sold).

I started taking it about two weeks after I was diagnosed. I had one chemo treatment. At that point my doctor noticed that the tumor on my groin lymph node was soft on top. Over the space of 3 or 4 weeks, it went from a hard tumor to a soft mush object. It eventually broke through the skin like a boil and drained a bright yellow fluid (waste proteins from the dead cancer cells). The tumor completely dissolved.

I have other tumors in my abdomen that may still be active cancer, but it is not spreading and my doctor is not sure if they are live tumors or just lumps of dead ones that my body hasn't cleaned out.

Protocel is low cost and easy to use. I take a 1/4 tsp every 4 hours (or 1/2 tsp every 8). It costs about $90 for a 2-month supply (comes as a concentrated dark liquid).

The concept of how it works is really simple. Normal cells produce an excess of energy with their metabolism. Cancer cells are defective and produce a lot less. Protocel will lower the energy production of the cells causing the cancer cells to not produce enough to maintain themselves. They die. Normal cells, because of their excess production, are hardly affected.

It is totally ncn-toxic (been tested) and the only side effect normally is to get flu-like symptoms for a few days when you first take it. I am looking forward to reading your book and also am a collector of information. I have my own web page that has some links with more information you might want to look at. It is:

http://mywebpages.comcast.net/apreston

Just click on the FAQ link.

Tony Preston
SR. Principal Engineer/Scientist
Atlantic Sciences and Technology Corp.
Lockheed Martin NE&SS
Threat System, Modeling & Simulation Analysis
Building 13000 A205-L"

By all means, visit his web site. Ignore the cosmetics. He says it is under construction. However, he does cover, **in detail**, his experience with Protocel, **the sources, the exact dosage, and the history of the testing** of this substance. He even has a month-by-month "diary" which is very interesting (including his wife's strenuous objections to his taking the Protocel). Don't miss the link he calls the **"Conspiracy."** It covers in great detail the cover up of the actual National Cancer Institute testing and other evidence by NCI and other government agencies and private corporations.

Bottom line: We're all in this together, folks…and we must **learn from each other**. You can't rely on any sources in the traditional medicine system to give you the information you need. **Scary, I know, but true!**

Tony Preston – Update

In June, 2002, I received another e-mail from Tony with an update on his cancer. I posted his letter on my web site. You need to **read it all**. Just go to:

http://www.getandstaywell.com/prestonltr.txt

Knowing you, my beloved readers, are an inquisitive bunch, I asked Tony a couple of follow-up questions, which he was kind enough to answer:

1. Are you continuing to take the Protocel, and, if so, for how long?

Tony's answer: *"I am still taking it. My CA 19.9 [pancreatic cancer tumor marker] is 100 so the cancer is not 100% gone. I will probably still take it after it goes to zero, for at least a year or two. After all, just because it is zero doesn't mean there is no cancer, just that **medical science cannot detect it**."*

2. Were you taking any other CAM substances in the past year or so?

Tony's answer: *"I did take MGN-3 for a month with no apparent effect (probably not long enough and I had not found a lot of the information on it like stuff on your site at that point).*

*I did run a little experiment with **Pau D'Arco tea**. I added it and compared my blood work after about 1 1/2 months. It had **no effect**, no real improvement. I had made it as strong as suggested in the info I found.*

*Both the Tea and Mgn-3 are compatible with Protocel, although the tea has **similar anti-oxidant properties** and probably tries to do the same thing as Protocel, which is why I did not see any benefit.*

I never took the GE-132, Pancreatin, and Bromaline supplements that many other people take with Protocel, My doctor had no objection to Protocel, but did to them. Also, any studies I found did not show them being successful with fighting cancer."

Latest Update from Tony Preston

On December 26 2002, I received the latest update from Tony.

"...a small update on my 'condition.' Here it is a year after I am supposed to be dead...;) I use Protocel and Graviola. Now, since i did not die on schedule, my doctor is saying I must not have had Pancreatic Cancer at all and now the type must be 'pseudomyxoma peritonei' as a possibility (false mucinous tumor of the peritoneum). It does fit some of the symptoms better than Pancreatic Cancer does (I was Stage IV, had a tumor on a lymph node which Protocel got rid of...). After all, nobody survives very long with Stage III pancreatic cancer, let alone Stage IV...

Well, I am sure that in a few months, a year, they will be 'updating' my condition to a new type that fits my current survival...

The funny part of all this is that they are basing it on the growth rate of the tumors (mostly not growing at all). They refuse to believe that Protocel or Graviola have any effects or benefits and so look at only half the information.

I am an electrical engineer and if I only looked at half the circuit, I would also be lost to find out why it did or did not work!

Best regards.

Tony Preston
Cancer is Curable, Ask me why!
apreston@comcast.net
2002-12-26"

Steve Finney – Protocel & Graviola

Next I would like you to meet Steve Finney. Steve is a Major Account Manager for Cisco Systems. Here is his letter to me:

*"Bill - Just a note of thanks for your 'labor of love' and for your ongoing work despite losing Marjorie. You must be a great friend to many people. I stumbled on your site after searching info on **Graviola**, as the many folks I am involved with who use Protocel (aka Cancell) have recently been made aware of this amazing extract from the Brazilian rainforests."*

[I'll give you some details on Graviola in the next section.]

Steve's letter continued:

*"I am 39 and was diagnosed with Stage 3 Anaplastic Astrocytoma **brain cancer** about 16 months ago, and after **taking Protocel for only 5 months**, the tumor is absolutely*

141

dead and does not enhance whatsoever. Two neuro-oncologists have told me they have never seen my kind of result, and I hear that so often now from others I just take it for granted. I am so grateful for Protocel, but I am real excited about it being used **in conjunction with Graviola**. I have heard of 2-3 cases already in which the two were used in conjunction and there was tumor disappearance in **literally days — serious tumors**.

It would be good to hear from you, but I wanted you to know that I admire your tenacity and love of people to go to the effort to do what you are doing. God bless, Steve Finney,"

Steve has said you can contact him if you have questions. His e-mail address is: sfinney@cisco.com

Graviola

My good friend George Freaner, another 80+ year old and 20+ year cancer survivor, was kind enough to send me an article on Graviola. You may have heard of this substance before, but I would like to remind you of it, because it is readily available without a prescription and it is quite **inexpensive (cheap!).**

Here's the article. It's from *"The Doctor's Complete Guide to Conquering Cancer,"* published by Agora Health Books of Baltimore, MD:

"Natural Cancer Fighter From the Amazon May be 10,000 Times Stronger Than Chemotherapy

Native medicine men in the Amazon have known about the Graviola tree for centuries. But cancer patients are just starting to learn about the benefits of the natural medicine it provides us with, which some say is more powerful than chemotherapy.

In as many as 20 laboratory studies over the last 30 years, Graviola has been found to selectively kill malignant cancer cells—cells from breast, colon, prostate, pancreatic and lung cancers specifically. In a 2000 study at the Catholic University in South Korea, two chemicals extracted from Graviola seeds showed cytotoxic results comparable to those of Adriamycin, a common chemotherapy drug. Another study, published in the Journal of Natural Products in 1996, found that Graviola killed colon cancer cells at '10,000 times the potency of Adriamycin.' Research at Purdue University found that leaves from the Graviola tree killed six different kinds of cancer cells, showing particular effectiveness against prostate cancer, pancreatic cancer, and lung cancer cells.

Proponents of Graviola report that it is able to selectively kill cancer cells without damaging healthy cells—and without serious side effects. Some users have reported gastrointestinal upset at high doses; this may be avoided, however, by taking Graviola with food. As a nutritional supplement, it is not subject to FDA approval and is available by mail order from Raintree Nutrition; tel. (800) 780-5902. Raintree supplies Graviola leaves, which can be made into a tea, as well as Graviola capsules. The recommended dosage varies from 1 gram to 5 grams of Graviola per day, or six to eight capsules daily. The cost for Graviola is about 20 cents per capsule."

Original Research

I usually don't quote from original research papers. Here's a sample from one on Graviola **which will show you why**:

"They are potent inhibitors of NADH: ubiquinone oxidoreductase, which is in an essential enzyme in complex I leading to oxidative phosphorylation in mitochondria. A recent report showed that they act directly at the ubiquinone-catalytic site(s) within complex I and in microbial glucose dehydrogenase. They also inhibit the ubiquinone-linked NADH

oxidase that is peculiar to the plasma membranes of cancerous cells."

And Now – In English

However, here is a quote from that same report on Purdue University's research on Graviola, which is a little more decipherable to us normal humans, and which is **quite significant**.

"In 1997, Purdue University published information with promising news that several of the Annonaceous acetogenins not only are effective in killing tumors that have proven resistant to anti-cancer agents, but also seem to have a special affinity for such resistant cells.' In several interviews after this information was publicized, Purdue pharmacologist Dr. Jerry McLaughlin, the lead researcher in most of Purdue's studies on the Annona chemicals [Graviola], says cancer cells that survive chemotherapy may develop resistance to the agent originally used against them as well as to other, even unrelated, drugs. 'The term multi-drug resistance (MDR) has been applied to this phenomenon,' McLaughlin says. He explains that such resistance develops in a small percentage of cancer cells when they develop a 'P-glycoprotein mediated pump' capable of pushing anti-cancer agents out of the cell before they can kill it. Normal cells seldom develop such a pump.

'If having this pump was such a good deal, all cells would have it. But all cells don't,' McLaughlin says in a statement from Purdue. 'In a given population of cancer cells in a person, maybe only 2% of the cancer cells possess this pump. But it's those 2% of cancer cells that eventually grow and expand to create drug-resistant tumors.' McLaughlin and his colleagues say some studies have tried to bypass these pumps by keeping them busy with massive doses of other drugs, like the blood pressure agent verapamil. In this way, it was hoped that some of the anti-cancer drugs would enter the cell and destroy it. But

this only caused potentially fatal side effects such as loss of blood pressure.

In the June [1997] issue of Cancer Letters, the Purdue researchers reported that the Annonaceous acetogenin, bullatacin, [Graviola] preferentially killed multi-drug resistant cancer cells because it blocked production of adenosine triphosphate, ATP — the chief energy-carrying compound in the body. 'A multi-drug resistant cell requires a tremendous amount of energy to run the pump and extrude things out of the cell,' McLaughlin says. 'By inhibiting ATP production, we're essentially pulling the plug on its energy source.' But what about the effect on ATP in normal cells? 'Normal cells and standard cancer cells may be able to minimize the effect of this compound because they don't require vast amounts of energy needed by the pump-running cells,' the Purdue researcher says.

'The resistant cell is using its extra energy for this pump as well as to grow, so it is really taxed for energy. When we mess with the energy supply, it kills the cell.'"

A good web site for more info on Graviola is:

http://www.graviola.org

Check it out!!

Four More Easy Self-Treatments

I will close this chapter with four more inexpensive and readily available cancer treatments. In the next chapter, I'll cover those that I DON'T recommend you try, at least not on your own (without a medical professional's supervision).

Red Raspberry Capsules

Why? What are the benefits? Raspberries, like many other fruits, contain ellagitannins, compounds that have been shown to have many health benefits, but **raspberries have the most.** These benefits include:

- ✓ Prevention of certain types of cell damage by carcinogens that result in cancer.
- ✓ Slowing of tumor growth.
- ✓ Inducement of natural cell death for cancer cells.

Would you believe that the American Cancer Society has even published information on red raspberries? Knowing what I do about their propaganda, that doesn't give me the greatest feeling of confidence.

However, if you would like to read a **true testimonial** from one of my readers, just go to:

http://www.getandstaywell.com/RedRaspberryTestimonial.txt

Call or e-mail Bob & Jackie Hall for more information on how and where to buy the red raspberry capsules. You can reach them at:
Phone: (707) 435-8434; Fax: (707) 371-4946; Email: ventures@jccomp.com
Approximate cost: $21.95 per month. They have a special of 6 bottles of 120 tablets of 1,000 mgs each for $17.95 per bottle.

Artemesinin

In late 2001, two bioengineering researchers at the University of Washington published their discovery of a **promising potential treatment** for cancer. Originating in the ancient arts of Chinese folk medicine, the **wormwood** herb derivative has been used for 30 years to treat malaria.

In the journal Life Sciences, Professor Harry Lai and his assistant Narendra Singh described how they targeted breast cancer cells with artemesinin. The results were indeed surprising. While only 25% of the cells were killed in the first eight hours, **virtually all of them were killed in 16 hours**.

"Not only does it appear to be effective, but it's very selective," Lai said. *"It's **highly toxic to the cancer cells**, but has a marginal impact on normal breast cells."*

Artemisinin works against malaria by reacting with the **high concentrations of iron** found in the malaria parasite. When artemisinin comes in contact with iron, a chemical reaction ensues, spawning charged atoms that chemists call "free radicals." The free radicals attack the cell membranes, breaking them apart and killing the single-cell malaria parasite.

About seven years ago, Lai began to hypothesize that the process might work with cancer, too.

"Cancer cells need a lot of iron to replicate DNA when they divide," Lai explained. *"As a result, cancer cells have much higher iron concentrations than normal cells. When we began to understand how artemisinin worked, I started wondering if we could use that knowledge to target cancer cells."*

Lai's work has been funded by a grant from the Breast Cancer Fund of San Francisco. However, artemisinin's **value is hardly limited to breast cancer**. In fact, an earlier study involving **leukemia** cells yielded even more impressive results. Those cells were **eliminated within eight hours**. A possible explanation might be the level of iron in the leukemia cells.

"They have one of the highest iron concentrations among cancer cells," Lai explained. *"Leukemia cells can have more*

then 1,000 times the concentration of iron that normal cells have."

Here are web sites with articles that will get you completely up to speed on this interesting substance:

http://www.cat007.com/curecancer.htm

http://www.newswise.com/articles/2001/11/CANCER.UWA.html

http://news.bbc.co.uk/1/hi/health/1678469.stm

http://www.annieappleseedproject.org/artemisinin.html

http://members.tripod.com/~altmedangel/cancherb.htm

Unlike some Chinese herbs, this one has **30 years** of Western scientific studies behind it and is used widely to treat malaria and hemorrhoids (it is anti-inflammatory) and is certainly non-toxic.

Fortunately for you, the University of Washington has patented Dr. Lai's idea. This just means that a pharmaceutical company probably can't pick it up, develop a synthetic form and sell it for **twenty times** as much.

Personal recommendation from the author: I've tried this product for about six weeks. I happened to start it two weeks after a blood test where my PSA (Prostate Specific Antigen) came back as **12.6** (it has been between 9.5 and 12.9 for about 15 years. After 15 days on the artemisinin, I happened to have another blood test. The PSA was **6.9**, the lowest it had been in 15 years.

Interestingly, when I told my urologist of this sequence of events, he was **not happy.** He knew nothing about artemisinin and felt that by varying what I was taking, I made it difficult for him to determine when to suspect prostate cancer. He alleged that "shrinking the prostate and/or reducing the PSA does not mean you won't get prostate cancer."

Since that exchange, which I found rather obtuse, I have **changed urologists**.

OK, so you're convinced that this substance is an interesting development in cancer treatment. Next question. How do you get it? Good question. I've looked at several sources, including Dr. Donsbach's "Canburst" and Hepalin 25. I have actually ordered one bottle of the **Hepalin 25** (at $56 a bottle for 30 100mg capsules — a one-month supply) and finished taking it.

Thanks to Dr. Russell K. Griffith, one of my alert readers, here's a very **inexpensive source** for artemisinin.

Artemesinin (100mg, 90 pills) can be obtained from Vitanet (Item no. 72160) for **$16.80.** That's where I get mine now. This is an Allergy Research Group product. Order at:

http://www.myvitanet.com/index.html

Instead of almost **$2 a day** from the Hepalin 25 source, it works out to **nineteen cents a day** at the recommended dosage of 1 pill per day.

Thank you, Dr. Griffith!

With a little luck, we may be able to get OurHealthCoop (see above) to stock artemisinin sometime soon. Their superior quality control procedures would certainly give me more security about the quality of the product.

Calcium

Calcium is an essential part of life. Bob Barefoot, in his book *"The Calcium Factor: The Scientific Secret of Health and Youth"* describes it as "the silver bullet" that conquers all degenerative disease.

I have "slogged through" both of Bob Barefoot's books on this subject. The other is called *"Death By Diet."* I find them both pedantic and very difficult for anyone to read and follow. I think this amount of detail on a relatively simple subject is **counter-productive**. In particular, his protocol on page 107 of *"Death By Diet"* is way too complicated and inferior to several simpler treatments mentioned above. I'm not a fan of Bob Barefoot, his "Coral Calcium" or the other supplements he sells in his books and on TV "infomercials."

However, the concept he champions that **calcium supplements** promote the **healthy alkaline state** in our bodies is a good one.

A better and simpler view is one I heard recently from Art Brown (remember him? – a charter member of my "vibrant network" club). Here's what Art has to say:

"For those calcium freaks (like myself) ever on the lookout for a good, high quality, absorbable form of this absolutely essential mineral, I recently stumbled across Crystal Calcium from the KAL Company. (KAL was founded in 1932.)

Hard to contain my enthusiasm here! The importance of calcium's ability to alkalinize in cancer care is established. Not to mention the hundreds of other roles it has in the body.

Crystal Calcium is a ready-to-go pre-ionized form of calcium. So, the body doesn't need to work at breaking down supplements like calcium carbonate in the stomach trying to pry out the calcium ion. I know this is a significant problem with *many people - especially me. A loose white powder, it disappears in a glass of water. Talk about bang for the buck! Would you believe just $12 for 2/3 of a pound?!*

Personal experience alone, but results were noticed immediately. Best stuff I've found in 20 years."

Want to try some? Just go to:

http://www.myvitanet.com

...and enter a search for "Crystal Calcium." It sells at that site for $9.10 for a 300 gram bottle. A real deal!

[Again, neither Art Brown nor I have any financial interest in any of the products we recommend.]

Beta Sitosterol

If you are a human bean of the male persuasion, I have a suggestion for you. **Pay attention to your prostate!** Next to heart problems and lung cancer, prostate cancer is the leading cause of death among men. Most of us my age (71) are coping with an enlarged prostate, formally known as Benign Prostate Hyperplasia (BPH).

Thanks to my friend Cy Bursuk, a nutritional consultant in Tucson, I have discovered Roger Mason and his book "The Natural Prostate Cure." Every man should read this book. It is the **most complete explanation** of the effect of hormones and supplements on male health in general and prostate health in particular I have ever read. In just 72 pages, he explains **why** your prostate grows larger as you age. He also destroys many of the myths about hormone therapy (for both men and women) and the effects of various substances (including hormones) on your prostate.

What is most interesting about this book is that the author, uniquely among living or dead "experts," has **read EVERY study** on the subject ever published, regardless of language. He did this by reviewing every entry in Chemical Abstracts (known as the "chemist's bible"). This tome contains every published medical article of importance from every scientific journal in the world. In a year of **tough, grinding research**, mostly at the National Institutes of Health Medical Library (the largest such library in the world) in Bethesda, Maryland, he read every one, even getting those **translated** from a foreign language, where necessary. Well documented conclusions? You bet!

How much does this book cost? $6.95 from amazon.com. Or, nothing, if you order, as I did, a couple of bottles of **Beta Prostate**. This product, recommended by Cy, is apparently unique in its content of the key ingredient "Beta-sitosterol" needed for prostate health, whether or not you have detectable

Time needed to see improvement: less than an hour.

2) *GET TO VITAMIN C SATURATION*, which is indicated by bowel tolerance. That means, take a few thousand milligrams of vitamin C every ten minutes until you get, or feel like you are about to get, diarrhea. This will both clean you out and jump-start your immune system. Vitamin C in quantity is the best broad spectrum antitoxin, antibiotic and antiviral there is.

Time needed to see improvement: less than a day.

3) *GET TO WATER AND CAROTENE SATURATION*. This can be simultaneously achieved by twice daily juicing a big stack of vegetables, such as carrots and any green or orange vegetable. Yes, green as well as orange veggies are absolutely loaded with carotene. Yes, you really do have to drink it. What are you afraid of? When's the last time a person died of vegetable overdose? Saturation of carotene is reached when your skin turns a partial-pumpkin, lovely orange-tan color. Called 'hypercarotenosis,' it is harmless. Looks cool, too, much like a suntan. Abundant water intake is guaranteed by abundant juicing. When your tummy is full of juice and you have to urinate a lot, you are at water saturation.

Inside your skin, you are an aquatic animal. Water is good. Veggie juice is better. If you are worried about getting enough trace minerals, relax. Most are amply found in the vegetables.

Time needed to see improvement: less than a week.

If you think I have lost what's left of my marbles, think again. I have never been more serious. When I work with very sick people, the first 'homework' I give is to go flush, reach bowel tolerance, hydrate, and turn orange. Sounds preposterous, doesn't it. But people who do so feel better immediately. Their *tests improve immediately. And they learn something of lasting practical value."*

Go thou and turn orange!

$$$$ For Your Treatments

Virtually everything we have discussed in this chapter – supplements, tests, IPT clinical treatment, etc. – is **not reimbursed by insurance**. Here's some information that may help.

Have you heard of something called **"viatical settlements?"** Neither had I. A viatical settlement is the **sale of a life insurance policy** issued on the life of a person who, in this context, is called a "viator." It is based on a law passed by Congress that went into effect on January 1st, 1997. It is called "The Health Insurance Portability and Accountability Act of 1996."

The person on whose life the policy is written does not have to be the "owner" of the policy. For example, a spouse may be the "owner" of the policy and/or the beneficiary.

What is important is that there are options available to **get money NOW** out of a life insurance policy. That money may be more useful now than after the death of the person on whom the policy is written. What is really ironic is that the money obtained in this manner **may actually extend the life** of the "viator" for many years. [Hint: Don't let the people buying your policy know how effective the "alternative" treatments are that you will be taking!]

The procedure, which amounts to selling the policy to a third party, covers all types of life insurance policies — term, whole life, "key-man" policies, buy/sell agreement policies and so on. Basically, someone is **buying the life insurance** benefit at something less than the full amount payable on the covered person's death (50-85%, depending on life expectancy).

For "seniors" 70 or older, the policy can be sold **regardless of the insured's health**. Generally, the proceeds of the sale are **tax-free**. Obviously, some paper work and time is involved, so **don't delay**. If you are interested in further information, here's a toll-free number to call to get a brochure from one company that specializes in this (it's not the only one). The number to call is (888) 321-9057. It's a company called Viatical Settlement Professionals, Inc. in Richmond, Virginia. They also have a web site (who doesn't?). It's at:

http://www.vspi.com

Mexican Cancer Clinics

Several years ago, when I first began researching cancer causes and cures, I heard about all the clinics in Mexico. Frankly, I felt less than enthused about them. Probably quacks and charlatans preying on cancer victims, I thought.

Wrong!!

After reading dozens of testimonials written by ecstatically grateful cancer patients cured in Mexican clinics, I have become a believer. Read some of the stories of dedicated physicians like Drs. Clark and Gerson, who have been hounded out of this country by our FDA/AMA "gestapo," and opened clinics in Mexico. You will become a believer, too.

Here is some information from an article by Art Brown titled "Mexican Hospitals - Some of the World's Best for Alternative Cancer Care." It was written in January, 2001. The entire article can be found at The Cancer Cure Foundation's web site: http://www.cancure.org

"Most people do not tend to think of Mexico as a haven for cancer treatment, but there are approximately 40 clinics and hospitals there offering some of the finest alternative medical treatments for cancer today. They vary in size from one-doctor operations to modern, multi-story, full-service hospitals with an extensive range of doctors on staff. Most are located close to the Mexican/American border across from San Diego, California. Some are even within walking distance of the border which avoids the need to wait in line in your car for half an hour at the border to clear customs. Although a passport or visa is not necessary, valid identification identifying your country of birth, such as driver's license, is required.

Why do patients go to these clinics and hospitals?

In Mexico, the political system is such that the government credits and inspects clinics and hospitals, but does not attempt to get in between the doctor and patient. In short, it leaves doctoring to doctors. This means they are free to use treatments from countries around the world which have proven successful in battling cancer. They can also develop and perfect their own treatments and immediately use therapeutic breakthroughs as soon as they become available.

Not so in the United States where cancer treatments are usually limited to varieties of chemotherapy, radiation and surgery. This is unfortunate as there are about 100 other useful, non-toxic cancer treatments, almost all of which have well-documented scientific evidence to support them.

Having freedom-of-choice regarding treatments, Mexican doctors have been able to develop their skills in using both conventional and alternative therapies, schooling their staffs in them and setting up appropriate patient care facilities. In addition, over the years they've learned which treatments, or combination of treatments, work best for which conditions.

An unusual 'sub-specialty' in cancer care has arisen in Mexico out of all this. Although hospitals there get patients from around the world, the majority come from the United States (This is another reason they locate close to the border.) These people typically have received conventional cancer treatments where they live without success. Frequently they are very sick with bodies severely weakened by surgery, radiation or chemotherapy. As a result, Mexican clinics and hospitals have become accustomed to helping patients with extra burdens. Not only must they treat end-stage cancer for people coming to them as a last resort, which is a task far more difficult than in the earlier stages, but they must also undo the damage done by conventional 'therapies.'

Best of the Best

Not all clinics and doctors in Mexico are worthwhile of course. We recommend only the best of the best. That is, those we feel are the most experienced, reputable and reliable - large or small. We have toured many facilities, talked to the staff, are familiar with their operations and talked to patients. Typically, they've been around for many years. One in particular has treated over 100,000 cancer patients with alternative treatments in the last 35 years. A record like that speaks for itself. (Call us to arrange a free consultation with a doctor from that particular hospital.) For more information and recommendations, phone (800) 282-2873, or (805) 498-0185 M-F, 9-5, Pacific time."

You may want to look into tours of these clinics. There are at least two agencies in California who offer organized tours. Detailed information on each of these is in the book "Third Opinion." Here is some brief contact information:

Private Cancer Clinic Tours
P. O. Box 530218
San Diego, California 92153
Phone: (619) 475-3834

Gentle, non-toxic treatments

Contact person: Roberto Rodriguez

Tour of Tijuana, Mexico Clinics
P. O. Box 4651
Modesto, California 95352-4651
Phone: (209) 529-4697
Contact person: Frank or Rosario Cousineau

Free Medicine

Can't afford the expensive medication your doctor prescribes for you? Here's a solution from a new reader named Bill McLaughlin. Bill brought to my attention a web site called:

http://www.themedicineprogram.com

These wonderful volunteers are dedicated to helping you wade through the paperwork to get your prescription medication (not alternative stuff) free. The criteria:

- That you do not have insurance coverage for outpatient prescription drugs.

- That you do not qualify for a government program which provides prescription medication, e. g. Medicaid.

- That your income is at a level that causes a hardship when you are required to purchase the medication at retail.

That last can vary widely, depending on the drug company. Some cancer patients, for example, have incomes as high as $60,000 per year and still get free prescription medication from this program.

Yes, this is **drug company largesse**. And you can bet it is done for a purpose. The primary purpose is to convince lawmakers of their "sincerity" in looking out for your interests.

Hmmmm. Their view of the **naivete of our lawmakers** is not encouraging, but, unfortunately, probably true.

Here's a quote from an article about this program in the July 28, 2000 Wall Street Journal:

"'In my opinion, they want to keep it a secret,' says Cindy Hogg, administrator for The Medicine Program, a private advocacy group in Doniphan, Mo., which helps patients navigate the free drug application process. 'They do it so they can tell Congress, "We give away medicine for free," but then they don't tell anybody about it and make it hard for people to apply."

Well, Cindy Hogg and the other Medicine Program volunteers are dedicated to helping you navigate through this application process. Again, contact them at this web site:

http://www.themedicineprogram.com

Here's another quote from the Wall Street Journal article that will give you a feel for the size of this program.

"...the nation's drug companies gave away 2.8 million prescriptions (this doesn't include drug samples) valued at about $500 million in 1998. By comparison, U.S. prescription drug sales reached $125 billion last year, according to IMS Health."

Says Bill McLaughlin, *"It works. And free hearing aids are also available."*

CHAPTER 6 – OTHER TREATMENTS YOU SHOULD KNOW ABOUT

"First, do no harm"
Hippocrates (400 B.C.)

There are a whole slew of cancer treatments out there touted by **credible experts** and **not-so-credible amateurs**. Many of these are quite effective **IF** a medical professional at a clinic where you are under constant supervision administers them. Others are just not proven to be effective or they are inferior to other readily available treatments or they are too expensive.

You will probably hear about each of these at some time during your journey. It is just as helpful, in my opinion, for you to know about those that are not as effective or which require professional supervision as those above in the self-treatment chapter. The goal is to make you an **expert "co-doctor."**

Laetrile/Amygdalin/Vitamin B17

A good example is Laetrile. I believe that Laetrile has helped thousands of cancer patients since it was first discovered in 1953. First, some background.

World Without Cancer

The best book I have found on the subject of Laetrile is *"World Without Cancer"* by G. Edward Griffin, first published in 1974. It has been through **many updates** including 15 printings since then — the most recent in **March 2000**. He has exhaustively researched the **history and science of Laetrile**

(B17). He has personally researched the reason the FDA banned Laetrile. Once you read this book, you will no longer believe in the **"protection"** being provided you and me by agencies like the FDA, the American Medical Association (AMA), and the American Cancer Society (ACS).

If you would prefer to hear audio excerpts from this book, just go to:

http://www.cancure.org/audios.htm

You will find four 30-minute audio clips (using Real Player software, which you can download free) on the subject by Ed Griffin, the author of "World Without Cancer."

If you go to the cancure home page (above) and type in B17 in the search engine, a number of articles will come up. The first one covers both sources of the B17 capsules and apricot seeds and clinics all over the world that use this as part of their cancer cure protocol, complete with phone numbers.

Edward Griffin documents the suppression of Laetrile and its advocates for what it is — a **conspiracy** to prolong the superb profits of the **"cancer industry."** The book contains very persuasive evidence that **Laetrile works**. This includes many case studies with the **names and hometowns** of the individuals. I will quote just one to give you an idea of the power of this book:

"WILLIAM SYKES

In the fall of 1975, William Sykes of Tampa, Florida, developed lymphocytic leukemia plus cancer of the spleen and liver. After removal of the spleen, his doctors told him that he had, at best, a few more months to live.

Although chemotherapy was recommended — not as a cure but merely to try to delay death a few more weeks — Mr. Sykes chose Laetrile instead. In his own words, this is what happened:

'When we saw the doctor a few weeks later, he explained how and why Laetrile was helping many cancer patients, and suggested that I have intravenous shots of 30 cc's of Laetrile daily for the next three weeks. He also gave me enzymes and a diet to follow with food supplements.

In a few days I was feeling better, but on our third visit the doctor said that he could no longer treat me. He had been told that his license would be revoked if he continued to use Laetrile. He showed my wife how to administer the Laetrile, sold us what he had, and gave us an address where more could be obtained.

The next week I continued on the program and was feeling better each day. One afternoon the doctor from Ann Arbor called to ask why I had not returned for the chemotherapy. He said I was playing "Russian Roulette" with my life. He finally persuaded me to return for chemotherapy, so I went to Ann Arbor and started the treatments. Each day I felt worse. My eyes burned, my stomach felt like it was on fire. In just a few days I was so weak I could hardly get out of bed… The "cure" was killing me faster than the disease! I couldn't take it any longer, so I stopped the chemotherapy, returned to my supply of Laetrile and food supplements, and quickly started feeling better. It took longer this time as I was fighting the effects of the chemotherapy as well as the cancer…

In a short time I could again do all my push-ups and exercise without tiring. Now, at 75 years of age [20 years after they said I had only a few more months to live], I still play racquet ball twice a week.'"

In a letter to Edward Griffin, the author of "World Without Cancer," dated June 19, 1996, Mrs. Hazel Sykes provides this additional insight:

"After Bill had conquered cancer, a doctor came to him one day. (This was an M.D. who gave chemotherapy in a well-known hospital.) He wanted to know how Bill had conquered his cancer because his wife was quite ill with cancer. Bill said: 'Why don't you give her chemotherapy?' His answer was: 'I would never give chemotherapy to any of my friends or family!' He was not the only doctor who came to Bill with the same question."

The Doctor is "In"

A large number of M.D.s have weighed in with opinions on the use of Laetrile to control cancer. Here are a few examples:

In 1994, **P. E. Binzel, M.D.** published his results from treating cancer patients with Laetrile between 1974 and 1991. He used a combination of intravenous and oral Laetrile. Intravenous doses started with 3 grams and worked up to 9 grams. After a period of months, oral Laetrile, 1 gram at bedtime, was begun in place of he injections. Dr. Binzel also used various nutrient supplements and pancreatic enzymes, as well as a low animal protein, no junk food diet as part of his regimen for cancer patients.

Out of a series of 180 patients with primary cancer (non-metastasized or confined to a single organ or tissue), 138 were still alive in 1991 when he compiled his treatment results. At that time, 58 of the patients had been followed for 2 to 4 years, while **80 had a medical follow-up from 5 to 18 years**. Of the 42 patients who had died by 1991, 23 died from their cancers, 12 from unrelated causes, and 7 died of "cause unknown."

Among his **metastatic** cancer patients, 32 of 108 died from their disease, while 6 died of unrelated causes, and 9 died of "cause unknown." Of his 61 patients still alive in 1991, 30 had a follow-up between 2 and 4 years, while **31 had been followed for 5 to 18 years.**

Binzel's results are impressive. Some of the individual patients discussed in his book were still alive (and well!) **15-18 years** after their initial Laetrile treatment. Binzel also notes that **none** of the cancer **diagnoses** were made by him, a small town, "family doctor." All patients had diagnoses from **other physicians**. Many had already suffered the **ravages of standard "cut-burn-poison"** (surgery/radiation/chemotherapy) medicine before being given up as **hopeless** cases by orthodox doctors.

His book is called *"Alive and Well,"* by P. E. Binzel, M.D. published by American Media in 1994 at Westlake Village, California.

If you would like to read an extract from this book that includes Dr. Binzel's detailed instructions on how to administer B17 in both intravenous and capsule form, just go to this web site:

http://members.lycos.co.uk/g0cge/index.html

Manuel Navarro, M.D., former professor of medicine and surgery at the University of Santo Tomas in Manila wrote in 1971: *"I...have specialized in oncology for the past eighteen years. For the same number of years I have been using Laetrile-amygdalin in the treatment of my cancer patients. During this eighteen year period I have treated a total of over five hundred patients with Laetrile-amygdalin by various routes of administration, including the oral and the I.V. The majority of my patients receiving Laetrile-amygdalin have been in a terminal state when treatment with this material commenced.*

It is my carefully considered clinical judgment, as a practicing oncologist and researcher in this field, that I have obtained most significant and encouraging results with the use of Laetrile-amygdalin in the treatment of terminal cancer patients, and that these results are comparable or superior to the results I have obtained with the use of the more toxic standard cytotoxic agents."

This quote is from the book *"World Without Cancer"* by G. Edward Griffin, mentioned above and in Appendix A to this book.

Dr. Ernesto Contreras of Tijuana, Mexico has used Laetrile as a cornerstone of his cancer practice since 1963. He remarks that *"For the prevention of cancer and the maintenance of remission, there is nothing as effective as Laetrile...Its non-toxicity permits its use indefinitely while surgery, radiation and chemotherapy can only be administered for a limited time...the majority of cancers that occur more frequently, such as cancers of the lung, breast, colon, ovaries, stomach, esophagus, prostate, and the lymphomas, are much helped by Laetrile."*

This quote is from a book called *"An Alternative Medicine Definitive Guide to Cancer,"* published in 1997 by Future Medicine, Tiburon, California.

Dr. Hans Nieper is a world famous oncologist in Germany. He is the developer of the standard anti-cancer cytotoxic drug cyclophosphamide. In 1970, he co-authored a brief paper on Laetrile with Dean Burk, in which he stated that *"...in the treatment of cancer, the active principle of nitrilosides is to be used mainly in prophylaxis* [prevention] *and early protective therapy... On the other hand, the complete atoxicity* [lack of toxicity] *of this method of treatment, which is maybe nothing else but a rediscovered natural principle, permits the unlimited use of this substance."*

This quote is from a paper entitled *"Problems of Early Cancer Diagnosis and Therapy,"* published in 1970 in the German periodical Aggressologie, Volume 11, page 1-7.

In 1972, Dr. Nieper told reporters while in the U.S.: *"After more than 20 years of such specialized work, I have found the non-toxic Nitrilosides – that is, Laetrile – far superior to any other known cancer treatment or preventive. In my opinion it is the only existing possibility for the ultimate control of cancer."*

This last quote is from *"World Without Cancer,"* mentioned above.

Many of the physicians whose anti-cancer programs are detailed in "The Alternative Medicine Definitive Guide to Cancer," mentioned above, also report positive Laetrile results as part of their cancer treatment programs. **Robert Atkins, M.D.**, the "Diet Revolution" guru, notes that *"Amygdalin appears to neutralize the oxidative cancer-promoting compounds such as free radicals... It's just one more key component keeping cancer from growing or spreading. Contrary to what people have said about Laetrile...it should be considered an effective, entirely safe treatment for all types of cancer."*

Why Not Self-Treat With Laetrile?

In the face of the above evidence and doctor's recommendations, why don't I include Laetrile/Amygdalin/Vitamin B17 in the "Self-Treatment" chapter of this book? Here are the reasons:

Laetrile's use to cure cancer needs to be part of a **complete protocol** of diet, enzymes, exercise and supplements, AND supervised by a medical professional.

For example, a proper level of zinc in the body is required for Laetrile to be effective. It doesn't work without adequate Vitamin C. Vitamin A interferes with its effects. A build-up of vitamins, enzymes and a proper diet for at least two weeks before starting the Laetrile treatment is necessary. A full stomach lessens the effect of Laetrile. Finally, the dosage of Laetrile requires injections along with capsules. The reaction must be monitored closely and the dosage adjusted over a period of at least three weeks after the body has been prepared properly to receive the Laetrile. Definitely not a "do-it-yourself" operation.

Other treatments, which I do suggest to you as **universally necessary** for cancer patients include things you can do yourself with no supervision. These include: MGN-3, beta glucan, other immune system boosters like Oncolyn and BCI-26, flaxseed oil/cottage cheese, Vitamin C with L-Lysine and L-Proline, Protocel, Graviola, red raspberry capsules, artemisinin, enzymes, Ph testing and a strict, macrobiotic diet. (See Chapter 5 above.) None of these interfere with any other treatments you may be taking or with each other.

Please don't misinterpret me. I'm not saying that any cancer patient should **self-treat their cancer**. All of the above are treatments that would be appropriate for **all of us** – cancer patients or not — and cannot be harmful, no matter what else you are doing. It is treatment **"until the doctor comes."** Literally, while you are locating an appropriate physician or other medical professional with an acceptable treatment regimen, you can help yourself by doing all of the above, except the Laetrile.

In Summary

Laetrile (amygdalin) is an effective preventative and treatment for cancer. It should be used under the supervision of a qualified medical professional.

Shark Cartilage

Another treatment you should be familiar with, but which I would wait to discuss with your chosen CAM medical professional is shark cartilage. Beginning in October 1991, Dr.

Williams has published **numerous articles** on this subject in his *Alternatives* newsletter.

I feel the best way to familiarize you with this option, however, is to quote from an article by the **discoverer** of shark cartilage, **I. William Lane, Ph. D.** When I called Lane Labs, the sole source for both MGN-3 and shark cartilage, recently to check on their relationship to Dr. Lane, I got his son on the phone. He said that while his father had no financial interest in Lane Labs, he did consult with them frequently on the products they produce, including shark cartilage.

Dr. Lane began studying shark cartilage as a potential cancer therapy in September 1983. **Using his own funds**, he conducted studies in Belgium and Mexico. Studies in the United States were too expensive. However, in September 1992, he aroused the interest of the **Cuban Health Ministry**. They invited him to do a study on **non-responsive terminal** cancer patients. Here is an excerpt from an article he wrote in 1995 for *Alternative & Complementary Therapies — A Bimonthly Publication for Health Care Practitioners:*

*"The Cubans agreed to provide me with 29 patients and a team of five oncologists, seven nurses, and the best possible follow-up. The Cuban study has, as a result of **extensive coverage** and story by **Mike Wallace and '60 Minutes,'** become a legend.*

*These 29 patients were all **unable to get out of bed**, and all were designated as **terminal and dying**. They had **failed to respond** to all available conventional cancer therapy. I almost gave up on the first day. I felt that my **chances** with such advanced patients were **nil**, a belief shared by the Cuban oncologists, headed by Lt. Col. Jose Menendez, M.D.*

*There were 10 different tumors represented including five in the **prostate**, six in the **breast**, five in the **central nervous system**, two in the **stomach**, two in the **liver**, two in the **ovary**,* two in the **uterus**, two in the **esophagus**, two in the **tonsils**, and one in the **urinary bladder**. By the **fifth week** I learned via my telephone and fax that the Cuban team was becoming **very hopeful**. I was due to visit on the sixth week.

Earlier, I had been contacted by **CBS and '60 Minutes.'** The station wanted to go ahead with the story, which the station had **initially looked upon as a scam**. For the visit on the sixth week of therapy, I, thus, was accompanied by **David Williams, D.C.**, the editor of the health newsletter **Alternatives**, five people from '60 Minutes' (including the **producer Gail Eisen**, who was **medically oriented** and initially **very negative** about the story), and Charles Simone, M.D., a consultant who I had asked to help me evaluate the results. It was clear to all of us that a number of the patients were **already responding**.

Except for Dr. Simone, who joined us at 16 weeks, this same group visited again at **11 weeks** and again at **16 weeks**. We were joined at this time by **Mike Wallace**, who stayed with us in Cuba for three days to review the results and to do filming.

At this time, the Cubans had added Fernandez Britto, M.D., a **world-class pathologist**, to the team. He showed, for the first time, **autopsy pathologic slides** that demonstrated the action of the shark cartilage in stimulating the rapid growth of fibrin tissue **replacing and encapsulating the cancer cells**. His slides, which now include **'before' and 'after' biopsy** slides, add materially to the explanation of how and if shark cartilage works.

'60 Minutes' later showed **X-ray pictures** along with blood work records to Eli Gladstein, M.D., of the University of Southwestern Texas for collaboration; Dr. Gladstein **confirmed the findings** and he did so **without knowing that shark cartilage was the therapeutic agent**.

*The '60 Minutes' team was so **excited** about these results that it broadcast the show **within 10 days** after their tape was finished; and they **showed it twice**, something that is rarely done. The team also promoted the story each time for four days prior to the broadcast.*

*Fortunately, this show had a budget that was large enough to truly **study the effects**, **see the patients**, and then **report on the positive results** they themselves observed. The **National Institutes of Health** (NIH), on the other hand, surprisingly, **never took the time to hear the whole presentation, see the slides, talk to me, or talk to the interested doctors.***

Isn't this a classic case of "not invented here?"

"Of the original 29 terminal patients, nine (31 percent) died of cancer, all within the first 17 weeks; none have died of cancer since; six others have died of accidents, heart failure, or other natural causes; 14 (48 percent) are completely well and cancer-free after 34 months (almost three years) as of June 15, 1995. After the 60 gm/day of shark cartilage for 16 weeks, these patients went to the maintenance dose of 20 gm/day, which appears to have been keeping them well for almost three years. With stage IV cancer patients, this is very impressive, even incredible, even if one or two patients might have been at stage III rather than stage IV at the outset.

All cancers had been biopsy-confirmed. The head Cuban oncologist, Dr. Menendez, told me recently, 'In my history as an oncologist, I have never seen or experienced anything like this response with shark cartilage.'"

Here are Dr. Lane's own words on his discovery.

"I am proud that I was willing to put my own money on the table to develop the shark cartilage therapy, and I will defend the results as will others who have seen the responses.

Peer review is a cornerstone of our system but other results, if well documented and supported, should not just be discarded and ridiculed.

The poor results with conventional cancer therapy should suggest that any new therapy that seems promising should be investigated, especially if it is inexpensive, nontoxic, and noninvasive. In these times of uncontrolled health costs, and the cancer epidemic that does not seem to be abating, all possibilities deserve attention."

Summary

Shark cartilage is readily available in health food stores and on the Internet. My concern about your self-treatment with it has to do with **dosage and monitoring.** For both, you need the advice of a medical professional.

Essiac Tea

If you have been surfing the Internet at all looking for cancer treatments, you have no doubt heard of Essiac Tea. There are many testimonials of its effectiveness against **all types of cancer**. Here is some background on it.

Essiac tea is a blend of herbs. The formula had been passed up through the Ojibwa medicine men. In **1922**, it landed in the hands of an Ontario, Canada nurse named Rene Caisse. Although Rene was not ill at the time, she asked for the formula in case she might ever need it. Unfortunately and ironically, a member of her family had been diagnosed with cancer and was given six months to live. Sensing that she had "nothing to lose"

Rene decided to test the product she came to call "Essiac" (Caisse spelled backwards) tea on her dying aunt.

The result was that the woman **went on to live another 21 years**. She eventually died of natural causes.

Inspired by her aunt's success with Essiac tea, Rene Caisse began to offer the remedy's recipe to anyone who asked for it. Soon thereafter, Dr. Charles Brusch **(personal physician to former President John F. Kennedy)** learned of the success of Essiac tea and became a **research partner** with Rene.

The original formula of Essiac tea apparently had eight herbs. The common blend today contains Burdock Root, Sheep Sorrel, Turkish Rhubarb Root, Red Clover, Watercress, Blessed Thistle, Kelp and Slippery Elm bark. Although no formal, clinical studies have been performed to support the merits of Essiac tea, many, many people have **praised its effectiveness** for relief from ailments that include cancer, arthritis, circulatory problems, urinary tract infections, prostate irregularities and asthma.

From **1922 to 1978** Nurse Caisse helped thousands of people with her original herbal formula at her clinic in Bracebridge, Ontario, Canada. Although she **refused payments** for her services she accepted donations to help support her clinic. Rene Caisse dedicated her life to helping others alleviate their pain and suffering with the use of her Essiac® formula.

If you do a search on Google, you will find **34,200** or more references to "Essiac tea." One source which claims to have Nurse Caisse's original formula is:

http://www.myhealthpro.net

Another possibly good source is:

174

http://www.essiacsource.com

Nurse Caisse's own account of her experience can be found at:

http://www.comboweb/com/essiac/nurse.htm

Summary

I exclude Essiac tea from the "self-treatment" category only because it is **critical** to verify the **integrity of the source**. Since I have no objective evidence on which to base a recommendation, I leave this decision to you and your medical professional.

Pau D'Arco Tea

Lots of people have been cured of all kinds of cancer by drinking Pau d'Arco tea (also known as Taheebo tea). Obviously, it is something you should know about.

The best way to get up to speed is to explore Roger DeLong's web site:

http://www.pau-d-arco.com/

Roger is a retired airline pilot who cured himself of cancer using Pau d'Arco tea. He was so convinced it would help people that he set up a simple, inexpensive way for cancer patients to get it. For the last two years or so, Roger imported it by the ton and sold it (he even gave it away to those who couldn't afford it) at **$14.95 a pound**, which was just about his cost. A pound is about a one-month supply.

My wife took it for her candida and swore that it helped her. We gave some to a friend who had cancer. I wrote it up in my newsletter.

175

Unfortunately, in December 2002, Roger decided that the demand was too great for him to handle alone as he had been doing. I will quote you an e-mail he sent me explaining the current status.

"Bill,

It is a real dilemma to recommend a source to buy the tea. The reason that I initially started selling the tea is that no one sold the bulk herb in one pound quantities at a reasonable price. That is still the case…

The only reputable source that I know is http://www.healthweigh.com and they sell it at $50 per pound and throw in some free stuff. They have the best quality product that I have seen. They focus their sales toward health practitioners and medical clinics. They have quite a list of M.D.'s that are using and testing the tea plus their vast list of historical customers. They haven't marketed or advertised yet. I've received several samples from different sources. I can't recommend any of them. Also, no one is completely knowledgeable of Pau d'Arco as I am with 15 years experience communicating with the users of the tea and my complete research studies. The production and importing of the tea is minimal and is a study in itself.

My efforts now are to get the herb fully researched by proper authorities and published in medical journals. Very tough job with the state of our medical society controlled by big money interests. It has to be researched with the N.C.I. protocols in phase I, II & III clinical studies. The N.C.I. won't do it so will have to be through private sources."

With Roger out of the distribution picture, I feel there is **no reliable source** at a reasonable price. It's a shame, because the healing properties of this tea when it is harvested and processed properly are awesome indeed.

Grape Juice

Grape juice is one treatment I was considering putting in the "self-treatment" category. Here is an account from a "true believer."

"My experience with this grapeseed diet is good. About 5 years ago I came across it in a book called 'Magnetic Therapy' by Abbot George Burke, 1988, DeVorss & Compmpany, P.O.Box 550, Marina Del Rey, Ca 90294

In it the author describes the Grape Cure as suggested by Fred Wortman, of Albany, Georgia, and told by Joseph F. Goodsavage, and printed in this book, 'Magnetic Therapy.'

.

'The doctors,' Mr. Wortman said, 'refused to operate when they discovered the condition of my bank balance.' Being a wide reader, he remembered a simple remedy for cancer that was given in a book by a 'Mrs. Brandt,' and looked it up.

It was rather involved and cumbersome to follow, so he reduced it to its essentials, took the cure and was completely cancer-free within a month.

Wortman then had his experiences published in the 'Independent' and received hundreds of replies. Over two hundred cancer sufferers reported complete cures-total recovery. The grape treatment cured lung cancer in two weeks, he reported. Cancer of the prostate took a little longer—about a month. Only four cases of leukemia (cancer of the blood) were treated, but the judicious usage of grape juice cured them all.

The Self Treatment:

Start the treatment like this: Begin with twenty-four ounces of (dark Concord) grape juice the first thing in the morning. Do not eat until noon. Take a couple of swallows every ten or fifteen minutes (don`t gulp it down all at once). After twelve o` clock, live the rest of the day normally, but do not eat anything after 8 o`clock in the evening....Food seems to carry off the curative agent in the grape juice, which may be Magnesium, so stick to the fast between 8 PM and noon the following day.

Keep this up every day for two weeks to a month...The dark Concord grape juice treatment is reported to be nearly 100% effective.'

Later on Wortman collected information on four hundred cases treated successfully this way. (All this is found on pages 52 and 53 in the above named book.)

When I took it myself for general health several times, I felt great, lost some weight (about five to eight pounds over a month) and it was easy to do. I am grateful for having found this 'diet,' because I remember the old Italians always saying, 'Se vuoi stare bene devi fare una mangiata di uve per due settimane, ogni tanto.' {If you want to stay(be) healthy you have to eat a lot of grapes, [only grapes], for a two week period every now and then.} Hmmm....they seemed to know a lot back then, eh?...

*The danger of this diet may be that the Concord grape juice (or any dark grape juice) may be contaminated with pesticides, hormones (GMO), and/or may be grown in soil where there is fluoride in the water which is absorbed by the grapes. To minimize this risk, either buy organic grape juice, Kosher grape juice, or know the farm where the grapes are grown and make your own grape juice. (Also, **excess sugar** is now found in a lot* *of grape juices made from concentrates, 'to make it taste good'/supermarket brands… etc.)*

This search for good grape juices could be a bit awkward at times but can be more effective as a self help treatment and certainly worth the extra effort. Good luck."

Caution

The above seems to indicate that this common staple might be worth a try. It's food, after all. The **caution** I advise is the result of the following e-mail I received a few weeks after first publishing the above in one of my newsletters.

"Hello,
My name is Bob Rabel. My wife has been battling ovarian cancer for three years now. We've tried many supplements and diet changes, some successful, some not. I appreciate your newsletters greatly. However, you might want to tell your readers what my wife experienced. She tried the grape juice therapy in your newsletter. She used pure organic 100% Concord grape juice just as the therapy advised. Many know that cancer cells grow 3 to 5 times faster in high levels of glucose. We were a little bit skeptical about the fructose content in grape juice. Turns out we were correct. Her tumor marker almost jumped 100%. In her 3 1/2 years it has never jumped higher than 25%. Keep in mind this was just one month's time. A word of caution might be given with this therapy because, in my opinion, the grape juice was the culprit.

Sincerely,

Bob Rabel"

Thank you, Bob. I can only hope the effect on your wife's condition was temporary. Because of the **adverse effect of sugar on cancer**, I'd suggest if you want to try the grape seed treatment, you order "O.P.C. Grape Seed Extract," 50mg, 60 capsules for $7.47 from www.ourhealthcoop.com

Cesium Chloride

An item I read recently reminded me of the difficult time we had trying to get my former wife's doctor to control her pain. I finally discovered a pain clinic at our University of Texas Health Science Center. A wonderful doctor there got it under control using MS-Contin, a form of time-release morphine. That was in 1994.

But now, there may be a much better solution! A natural, non-prescription substance called cesium chloride that controls severe cancer pain.

Here's the excerpt which caught my attention:

Beginning on page 313 of the book *"Painfree in Six Weeks"* by Dr.Sherry Rogers:

"The Pain of Terminal Cancer

No pain is scarier than that of terminal cancer. And you will be as amazed as I was to discover that researchers have shown that it can be terminated in some cases in less than one day, in fact within a matter of hours with a simple over-the-counter mineral. This is in spite of these cases being resistant to morphine and other standard narcotic treatments. And even more excitingly, persistent use of this common mineral has been part of a program where inoperable or metastatic end-stage tumors have even shrunk and totally disappeared.

Cesium (pronounced seez' e um), is the non-toxic mineral, that in some folks has stopped cancer pain within 12-24 hours in many cases. And when combined with other minerals and vitamins, all non-prescription, it has caused complete

disappearance of tumors within 3 months to two years in some cases (again, it depends on each person's total load and individual biochemistry).

Why haven't we heard of it? The same reason the media does not feature the stories of folks with end-stage cancer who have totally healed themselves of all cancer and metastases with diet and other non-prescription treatments. There is no money in it and, more importantly, it does not deify and empower those who want total control over your pain and health.

Normal cells get transformed into cancer cells via the combination of (1) environmental chemicals that generate free radicals and (2) nutrient deficiencies from a poor diet. Even government studies show that 95% of cancer is caused by diet and environment. The free radicals in turn damage genetics and other regulatory mechanisms and membranes. With damaged cell membranes, as one example, oxygen can no longer readily enter the cancer cell, but glucose or sugar can. In fact, sugar is like fertilizer for cancer cells.

To better understand how cesium works, let's look briefly at the inside of a cancer cell and see what else makes it different from normal cells. Normal healthy cells live, breath and make energy via a process called aerobic (with oxygen) metabolism. They rely on oxygen. The cancer cell does not rely heavily on this process, having switched its chemistry to a fermentative process using much less oxygen, but lots of sugar (anaerobic). Now you can see why taking a box of candy to a cancer patient is like pouring gasoline on a fire. Sugar and alcohol are like fertilizer for cancer."

Cesium chloride (the only form suitable for human consumption) is available from:

http://www.TheWolfeClinic.com/cesium.html

They have tablets in various sizes — 10 mg, 50 mg, 100 mg, 500 mg and 1,000 mg. A bottle of 100 of the 500 mg tablets, for example, costs $75. A bottle of 100 of the 10 mg tablets costs $29.95. Dr. Wolfe is available for telephone consultation on dosage. The pain relief from this substance is, quite obviously, not limited to terminal cancer patients.

They cannot ship this product to an address in Canada. They can ship to the U.S. Shipments to other countries will depend on customs regulations.

There is a **minimum order of three bottles** at one time. They can be of various sizes. They ship them in 4-6 business days or overnight, if you ask for it. The clinic is located in British Columbia, so they are in the Western time zone. You can reach them at (800) 592-9653 or (250) 765-1824.

Caution

A reader with some experience with this substance warns that you have to take it **with food**. She said it can cause **stomach bleeding and irritation** otherwise. You should also take it with **potassium** and **other supplements** to avoid heart palpitations.

Another reader (an RN) with some experience with it warned **not to** trust Dr. Wolfe's advice and not to **try self-treatment**.

Based on the above, I suggest you try cesium chloride **only** under the supervision of your own medical professional.

PolyMVA

Several readers have alerted me to a very helpful substance called PolyMVA. From what I have been able to learn from my own research, I'm convinced this is a valid substance, both as a **preventative and a self-treatment**.

Poly-MVA (MVA = mineral, vitamins and amino acids) is a non-toxic antioxidant composed of alpha lipoic acid and the element palladium. Developed in the U.S. by Dr. M. Garnett, the discoverer of the Second Genetic Code, it has already proven effective against many degenerative diseases, including cancer.

My research on the Internet turned up the Advanced Brain Tumor and Cancer Poly-MVA Hospital in Tijuana, Mexico as one of the first treatment centers for this therapy. Starting 20 years ago with treatment of brain tumors, they have now determined that the therapy is just as effective for **virtually all types of cancer**.

At their web site (just click on the link below), you'll find many testimonials and a lot more information on this treatment. Take a look at:

http://www.brain-cancer-treatment.com/

For more testimonials and to order it online, check out both of these sites:

http://www.polymva.net

http://www.polymvasurvivors.com

The Catch

So, what's the catch? Why wouldn't this qualify as a good self-treatment? In a word – **expensive!!** A one-month supply (8 oz. Bottle) costs about **$330.** There are much simpler and cheaper alternatives, which, in my opinion, are equally effective.

OTHER CANCER CURES

In this section, I will summarize all the other "alternative" cancer treatments I have found in my years of research. In studying these, ask yourself the obvious question: "Why hasn't at least one of these inspired the official cancer research community to explore it further?"

Rife/Bare Electrical Resonance

Cancer therapy and electrical frequency resonance met first in the 1930's. Dr. Royal Rife built the device. In 1934, physicians from the University of Southern California allegedly conducted clinical trials. They used it on 16 cancer patients at the Scripps Ranch in California. The results? Within 60 days, 14 of the 16 people were pronounced cured of their cancers. The remaining two people were pronounced cured within the next 60 days.

The Rife Device, using electrical resonance, had the ability to destroy or devitalize specific cells and microorganisms. It is alleged to have the ability to remove cataracts from patients' eyes.

James E. Bare, D. C., picked up the torch. He published a book and videotape in 1995. The book, *Resonant Frequency Therapy — Building the Rife Beam Ray Device,* includes instructions on how to build the device. Mr. Bare claims that anyone can build it in about four hours.

The videotape includes examples of the device's effect on blood samples containing disease microorganisms. There is also available an audio tape of a lengthy interview of Mr. Bare on The Laura Lee Show, a radio talk show, in 1996.

You can find all the above materials and a lot more information at:

http://www.lauralee.com/rife.htm

By all means, check out Dr. Jon Brooks' article on this subject at:

http://www.cat007.com/rife.htm

You'll even find information on how to download free a frequency generator that works on your PC computer along with a list of all the frequencies to use for specific maladies. Amazing stuff.

"The Cure For All Cancers" (?)

Hulda Regehr Clark, Ph.D., N.D., is a **remarkable person**. I'm sure you will find her book, *The Cure for All Cancers*, as fascinating as I did. Published in 1993, this book documents not only 100 cancer cases she treated personally but also instructions on building an **electronic device** to replicate her tests.

Dr. Clark's hypothesis is that parasites, or intestinal flukes cause all cancers. Her Doctorate is in biophysics and cell physiology. After working on Canadian government research projects for eleven years, she began private consulting in 1979.

In 1990, she put together her theory on **cancer cause and cure**.

The parasites Dr. Clark claims to have isolated come from all manner of **toxins** in our food, our water, our cosmetics and even the **fillings in our mouths**. Eating out of Styrofoam containers is a "no-no." In fact, she lists multiple everyday items which contain traces of 33 **"unnatural chemicals"** harmful to our bodies (arsenic, barium, cobalt, lead, radon, tin and so forth).

The **constraints** she suggests on your life to avoid all these **"cancer causers"** are so severe, most of us would simply throw up our hands in despair, as I did. For example, you must stop smoking (good idea!); change your **copper** water pipes to **plastic**; remove all **chemicals** from your house; board your **pets** with a friend; get rid of any possible **asbestos** sources (hair dryer and clothes dryer); have your house tested for **radon**; remove all possible **formaldehyde** ("if your bedroom is paneled, move out of it and keep the door locked."); remove all possible **arsenic** (wallpaper glue, roach killer, lawn chemicals, etc.); check your home for exposed fiberglass; and check your **gas** heat and gas water heater for **leaks**.

She's not done. You also have to remove all **metal fillings** from your mouth and have infected teeth removed and **"cavitations"** on your jaw by an **oral surgeon**. I agree with her that **toxins leaching out of our teeth** are the **unrecognized (by the "establishment") cause** of many diseases. I'll have to cover this in the next book.

Dr. Clark's theories about the cause of cancer are not that "radical." She mentions **cell "mutations",** just as Dr. Roizen [in Chapter 3] did. Her contention is that she has discovered the CAUSE of the mutations. It is **"intestinal flukes"** which migrate primarily due to the presence in our bodies of isopropyl alcohol.

Dr. Clark uses **247 pages** of this book to cover the **103 case studies**. Fascinating reading. At least **three dozen** of her case studies followed her instructions meticulously and were **cured**. In fact, one of the most convincing features of her book is the inclusion of dozens of cases of patients who **did not** follow her regimen and, in most cases, came for only a single visit.

Dr. Clark has **added much** to the understanding of **causes and cures** for cancer. No study of alternative/complementary cures is complete without looking at her work. Like other pioneers, she has been **persecuted** by our medical "system." In 1999, the FBI **arrested her** in San Diego and extradited her to Indiana where she was tried for "practicing medicine without a license." After she had spent **several months in jail**, all **charges were dismissed** in a trial in April, 2000.

She wrote another book in 1995 called *"The Cure For All Diseases."* Either of her books is available at many health food stores or on amazon.com.

You can get the full story on Dr. Clark, including her brief stint in jail in 1999 at: http://www.drclark.ch/

Included at this web site are **47 detailed testimonials** of cancer patients cured using her methods.

Her electronic "zapper" which kills parasites in your body has spawned a mini-industry on the web. If you want to buy one of the "zappers" she recommends, here's one source for a "hands free" Multi-Zap HF Zapper. It costs $79.00 and again, I get no cut off this or any other recommendation. To investigate it further, go to: http://www.ess-in.com/Zapper_HF.htm

On Our Own Terms – An "Aside"

In 2000 I saw Bill Moyers' six hour TV special on **death and dying** called *"On Our Own Terms."*

The intimate interviews with dying people and their caregivers and doctors were **extremely moving** for me. It brought back **many memories** of my own experience with my former wife, Marjorie. It also caused me a great deal of **frustration** to see the **needless suffering and death** that is occurring every day because of ignorance of what you are reading here.

None of the alternative therapies we are covering here actually **shorten your life**, as do most chemotherapy and radiation treatments. They do not **destroy your immune system**, as do most chemotherapy and radiation treatments. They are **non-invasive and non-toxic**. They don't kill patients, even when they don't cure them.

"Most cancer patients in this country die of chemotherapy," observes Dr. Alan Levin of the University of California Medical School. *"Chemotherapy does not eliminate breast, colon or lung cancers. The fact has been documented for over a decade…Women with breast cancer are likely to die faster with chemotherapy than without it."*

As you read about the various therapies in this book, remember that they are included here because they have cured at least some cancer patients. Unlike conventional medicine, I don't define "cured" as **survival for four years**. I define "cured" as being able to return to a **normal lifestyle and maintain it indefinitely.**

Antineoplaston Therapy

The following is a **classic example** of how our medical system reacts to a discovery that may fundamentally alter current beliefs. This negative reaction parallels the **public punishment** of medical pioneers down through the ages.

"The body itself has a treatment for cancer," says Dr. Stanislaw Burzynski. The Polish-born physician-biochemist, based in Houston, Texas, discovered that a group of **peptides** (short chains of amino acids) and amino-acid derivatives occurring naturally throughout our bodies **inhibit the growth of cancer cells**.

In his view, these substances are part of a biochemical defense system **completely different** from our immune system. Unlike the immune system, which protects us by destroying invading agents or defective cells, the biochemical defense system **reprograms**, or corrects, defective cells. It carries "good" information to abnormal cells, instructing them to develop normally. Does this remind you of the "proofreader" cells we discussed above. Our bodies are **wonderfully complex** creations.

Dr. Burzynski named these peptides **anti-neoplastons** because of their ability to inhibit neoplastic, or cancerous, cell growth. He discovered that cancer patients have a **drastic shortage** of these compounds in their bodies. Blood samples of advanced cancer patients reveal only 2 to 3 percent of the amount typically found in healthy individuals. By simply reintroducing the peptides into the patient's bloodstream, either orally or intravenously, he brings about **tumor shrinkage or complete remission**. In many cases, just weeks after the start of treatment, tumors have shrunk in size or disappeared.

Since the Burzynski Research Institute (BRI) opened in 1977, Dr. Burzynski has treated some 3,000 cancer patients, most of them in advanced stages. There is no doubt from the peer-reviewed literature he has published **(150 scientific papers)** that his treatment works, at least for some patients. In fact, he holds **20 patents** for antineoplaston treatment covering **16 countries**. Dr. Burzynski advises that antineoplaston treatments are neither effective against all types of cancer nor for all patients.

Burzynski's breakthroughs are being eagerly pursued abroad. Clinical studies are underway in **Japan, Poland, Great Britain, Italy and China**. In September, 1990, the Burzynski Research Institute entered into a letter of intent with Ferment, a major Soviet pharmaceutical firm, to conduct **clinical trials** with antineoplastons on cancer patients **in Russia**.

How has his work been received in the United States by the cancer "establishment?" Well, you probably guessed it. His work has been dismissed as **quackery** by such interlocking government agencies as the Food and Drug Administration and the American Cancer Society. Oncologists, when asked by patients about Dr. Burzynski, respond that he **hasn't published anything**.

The FDA **filed suit** against Dr. Burzynski in March 1983 in an attempt to drive him out of business. It ordered Burzynski and his Institute to stop all further research, development, manufacture, and use of antineoplastons. A federal judge allowed the doctor to continue his research and treatment **within Texas** but ruled he could not ship the drugs across state lines.

In July, 1985, **FDA agents** and federal marshals, armed with an illegal search warrant to look for vague "violations," **raided** the Burzynski Research Institute and seized over 200,000 **confidential documents**, including private medical records. They went through Dr. Burzynski's personal correspondence and rifled his briefcase. The federal officers loaded **eleven** of his filing cabinets onto their truck in an outrageous violation of his (and patients') constitutional and civil liberties. Dr. Burzynski sued the FDA for the return of his records, but all the documents remain in the FDA's hands to this day.

The Texas State Board of Medical Examiners tried to revoke Burzynski's medical license in 1988 on hairsplitting technical charges that had **no connection** with the quality of care he provides. Hundreds of letters of support were sent to the board by Burzynski's patients and their families and friends. The following letter from a Midwestern teenager was typical:

"I am 13 years old and I have a 7 year old brother. We love our father very much. Thanks to Dr Burzynski's treatment, my father's tumor has stopped growing. All of the doctors in my home state of Missouri said there was no cure for my father's disease. Dr. Burzynski gave him a chance for life again. Please don't take that away from us."

There's more to this story. If you want the **complete story** and several more case studies, please get the book *"Options – The Alternative Cancer Therapy Book"* by Richard Walters, copyright 1993 published by Avery. It is available from amazon.com.

The bottom line is that to the American medical monopoly, Dr. Burzynski and his therapy are a **threat** in at least three ways. First, if his theory about a biochemical defense system separate from the immune system is correct, the biology textbooks will have to be rewritten. His theory is **revolutionary** in its implications and he has **impeccable credentials**.

Second, although he is an alternative healer, Burzynski **plays by the rules**. He publishes his findings openly and widely in the **peer-reviewed medical literature**. This makes it harder, but obviously not impossible, to smear him as a quack.

Third, and most important, his **safe, non-toxic** cancer treatment, with its tremendous promise, is perceived as a threat by the **mega-billion-dollar cancer business** with its vested interests in toxic chemotherapy, radiation and surgery. Orthodox doctors and the huge drug companies would not welcome a safe, relatively inexpensive cancer cure – such as naturally occurring peptides, an herbal brew, or something similar – that can't be marketed to reap **super profits**.

Contact information for Dr. Burzynski's Houston clinic is in Appendix A to this book.

My Personal Experience

My information about the Burzynski therapy is second hand. A close personal friend who I will call "Paula" (not her real name) had a hysterectomy on September 17 2001. The pathology report showed endometrial cancer cells in the lining of the uterus. In a few days after the operation, she began taking magesterol, a hormone.

Recovering nicely, she began taking several CAM products — MGN-3, beta glucan, shark cartilage and acidophilus. She was feeling good.

Paula and her husband read lots of literature on cancer, including my book. They decided to try the Burzynski Clinic in Houston, Texas. After sending Paula's records a couple of weeks before, they visited the clinic at the end of October 2001. Their experience was anything but positive.

After waiting one hour beyond their appointment time, they were seen by one of the physicians. Paula commented to him that they probably wouldn't have had to wait an hour if she had been Jane Seymour or one of the other celebrities whose pictures filled the walls of the fancy clinic building.

Their interview with the physician proved that he had not looked at Paula's records. This, of course, bothered them.

Paula had a discussion with Dr. Burzynski, himself. She asked him if he had statistics on the treatment's success with ovarian cancers like hers. He said they **didn't have enough** to compute valid success rates. She also asked him for names of CAM-sympathetic doctors in San Antonio. He said he would get her some names.

As for Paula, she was given a large number of pills called PBN (sodium phenylbutyrate). She was told to begin with 1 every two hours, six times a day. That was to be built up to NINE every two hours. They said to continue taking the MGN-3, but stop taking the beta glucan and acidophilus because they interfered with this treatment.

By the time she reached the **FIFTY FOUR** pills per day level, Paula was **very sick**. She was so nauseous, she could not hold down either the Burzynski pills or any other medication or food. She called the Burzynski Clinic. The physician said stop taking the PBN until the nausea went away, then begin at a lower level again.

When Paula asked for the names of CAM-competent doctors that Dr. Burzynski had promised her, the physician said Dr. Burzynski was out of town and he didn't know anything about that.

The **statistics** that Burzynski publishes are **not very impressive**. For example, they showed that as of July 2001, the **"objective response"** rate for both colon and breast cancer was **57.2%**. The rest had either "stable disease" or "progressive disease." Objective response means **"complete response, partial response or substantial decrease in tumor size."**

The cost: **$4,500 PER MONTH**. They handle only outpatients. The payment seems to cover only **office visits** (about every six weeks, in Paula's case) and the **medication**. While a few insurance companies will reimburse for the treatment, Medicare will not.

Obviously, I'm not a great fan of the Burzynski treatment. I would consider it only as a **last resort for brain tumors**.

The 714-X Compound and Gaston Naessens

A French biologist now living in Canada, Gaston Naessens developed a non-toxic treatment for cancer and other degenerative diseases. Called 714-X, the compound is an aqueous solution of nitrogen-enriched with camphor molecules. Camphor is a **natural substance** derived mainly from the camphor tree of East Asia. The camphor-nitrogen compound is injected into the body's lymphatic system. It is said to strengthen the patient's ravaged immune system, which then **rids the body of disease**.

Based on **forty years** of microscopic and biological research, Naessens' treatment has restored health to **hundreds** of cancer patients, many of them **diagnosed** by orthodox doctors **as terminal**. Many patients experience dramatic benefits, including **relief of pain**, improved appetite and weight gain, increased strength, cessation of vomiting, and feelings of well-being. A course of treatment consists of daily injections for at least three 21-day periods, with a 3-day rest between each period. For advanced or metastatic cancer, an average of seven to twelve periods is recommended. Patients can be taught to **self-administer** the treatment.

Again, detailed information on the science of this remedy and case studies are available in Richard Walters' book *Options*, mentioned above. You can also find there detailed information on **sources** for the substance and treatment. I will not elaborate on it further, because I believe other substances mentioned above (MGN-3, beta glucan, et al) are much more readily available and at least as effective.

It's no surprise that the Canadian medical establishment hounded Naessens. Quebec's medical-drug complex has dismissed his treatment as worthless. Nevertheless, Canadians can obtain 714-X through the emergency drug branch of the federal government for patients suffering from degenerative diseases (cancer, AIDS, etc.)

His research shares much **common ground** with that of other cancer researchers. His discovery of pleomorphic (form-changing) organisms in the blood **tracks with the immune theories** of Virginia Livingston, M.D. (see below) and the electromagnetic frequency generator developed by Royal Rife (see above).

Once again, the establishment dismisses promising research as quackery.

Revici Therapy

Dr. Emanuel Revici has developed another original approach to the treatment of cancer. His non-toxic chemotherapy uses **lipids** and other substances to correct an imbalance in the patient's chemistry. Lipids – organic compounds such as fatty acids and sterols – are **important parts of all living cells**.

The Romanian-born physician, who practiced in New York City, had applied his wide-ranging discoveries for over **sixty years** to the treatment of cancer. The great majority of his cancer patients were in **advanced stages** of the illness. Many years after receiving his treatment, some of these patients were in remission with **no signs of active cancer**.

Commenting on Revici's 1961 book, *Research in Physiopathology as a Basis of Guided Chemotherapy with Special Applications to Cancer*, Dr. Gerhard Schrauzer, a leading authority on selenium, wrote, *"I came to the conclusion that Dr. Revici is an innovative medical genius, outstanding chemist and a highly creative thinker. I also realized that few of his medical colleagues would be able to follow his train of thought and thus would be all too willing to dismiss his work."*

Dr. Revici tailored his treatment to the individual. One patient, a forty-three year old man, was diagnosed with an invasive, high-grade of cancer of the bladder at Memorial Sloan-Kettering Cancer Center in September 1980. *"They said, 'The only way you can be treated is if we **take your bladder out** and give you a **colostomy** on the side.' He said no."* The patient visited Dr. Revici in October and went on his therapy. He has had no other treatment. In 1987, he returned to Sloan-Kettering for a cystoscopy, which revealed him to be **cancer-free**.

Another patient, a twenty-nine year old woman, was operated on at Memorial Sloan-Kettering in October 1983 for a chordoma, a **brain tumor**. The tumor was incompletely removed, and she was given a course of **radiation therapy**. Her condition progressively worsened during the twelve months following the surgery. Dr. Revici first saw her in May 1984. At the time, she was confined to a wheelchair with **limited function**. She started the Revici program. She subsequently had **two babies** and functions well. Her only problem is that she **walks with a cane**.

Revici's non-toxic cancer therapy never received fair testing or funding in the United States. That should come as **no surprise** to any of you who have read this far. His methods have been formally studied and put into practice in **France, Italy and Austria**. He was a distinguished physician who graduated **first in his class** at the University of Bucharest.

The American media portrayed him as a quack that should have been **put out of business**. The American Cancer Society put Revici's therapy on its Unproven Methods blacklist in 1961. In 1984, the State of New York tried to revoke his medical license **permanently** on the grounds of deviation from standard medicine, negligence, incompetence, fraud, the use of unapproved experimental drugs, and similar charges. After **four years** of struggle, Revici won in July 1988. The court decision allowed him to **continue treating cancer patients.**

To save his license, Revici's patients and several medical civil-liberties groups undertook **extensive lobbying** at the state capitol. At the federal level, New York Congressman Guy Molinari held an **all-day hearing** in March 1988 to address the Revici matter and the whole field of alternative cancer therapies. Dr. Seymour Brenner, a respected radiation oncologist in private practice in New York, testified **on Revici's behalf**.

Dr. Brenner had investigated a number of patients in very **advanced stages** of cancer, **incurable** by orthodox means. Revici had put **each of them** into long remissions. Dr. Brenner had an **independent panel of pathologists** confirm the diagnosis and stage of illness prior to each patient's initial visit to Revici. He testified that his personal findings strongly suggested Revici has a cancer treatment **deserving further study**, and he proposed that the **FDA conduct such an evaluation.**

In a letter to Congressman Molinari, Brenner outlined a protocol in which a **panel of doctors** would monitor cancer patients placed on alternative therapies. All of these patients would have been **declared untreatable** by conventional means. The letter contained **detailed case histories** of ten advanced cancer patients whom Revici had healed.

It is now almost **fifty years** since Revici developed his non-toxic chemotherapy. An open-minded, unbiased evaluation of it by the cancer "establishment" has **never been done**. Once again, the cancer industry succeeded in suppressing an alternative non-toxic treatment that showed promise to **replace, or at least enhance**, toxic chemotherapy and radiation.

If this type of suppression and ridicule of promising cancer cures interests you, you will find ten painstakingly documented cases in Daniel Haley's book *"Politics In Healing."* I strongly recommend it to you.

Fighting Cachexia With Hydrazine Sulfate

Cachexia (pronounced ka-KEK-si-a) is the wasting away process that kills **two-thirds** of all cancer patients, including my former wife, Marge. Hydrazine sulfate **dramatically reverses** this process. It is an inexpensive drug, with **no side effects**. It has a clinically documented anti-tumor action. It causes malignant tumors to stop growing, to reduce in size, and, in some cases, to disappear.

About **half** of all patients who take hydrazine sulfate experience **weight gain**, restored appetite, **extended survival time**, and a significant **reduction in pain and suffering**. Many patients report an increase in vigor and strength and the disappearance of symptoms of the disease, along with feelings of well-being and optimism.

While hydrazine sulfate may not be a sure-fire cancer cure (and what is?), **large-scale clinical trials** suggest that it affects every type of tumor at every stage. It can be administered **either alone or in combination** with cytotoxic chemotherapy or radiation to make the cancer more vulnerable to the standard forms of treatment.

Dr. Joseph Gold discovered the effects of hydrazine sulfate in **1968**. Cancer has two principal devastating effects on the body. One is the **invasion** of the tumor into the vital organs and the destruction of the organs' functions. To the general public, this sounds like the most common cause of cancer death. In fact, it accounts for **only 23%** of the cancer deaths each year.

The other devastating effect of cancer is **cachexia**, the terrible wasting away of the body. It means weight loss and debilitation. In cancer, as in AIDS, patients **die from the accompanying illnesses**, which they would otherwise survive if not for the wasting syndrome.

"In a sense, nobody dies of cancer," notes Dr. Harold Dvorak, chief of pathology at Beth Israel Hospital in Boston. *"They die of something else – pneumonia, failure of one or another organs. Cachexia **accelerates that process of infection and the building-up of metabolic poisons**. It causes death a lot faster than the tumor would, were it not for the cachexia."*

But what causes cachexia? Cancer cells **gobble up sugar** ten to fifteen times more than normal cells do. The sugar consumed by the cancer cells is generated mainly from the liver, which **converts lactic acid into glucose**. (Normal cells are far more efficient users of glucose, which they derive from the food we eat, **not from lactic acid**.)

When cancer cells use sugar (glucose) as fuel, they **only partially metabolize it**. Lactic acid – the **waste product** of this incomplete combustion – spills into the blood and is taken up by the liver. The liver then **recycles** the lactic acid (and other breakdown products) back into glucose. The sugar is consumed in ever-increasing amounts by **voracious** cancer cells.

The result is a vicious cycle, what Dr. Gold calls a **"sick relationship"** between the liver and the cancer. The patient's **healthy cells starve** while the cancer cells **grow vigorously**. Some healthy cells even dissolve to feed the growing tumor.

To break this sick relationship, Dr. Gold reasoned, all he needed was to find a **safe, non-toxic drug** that inhibits gluconeogenesis (a big word meaning the liver's recycling of lactic acid back into glucose). In 1968, he outlined his theory in an article **published in Oncology**. *"The silence was deafening,"* he recalls.

A year later, by remarkable coincidence, Gold heard biochemist Paul Ray deliver a paper explaining that **hydrazine sulfate** could shut down the enzyme necessary for the production of glucose from lactic acid. Gold had chanced upon an **eminently logical way** of starving cancer. He immediately tested hydrazine sulfate on mice and found that in accord with his theory, the drug **inhibited both gluconeogenesis and tumor growth.**

Here is just one of many case studies of hydrazine sulfate's dramatic effects. In 1987, Erna Kamen, a sixty-three year old lung cancer patient, was administered hydrazine sulfate after her discharge from a Sarasota, Florida hospital. *"Basically, my mother was **sent home to die**,"* says Jeff Kamen, an Emmy-winning television reporter. *"She'd lost a significant amount of weight by then, and she had **no appetite** and virtually **no will to do anything**"* (eerily reminiscent of Marge's condition in 1994).

A doctor had told Jeff's father, Ira Kamen, that hydrazine sulfate offered at least **"a shot in the dark."** So one Monday in August 1987, a home nurse gave Mrs. Kamen **one hydrazine sulfate pill** shortly before serving lunch. *"On Tuesday morning,"* recalls Jeff, *"there was a commotion in the house. My mother had **risen from her bed** like the phoenix rising from the ashes. She was demanding that the nurse bring her downstairs so that she could have breakfast with me…When people you love get into this kind of facedown with death, you're just **incredibly grateful** for each moment."*

As Jeff describes his mother's recovery, *"her **searing pain was gone**; her appetite returned at a gallop."* Within three weeks, her racking cough had vanished and she could **walk unaided**. *"In the months before her death, she went on television with me to **tell the nation** about hydrazine sulfate. The National Cancer Institute stopped trashing hydrazine sulfate and began referring inquiries to the UCLA Medical School team whose work had **validated the effectiveness of the drug** long before Erna Kamen began taking it."* Jeff attributes his mother's death months later to her being *"mistakenly taken off hydrazine sulfate and subjected to an **unproven experimental substance.**"*

With cancer patients, hydrazine sulfate is usually administered orally in 60-milligram capsules or tablets, approximately one to two hours before meals. It is given first once a day for several days, then twice a day, then three or four times daily, depending on the patient's response and the **physician's judgment**. On such a regimen, many terminal and semi-terminal patients have derived considerable benefit. Patients in the **early stages** of cancer derive the most benefit.

About half of the patients who get the drug administered in the early stages of cancer show an **almost immediate** weight gain and reversal of symptoms. In some instances, the tumor eventually disappears.

The common types of cancer most frequently reported to benefit from hydrazine sulfate therapy are recto-colon cancer, ovarian cancer, prostate cancer, lung cancer, Hodgkin's disease and other lymphomas, thyroid cancer, melanoma, and breast cancer. These account for over **90 percent** of the cancers reported in this country.

Again, for further information on how to obtain this drug or research it further, do your own search on the Internet or look at Richard Walters book, Options.

My Concerns

I do not recommend hydrazine sulfate as a self-treatment regimen because it does not have a proven safe dosage level and treatment regimen. You, of course, are free to form your own opinion. Certainly, it is cheap and readily available.

Immune Therapies

Long before Dr. Ghoneum discovered MGN-3, researchers have been working on ways to use the body's immune system to fight cancer. Right now, much of the research is centered on **vaccines**. You may hear about some of these, so it pays to be familiar with some of the terms.

Monoclonal antibodies are **synthetic cells** created through gene-splicing. The cancer patient's white blood cells are fused with his or her cancer cells. When the resulting *hybridomas* are reintroduced into the patient's body, they manufacture specific antibodies. These attack only cancer cells. Attached to anti-cancer drugs or natural toxins, **monoclonals serve as "guided missiles"** by directing he antibodies they manufacture toward their malignant prey.

Still in the research stage, monoclonals promise to be **tremendously expensive**. They will be a boon to the pharmaceutical-medical monopoly if they are ever used for cancer treatment. The media frequently touts them as the next cancer breakthrough.

The American Cancer Society freely admits that it will take "many years to find the proper role of these [orthodox immunotherapy] agents in cancer treatment." Knowledgeable observers say this means **another twenty years or more**. Meanwhile, the ACS continues to use its enormous power to **restrict or suppress** safe, non-toxic cancer therapies using immune system therapy that have produced **remarkable**

clinical results in human beings. Some examples are, of course, MGN-3, beta glucan, IP-6 (not covered in this book), Oncolyn, BCI-26 and earlier immune therapies such as that of Lawrence Burton, Ph.D. (discussed below) and Virginia Livingston, M.D.

Coley's Mixed Bacterial Vaccine

Ironically, *Coley's mixed bacterial vaccine*, which has perhaps shown a greater cure rate than any other cancer treatment, is totally unavailable. Dr. William Coley (1862-1936) was an eminent New York City surgeon and Sloan-Kettering researcher. In the **1890s**, he developed a **vaccine** made of bacterial toxins that **activated immune-resistance mechanisms in cancer patients** and cured hundreds.

His daughter, Helen Coley Nauts, D.Sc., has preserved and carried forward his important work. Yet, despite the successful use of bacterial vaccines amply reported in the medical literature since the turn of the century, today's big drug companies have **no interest** in what they view as merely an **unprofitable** item.

The bottom line, dear readers, which is rather horrible to consider, is that at any one time, there are **thousands** of patients in the United States getting **aggressive chemotherapy** who would benefit from **any** immune-enhancing measures, even supportive nutrition or vitamin supplements. Do they get it? Unless they seek it out through publications like this one, **the answer, sadly, is no**.

Burton's Immuno-Augmentative Therapy

Dr. Lawrence Burton uses four blood proteins – substances occurring naturally in the body – to treat cancer. His Immuno-Augmentative Therapy (IAT), developed while he was a senior oncologist at St. Vincent's Hospital in New York City in the **1960s**, does not "attack" the cancer. Instead, it aims to **restore normal immune system functioning** so the patient's own immune system will destroy the cancer cells. Sound like Dr. Ghoneum talking about MGN-3? Sure does. Ask yourself what happened to the following evidence in the ensuing forty years.

Burton discovered that the components of the blood, which he called **blood fractions**, are deficient in the cancer patient. When they are present in correct balance, they work **synergistically** to control cancer cell growth and kill tumors.

His therapy involves replenishing the deficient blood fractions by injecting patients with them in amounts based on **daily or twice-daily blood analyses**. Patients continue to self-administer the injections from serum for whatever length of time is necessary, much like a diabetic takes insulin. IAT is **non-toxic and has no side effects.**

Dr. Burton does not claim that IAT is a cure. He describes it as a means to control and combat cancer. Yet, according to clinical records, **50 to 60%** of patients experience **tumor reduction**. Many undergo long-term regression. Some, even those with **terminal cancer**, have achieved **complete remission**.

Many cases of **metastatic cancer** of the colon and abdomen, treated with Burton's IAT, have gone well beyond five years of recovery. This is a remarkable achievement since the National Cancer Institute says these types of cancer have a **zero** five-year survival rate.

*For more on Burton's experience with the **cancer "system"** in the United States, read the book* "Options – The Alternative Cancer Therapy Book" *by Richard Walters.*

Cytoluminescent Therapy (CLT)

One of the newest wrinkles in cancer treatment is called "Cytoluminescent Therapy" (CLT). This has been known as Photodynamic Therapy (PDT), which was similar but used a different "sensitizing" agent. A clinic in Ireland specializes in CLT. Dr. Ralph Moss has visited them and was quite impressed. He published a report that was **quite enthusiastic** about the efficacy of this treatment. Recent rumors are that it is being introduced in the U.S. Here is a web site where you can learn all I know about it quite quickly:

http://www.cancerclt.com

I will also quote for you an e-mail from a lady who visited the Ireland clinic for the treatment in late 2002. Here's how she described the treatment:

"...the theory behind CLT (PDT with a new agent) is that one ingests a sensitizing agent, this one is made from spirulina, which binds almost exclusively to cancer cells, and then infrared and LED light shined on the body will activate the agent through the blood (as it kind of rides to the cancer cells on the cholesterol-like substances in the blood), causing cellular excitement and creating singlet oxygen, an oxidative process, which in turn causes the cancer cells to basically blow up.

Lynnette"

Problems

In addition to the **exorbitant cost** ($20,000) and the fact that the Ireland clinic is booked for several months in advance, Lynette reports that they have been receiving many complaints about their **lack of follow-up** after the patient returns home – an essential part of this treatment.

Cancer "Cures" A-Plenty

The wide variety of cancer therapies that have proved effective over the past 50 years **boggles the mind**. I will simply list some more of them here to give you the words you need to research them further on the Internet, if you are interested, using your favorite search engine (Google, Yahoo, etc.).

Asian herbs

Ayurveda

Bioelectric Therapies

Bovine Colustrum

Carctol

Chaparral

Chelation

Chinese Medicine

Chlorella

Co-enzyme Q10

Colloidal Silver

Concentrated Aloe Vera

Detoxification

DMSO Therapy

Far Infrared Therapy

Germanium

Gerson Therapy

Hans Nieper, M.D.

Haelan 95

Homeopathy

Hoxsey Therapy

Hyperbaric units

Hyperthermia

Immunocal

IP6

Issels' Whole-Body Therapy

Kelley's Nutritional-Metabolic Therapy

Lactoferrin

Live-Cell Therapy

Livingston Therapy

Lymphotonic PF2

Magnetic Sleep Pads

Mind-Body Treatments

Mistletoe (Iscador)

Moerman's Anti-Cancer Diet

MycoSoft

N-Tense

Noni Juice

Oncotox

Ozone Therapy

Psychohtherapy

Peroxide Therapy

Rain-forest herbs

Selenium

T-Plus

Transfer Factor +

Ukrain

VG-1000

Wigmore therapy

....and many more....

Check a few of those out on your favorite search engine. You'll be amazed at the wealth of material on them. I have tried to **avoid information overload** in this book by covering in detail the treatments you should seriously consider. Obviously, this is a judgment call. I am **not dismissing** any on the above list. Some cancer patients have been cured by each of them.

Conclusion

Do not trust the "system" to take care of your or your loved one's cancer. Get **proactive**. Do the research. Get knowledge. **Knowledge is power**.

Know this. Many different promising approaches to curing cancer and/or preventing its recurrence **now exist**.

You may want to travel to the Bahamas or Mexico or Ireland or Germany but you don't have to any more. Your local health food store carries the things you need or you can order them from the sources I list in this book.

Your most difficult search may be to find a doctor who will help you use these treatments to augment "conventional" therapy and test your progress. **Keep looking**. These doctors are out there in the United States, Canada, Mexico and other countries.

Don't Wait For More Proof

Many of these "alternative" therapies are **urgently** in need of more research to bring out their full potential. Do not hold your breath waiting for that to happen.

Dr. Robert C. Atkins, who many of you may know because of his nutrition books, puts it quite succinctly. He says:

*"There have been **many** cancer cures, and all have been ruthlessly and systematically suppressed with a Gestapo-like thoroughness by the cancer establishment. The cancer establishment is the not-too-shadowy association of the American Cancer Society, the leading cancer hospitals, the National Cancer Institute, and the FDA. The shadowy part is the fact that these respected institutions are very much dominated by members and friends of members of the*

pharmaceutical industry, which profits so incredibly much from our profession-wide obsession with chemotherapy."

It is hard for most Americans to believe that life-saving and valid therapies are being **suppressed deliberately**. It just doesn't seem possible in modern America. Unfortunately, most Americans are **dead wrong**. The cancer establishment has a **eighty-year history** of corruption, incompetence, and **deliberate suppression** of cancer therapies that actually work. This includes the rigging of clinical trials at major institutions in order to **discredit non-toxic, natural therapies**. Barry Lynes has documented this well in his book *The Healing of Cancer* as has Daniel Haley in *"Politics In Healing."* See Appendix A for more information on these books. As Lynes says, *"The American Cancer Society is not interested in a cure. It would go out of business."*

Cancer Research Is Fraud

Two-time Nobel laureate Linus Pauling summed up the situation well when he said, *"Everyone should know that the 'war on cancer' is largely a **fraud**, and that the National Cancer Institute and the American Cancer Society are **derelict in their duties** to the people who support them."*

According to Barry Lynes, *"At a minimum, the American Cancer Society…should be investigated by the U. S. Justice Department for **fraud**, false advertising, **conspiracy** and a variety of other anti-trust, monopolistic crimes."*

Closely linked to the ACS through interlocking directorates is the National Cancer Institute. Funded by the government, this agency currently has a budget of over **3 billion dollars a year**. Wouldn't you expect such an agency to be a catalyst for **innovation**? Shouldn't they openly encourage any new technique or method that might slow the death count in the **cancer epidemic** that claims 10,000 American lives every week? NCI is **just the opposite**. It is a repressive guardian of the status quo that funds an **"old boys' network"** committed to chemotherapy and radiation. They actively conspire with other government agencies to **harass or thwart** innovative alternative cancer therapies.

Instead of serving the public, *"NCI created a bureaucratic haven for scientism, filled with **committee procedures**, payoffs, **collusion with drug companies** and **interminable roadblocks** for the truly innovative cancer fighters,"* as Barry Lynes observes in *The Healing of Cancer*.

What the NCI does with their $3 billion in taxes each year is a unique form of **corruption** in the history of science. NCI distributes these billions in research grants and, together with the ACS, sets the dominant trends in research. Incredibly, **90 % of the members** of NCI's peer review committee get NCI money for **their own research**. **70% of ACS's research budget** goes to individuals or institutions with which the ACS board members are **personally affiliated.**

*"In any other part of government, it would be a **corrupt practice** for the persons giving out the money and the persons getting it to be the same people,"* says Irwin Bross, Ph.D., former Director of Biostatistics at the famed Roswell Park Memorial Institute, the nation's oldest cancer research hospital. Testifying before a congressional subcommittee, Dr. Bross added, *"It is a corrupt practice even when it is called 'peer review' or 'cancer research'…This set-up is not worth revamping and should **simply be junked**."*

Don't Be A Statistic

You need look no further than the **statistics on cancer deaths**. The death rates from the six major killer cancers – cancers of the lung, colon, breast, prostate, pancreas, and ovary – have either stayed the same or increased during the past **sixty years**. If this is a "war on cancer" it has **long since been lost**.

Unlike many other countries, the United States supports only **one kind of medicine**. Because of this, Americans have been denied many vital aspects of the **science and art of healing**. *"Your family doctor is no longer free to choose the treatment he or she feels is best for you, but must follow the dictates established by physicians whose motives and alliances are such that their decisions may not be in your best interests,"* says Alan Levin, M.D.

Your Right Of Choice

Patients' most fundamental right – **medical freedom of choice** – has been lost in this country. The medical monopoly's **right to make money** comes before your right to decide – in consultation with your doctor – which cancer therapy would be **best** for your particular condition. The following letter eloquently and movingly illustrates the **dilemma faced** by the cancer patient. The author is a psychologist.

"My wife was diagnosed as having terminal ovarian cancer five years ago. She is alive, well and healthy because of non-approved and unconventional cancer treatment.

I am writing this as a letter of protest and in an attempt to educate you and possibly save your life or that of your wife or child. I am not a crazy fanatic, but I am a 48-year-old man who, five years ago, had to decide what to do in order to try to save my wife's life. We investigated and researched our options and

213

made an informed and intelligent decision to seek something other than what was offered by traditional medicine in this country.

I am angry, frustrated, and mad as hell that I have had to take my wife out of this country, had to struggle with my health insurance company because her treatment was 'not approved,' and had to struggle to obtain her medications because they are 'not approved' and subject to confiscation. It has been a battle to provide her with alternative cancer treatment.

I now know that there is a financial war going on, and the victims are the millions of people who have been denied alternative cancer treatments because the AMA or FDA or someone has decided that we can only undergo an approved treatment…There are no rights to life or liberty in this country when it comes to freedom of choice in medicine. There is only coercion and subversion and greed – and people dying. We are the financial prisoners of the AMA and FDA, and they are killing us in the name of approved treatment.

My wife was almost a victim; and if you allow this to continue, then one day you will become a victim, too.

Please help to do something to bring truth, sanity and morality back to health care in America."

A Great Wrapup

Here, finally, is a great e-mail I read the other day. It was on one of the forums I monitor. The writer, Peter Lorenz, is quite knowledgeable about cancer treatments. But his message, I think, sums up the main message of this book quite well. Peter was responding to a plea from another forum contributor called Ernie, who had lamented that there was not more "proof" of the efficacy of the treatments we have been discussing. Here's Peter's message:

"Hi Ernie!

As you may already know, with cancer there are no guarantees, regardless of treatment type. If you were to pose the same question to your oncologist, and he or she were disposed to tell the truth, you would find that the treatments that mainstream medicine has to offer you have no proof of effectiveness, cure, or life extension.

But there is a very important difference. Once you have gone down that road of surgery, radiation, and chemotherapy, there is no turning back. The collateral damage is permanent. If these methods do not work, you would be a very poor candidate for alternative approaches. Mainstream treatment would simply continue with more of the same until you die. Forgive me for being so blunt. But this is the sorry state of conventional cancer treatment in the U.S.

Whereas when you obtain non-toxic treatments, and this generally means a number of treatments simultaneously meant to work synergistically, if they do not control or cure, you simply move on to other alternatives with your immune system and DNA intact.

Do not let your doctor pressure you into any quick decisions. Get second and third opinions. Do some research over the Internet. Take a look at www.alkalizeforhealth.net and other sites.

Consider this: When the only tool you have is a hammer, everything begins to look like a nail.

I wish you the best of luck in your search.

Peter Lorenz
A comrade-in-arms"

Live Long and Die Young!

Thank you for reading this book. Please read the booklets on **prevention** of cancer and other degenerative disease with proper **diet and exercise**. Let's avoid becoming victims.

If you or a relative or friend suffer from either a **sore back** or **diabetes**, please read those booklets, also.

If you already are engaged in the battle of survival with cancer, I sincerely hope that I have given you **ammunition and hope**.

May God Bless You with a long and healthy life!!

Bill Henderson
Author, Cure Your Cancer
http://www.GetAndStayWell.com
E-mail: bhenderson@getandstaywell.com

APPENDIX A – RESOURCE SUMMARY

Following is a summary of the sources mentioned in this book and some others of interest.

1. *REAL AGE – Are You As Young As You Can Be?*, by Michael F. Roizen, M.D., copyright 1999. Website: http://www.realage.com

   Learn how each part of your lifestyle affects your lifespan. Is your "Real Age" older or younger than what's on your driver's license? Once you take the test, you will have perfect knowledge of what changes in your lifestyle will be the most beneficial. At the website, you can also subscribe to a free e-mail service that will deliver daily tips on improving your health and longevity to your e-mail box.

2. *Antioxidants Against Cancer* by Ralph W. Moss, PhD, copyright 2000. Website: http://CancerDecisions.com

   This book should be "required reading" for everyone, not just cancer patients. All of us need to be familiar with the antioxidants. This book has lots of detail about specific compounds and their effects on different types of cancer. Many of them have an anti-cancer effect as well. At his web site, you will be able to order any of his 10 books on cancer plus a 500+ page report on each of over 210 cancer diagnoses. These cover both conventional and alternative treatments; supplements you should take, or avoid; and information on European and Mexican clinics. A monthly telephone or e-mail update on each report is also available.

3. *Alternatives* newsletter by David G. Williams, M.D. Website: http://www.DrDavidWilliams.com

   Dr. Williams is quoted extensively in this e-book. For over 20 years, he has traveled the world in search of the best cures for all common diseases. His website has a complete catalog of his newsletters, organized by subject. You can read a synopsis of each article and order those that interest you. I have subscribed to his newsletter since 1985. You can send him e-mail questions at his website. I have found no better source for a wide variety of health information.

4. *Ultra-Fit*, by Joe Davis, M.D. with Lucille Enix, copyright 1991.

   This paperback may be out of print. If you can find it, I recommend it. You'll find information on the cellular mechanics of healthy exercise plus diets and specific exercises to achieve and maintain what Dr. Davis calls "The Ultra-fit State." Works for me.

5. *Questioning Chemotherapy*, by Ralph W. Moss, PhD, copyright 1995. Website: http://www.CancerDecisions.com

   A complete discussion of the limitations of chemotherapy for the treatment of cancer. If you or a loved one or friend have cancer, you must read this book. It gives you detailed information on each medication used and how effective it is for each type of cancer. Do not agree to any chemotherapy treatment until you read this book cover to cover plus the 500-page "Moss Report" on your type of cancer available at the website above.

6. *World Without Cancer – The Story of Vitamin B17*, by G. Edward Griffin, copyright 1997 and 1974 – Fifteenth printing: March 2000. Website: http://www.lifewithoutcancer.com/aboutlaetrile.htm

   The first half of this book presents a detailed and documented history of Laetrile (Vitamin B17) and its use in cancer treatment. It describes in detail the suppression of this compound by the Food and Drug Administration (FDA) and the "cyanide scare" used to justify it. The second half covers "The Politics of Cancer Therapy." The author describes a conspiracy involving American moguls, Nazi officers in Hitler's Germany and the drug industry in general. Fasten your seat belt. This is a very well-written but controversial book. There are several reader reviews available at http://www.amazon.com

   To order apricot seeds and Laetrile/Amygdalin/B-17 tablets, go to: http://www.smart-drugs.net/ias-laetrile-cancer.htm

7. *The Healing of Cancer*, by Barry Lynes, copyright 1989 distributed in the United States by Vitamart, K-Mart Plaza, Route 10, Randolph, NJ 08869; (201) 366-4494.

   A hard-hitting expose of the medical establishment's fifty-year history of suppressing alternative cancer therapies. American journalist Barry Lynes discusses various alternative treatments in this incisive analysis.

8. Remarkable Recovery – What Extraordinary Healings Tell Us About Getting Well and Staying Well, by Carlyle Hirshberg and Marc Ian Barasch, copyright 1995.

219

An inspiring documentation of the history of "spontaneous remission," primarily of cancer patients. The original research done here attempts to isolate what these remarkable recoveries have in common. If you want an exciting exposure to a phenomenon witnessed by virtually every doctor who has treated cancer patients. Included in one of the appendices is a form for you to submit to a "Remarkable Recovery Registry" if you have witnessed or experienced such a recovery.

9. *Resonant Frequency Therapy – Building the Rife Beam Ray Device*, by James E. Bare, D.C., copyright 1995. Website: http://LauraLee.com/Rife.htm

I recommend you check out the website first. It includes a 45-minute interview of James Bare by Laura Lee. If you are interested, you can, of course, purchase the book. The book includes detailed instructions for building the Beam Ray Device. My personal opinion is that this device has been made obsolete by several of the natural cancer therapies discussed in this e-book. If you have some talent as a do-it-yourself electrician, check it out.

10. *The Cure For All Cancers*, by Hulda Regehr Clark, PhD, N.D., copyright 1993.

This book documents Dr. Clark's treatment of over 100 cancer cases. She uses an electronic device to isolate the cancer sites. The instructions for building it are in the book. Her theory on the cause of cancer by parasites or intestinal flukes is not completely original. It is interesting and controversial.

For more information on Dr. Clark, go to the web site: http://www.drclark.net

11. *Creating Health – How to Wake Up The Body's Intelligence*, by Deepak Chopra, M.D., copyright 1987. Website: http://www.chopra.com

This is Dr. Chopra's "breakthrough" book – the first in which he created a new understanding of health and illness and the healing power of the mind. He has since written over 25 books, translated into 35 languages, plus over 100 audio and videotape series. In 1999, Time Magazine selected Dr. Chopra as one of the "Top 100 Icons and Heroes of The Century." You will understand his later work better if you read this book first. His theories about mind-body interaction have now been proven. The scientific proof is covered in the next book on this list.

12. The Balance Within – The Science Connecting Health and Emotions, by Esther M. Sternberg, M.D., copyright 2000.

Dr. Sternberg is a leading expert on the interaction of the endocrine and immune systems, with impressive credentials. She takes us from the origins of medicine in Greece, to the early medical schools in Padua, to modern research in Montreal and the U.S. She clearly describes how we came to appreciate the physiology of stress, how the mind influences the body, and how the body affects the mind. This area of research, in which Dr. Sternberg has been one of the world's leading scientists for at least a decade, is leading to new understandings and treatments of the stress-related diseases of modern life.

13. *Eat Right 4 Your Type – The Individualized Diet Solution to Staying Healthy, Living Longer & Achieving Your Ideal Weight*, by Dr. Peter J. D'Adamo with Catherine Whitney, copyright 1996. Website: http://www.dadamo.com/

This book gives you specific recommendations on which foods you should eat and not eat based on your blood type. It is based on 40 years of research by Dr. D'Adamo and his father. In the years from 1982 through 1996, the author challenged samples of each blood type (O, A, B and AB) with hundreds of foods, vitamin supplements, condiments and beverages. My family has used this book to avoid certain foods, supplements, etc. and seek out others for the last three years. It has been very helpful in eliminating my wife's gastritis and my flatulence. The book includes specific case studies and recommendations on cancer and other diseases.

14. *Dr. Atkins' New Diet Revolution*, by Robert C. Atkins, M.D., copyright 1992 (updated in 1999). Website: http://www.atkinscenter.com

This website includes an enormous amount of detail on Dr. Atkins and his diet and supplement recommendations. His focus has shifted from his earliest books that were mainly concerned with helping people like me to lose weight quickly and easily. His latest books, including this one, are more concerned with long-term wellness and healing through natural therapies, including the use of an ongoing enjoyable and healthy low-carbohydrate maintenance diet and vita-nutrient supplementation. This book and Dr. Atkins Age-Defying Diet Revolution detail how to prevent what once were considered inevitable signs of aging through a diet of phytonutrient-rich vegetables (and, yes, fruit!) and use of anti-aging supplements. Dr. Atkins says, *"After over 40 years as a practicing physician and over 30 years as Medical Director of The Atkins Center, I have found these are the most effective methods for treating the vast majority of chronic conditions as well as for staying vigorously healthy and forever youthful."* Get this book and explore his website!

15. My website: http://www.GetAndStayWell.com

At my website, you can order this book. You can subscribe to my free newsletter. All the previous editions of the newsletter are archived if you missed one.

16. American Holistic Health Association, P. O. Box 17400, Anaheim, CA 92817. Phone: (714) 779-6152. Website: http://healthy.net/ahha

At this website, you can enter search criteria (zip code, telephone area code, state, specialty, etc.) and get a list of "holistic" doctors with their specialties in your area.

17. American Holistic Medical Association, 6728 Old McLean Village Drive, McLean, VA 22101. Phone: (703) 556-9728 FAX: (703) 556-8729. Website: http://www.holisticmedicine.org/

At this website, you will find information about this group. If you want a directory of their members, you will need to send them $10.

18. The Simonton Cancer Center, P. O. Box 890, Pacific Palisades, CA 90272. Toll free: (800) 459-3424; Local: (310) 457-3811; FAX: (310) 457-0421. E-mail: simonton@lainet.com.
Website: http://www.simontoncenter.com/

Dr. Simonton is famous for pioneering studies in the use of the mind to overcome cancer and other diseases. You may also want to read his book *Getting Well Again*. It covers the mental processes essential in recovering from advanced and terminal cancer and other serious ailments.

19. WebMD Health. Website: http://my.webmd.com

A **very** comprehensive website covering all aspects of health care – conventional and alternative/complementary. This website is a perfect example of the information available through the Internet. Search capability, chat rooms, research results, etc. All-encompassing and **complete**. It is also an example of one of the **main reasons I wrote this book**. Laymen need a guide to the vast amount of information available. Without that, it can be **overwhelming**.

20. American Diabetes Association. Website: http://diabetes.org

Another comprehensive website for diabetes sufferers. It covers both Type 1 and Type 2 diabetes. Emphasis is on **diet and exercise**. If you have diabetes or suspect you have it, **go here**. Same comments about comprehensive nature of this site as those for WebMD Health above.

21. Third Opinion: An International Directory to Alternative Therapy Centers for the Treatment and Prevention of Cancer and Other Degenerative Diseases, by John Fink, Avery Publishing Group (120 Old Broadway, Garden City Park, NY 11040; 800-548-5757), revised edition, 1991.

Provides basic information on about 160 alternative and complementary therapy centers, practitioners, support groups, educational centers, and information services for the treatment and prevention of degenerative diseases, mainly cancer. It contains a concise description of each clinic's approach and method of treatment as well as contact names, addresses and phone numbers; prices; and a large listing of relevant books. For the cancer patient seriously investigating alternative or adjunctive treatment, this book is a user-friendly, extremely helpful resource. Unfortunately, it is out of print, but you can get it on amazon.com from one of their alternative sources.

22. The Complete Encyclopedia of Natural Healing, by Gary Null, September, 2000.

Gary Null has been updating this reference book since it was first published in 1988. It is written for the layperson but written by an expert. The listings are by ailment, so you can look under whatever ails you – asthma, heart disease, arthritis, diabetes, allergies, cancer, etc. – and take whatever vitamins or herbs are helpful for that specific condition. This book is also available from amazon.com. The last time I checked, it was $16.

23. *An Alternative Medicine Definitive Guide to Cancer* by W. John Diamond, W. Lee Cowden and Burton Goldberg, March, 1997.

This massive (1,116 pages) book is published by the editor of the magazine *Alternative Medicine*. The first section consists of richly detailed accounts of the successful cancer treatment plans of 23 respected alternative physicians from Robert C. Atkins to Charles B. Simone. Part 2 is a fundamental explanation of the nature, causes, politics and prevention of cancer. The final section presents alternative therapies from a to z. It is meant for those who have cancer, their friends and family and (who knows?) maybe even their doctor! It is also available from amazon.com for (gulp!) $49.95. They have used ones available for $29.95. I recently discovered a slimmed down version of this hefty tome. It is called *Cancer Diagnosis – What to Do Next* by the same authors. Only $14.95.

24. Racketeering in Medicine: The Suppression of Alternatives, by James P. Carter, September 1992.

Carter describes in detail how, for years, the AMA, FDA and pharmaceutical industry have tried to discredit alternative, less expensive, less invasive and often more effective methods of treatment. He does not sensationalize the topic but documents with evidence how the governing bodies of modern medicine have a vested interest in suppressing these treatments and making sure that average folks never know about them. If you have any doubts about this after reading my book, get James Carter's. If he doesn't convince you, I doubt that anything will. This one, too, is available from amazon.com, price: $10.36, with used ones for $7.95.

25. *Options – The Alternative Cancer Therapy Book*, by Richard Walters, copyright 1993, published by Avery.

A comprehensive guide to all forms of alternative cancer therapy known at the time this book was published (1993). Walters has thoroughly documented 28 such therapies. In much more detail than I can do here, he lays out the case that suppression of valid cancer therapies has been a common practice of the American cancer "establishment" for at least the last 50 years.

26. Lorraine Day, M.D. Website: http://www.drday.com

Dr. Day is an orthopedic surgeon. She spent 15 years on the faculty at the University of California at San Francisco School of Medicine. She was also the Chief of Orthopedic Surgery at San Francisco General Hospital.

At her website, you'll be able to see a streaming video of her describing how she cured herself of metastasized breast cancer. There are remarkable photos of her **grapefruit-sized tumor** protruding from her chest. Many of her videos on cancer can be purchased at her website. [Again, I feel the need to repeat that I get no cut or any other remuneration from these recommendations.] The video titles will give you an idea of her **wonderful healing message**:

"Cancer Doesn't Scare Me Anymore"
"Drugs Never Cure Disease"
"Diseases Don't Just Happen"
and
"Sorting Through The Maze Of Alternative Medicine"

Don't miss this website.

27. Moderated chat room. http://aoma.com/cs

The "cs" in the site name stands for "cancer survivors." This is a "real time" chat room. Here you will find others with an interest in cancer therapy. The advantage of a moderated chat room is that you usually get a relatively "instant" answer to your question.

28. A Dietician's Cancer Story, by Diana Dyer.

This lady self-published her 54-page cancer and nutrition booklet in 1997. It is now the best-selling cancer and nutrition book on amazon.com. She has set up an endowment with proceeds from the booklet to help underwrite research about how good nutrition can prevent the recurrence of cancer. For more information, go to:

http://www.DianaDyerMSRD.com

29. The Cancer Cure Foundation

Once you have read this book, you need to explore this company's site. It is a non-profit organization dedicated to providing information on alternative cancer therapies. At their web site, you will find detailed descriptions of multiple clinics all over the world. They are divided into "Clinics in the U.S.," "Clinics in Mexico," and "Clinics Outside the U.S. and Mexico." They include contact names, phone numbers, addresses, web sites, e-mail addresses, pictures of providers, pictures of the clinics, and pictures of patients with their testimonials. They give a detailed description of the type of treatment given by each clinic, including glossaries of terms. Finally, they give you a list of 8 or 10 of the "Most Popular" clinics. They ask for feedback from their users and obviously they get it. They have been doing this since 1976, but they have adapted their service very efficiently to the Internet Age. Go to:

http://cancure.org

30. Annie Appleseed Project

An awesome lady. Ann Fonfa has taken up the torch for all cancer patients in a very courageous and vivacious way. You need to get to know this lady. At her web site, among dozens of other resources, you will be able to read her three-week diary kept during her successful treatment for breast cancer at the Gerson Clinic in Tijuana, Mexico. She lobbies constantly for more research into Complementary & Alternative Medicine (CAM). She is championing your interests. Don't miss this site:

http://www.AnnieAppleseedProject.org

31. Forbidden Medicine

Here is a web site that is an absolute mother lode of information on alternative cancer cures. Part of it is available free. The rest requires a "membership" fee of $97 (or $15, if you can prove you cannot afford the $97). Don't blow this one off. It has lots of valuable information and consultations with CAM doctors are available at "reasonable" prices. They will also help members find a qualified CAM doctor in their area. Worth a close look.

http://www.ForbiddenMedicine.com

32. Dr. Ron Kennedy's web site.

This wonderful doctor's web site contains an encyclopedic summary of all the alternative treatments. There is even a search engine where you can enter your Zip Code and get a list of doctors or dentists in one or more of the "alternative" specialties in your area of the country.

http://www.medical-library.net/sites/adjunctive_therapies_for_cancer.html

33. Dr. Matthias Rath's web site

This outstanding German doctor has one of the more complete and educational web sites I have ever seen on the causes and cures for cancer. You can download his books free and read them in the language of your choice. There are videos showing how cancer spreads at the cellular level and how to control metastasis and eradicate the cancer cells. Don't miss this one!

http://www.naturally-against-cancer.org

34. Insulin Potentiated Therapy (IPT).

If you have cancer, you need to consider this form of low-dose chemotherapy. Side effects are minimal and the effects of the chemo are magnified several thousand times by using an insulin shot 30 minutes or so before administering the chemo drug (in a very weak dose). This web site includes a list of all the physicians (about 80 at this writing) who are qualified in this important therapy.

http://www.iptq.org

35. Art Brown's web site.

Art Brown has written a book similar to mine. He is an active participant in several on-line forums concerning cancer treatments. Art is a former employee of the Cancer Cure Foundation. His web site is:

http://www.alternative-cancer.net

36. National Cancer ResearchFoundation

At Fred Eichhorn's interesting web site, you'll find lots of testimonials from cancer survivors – all types of cancer. Fred works hard and charges little to help heal lots of cancer patients. His web site is:

http://www.ncrf.org

37. CancerEducation.com

One of the best sites for comprehensive cancer information. You can see lectures by famous cancer experts. One example: A 71-minute slide show and lecture by Dr. William Fair. Dr. Fair has been on the staff of Memorial Sloan-Kettering Cancer Center in New York for 18 years as a urologist. He was diagnosed with colon cancer in the early 90's. After two bouts with chemo, and two recurrences, he cured himself with "alternative" methods and has become a zealot about informing people about the inadequacy of the cancer treatments in the allopathic (conventional) medicine system.

http://www.CancerEducation.com

38. Life Extension Foundation

One of the best sources for information about prevention of all degenerative disease, including cancer. They publish a monthly magazine and (of course) a line of supplements. Their prices don't come close to Our Health Coop, so use this as an information source only.

http://www.lef.org

39. *Beating Cancer With Nutrition* by Patrick Quillin, copyright 2001.

An enormously useful book for cancer patients to understand their diet choices and a slew of great recipes to help you implement them.

40. *The pH Miracle* by Dr. Robert Young, copyright 2002.

    Here is the ultimate logic behind your body's need to alkalize to stay healthy.

41. 10 Natural Remedies That Can Save Your Life, by James Balch, M.D., copyright 2000.

    Dr. Balch discusses enzymes and other natural treatments in detail. $19 in paperback from amazon.com. Also available in an audio playback download for $12.95.

42. *Lessons From The Miracle Doctors*, by Jon Barron, copyright 2002.

    A 169-page PDF download e-book that is chock full of information on getting and staying well. Covers all types of illness from the CAM viewpoint. You can download it free at:

    http://www.drtabor.healingamerica.com/.

43. Saving Yourself from the Disease-Care Crisis, by Walt Stoll, M.D., copyright 1996.

    A treatise on coping with common ailments and the effects of stress on your health.

44. Alive And Well – One Doctor's Experience With Nutrition in the Treatment of Cancer Patients, by Philip E. Binzel, M.D.

    An intriguing account of this conventional doctor's epiphany about the importance of nutrition in the healing of cancer.

45. National Foundation for Alternative Medicine

I think the best way for you to get a flavor of this organization is for me to quote from the introductory message from the founder.

"NFAM OFFERS HOPE TO YOU FOR FREE!

Welcome from NFAM's Founder and Chairman of the Board, former U.S. Congressman Berkley Bedell

Dear Friends,

Over 1,500 Americans will die TODAY from cancer. That's over 553,400 individuals in a year! Will someone you know or love be next?

Most people have no options for treatment other than conventional medicine. I am a cancer survivor. I was one of the fortunate few who learned about other innovative, safe, and effective treatments that are often only available outside this country.

Because of my experience and the dedication of others like me, The National Foundation for Alternative Medicine (NFAM) was created to scientifically study, validate, and publicize information about alternative and complementary treatments and to make the findings available to the public free of charge. Most of NFAM's research to date has been in cancer treatment. But as soon as we are able to raise the necessary funds, we will move forward in studying other chronic illnesses such as heart disease, AIDS, Lyme disease, Alzheimers, and diabetes."

Check out their web site and their 70 reports on investigative visits to cancer clinics all over the world at:

http://www.nfam.org/home/

46. Education Center for Prostate Cancer Patients

Right around New Year's Eve, 2001, Ed Van Overloop called me. Ed lives in Park Ridge, New Jersey. He is a cancer survivor. He has been helping cancer patients for 13 years. He runs a support group for about 100 cancer patients and survivors.

Ed co-founded a non-profit organization you should check out if you are a prostate cancer patient. It is called the Education Center for Prostate Cancer Patients. Just go to their web site:

http://www.ecpcp.org

I joined and they mailed me a lot of material: a book called *"The Reference Guide to Prostate Cancer;"* two periodicals called *"The Prostate Cancer Exchange"* and *"The Prostate Cancer Digest."* If you want to speed up the process, you may want to call them. Contact Bettye Rainwater at (516) 942-5000 between 9:00 AM and 3:00 PM Eastern time.

If you're in the New York/New Jersey area, I'd recommend you contact Ed and join his support group. It includes all kinds of cancer patients, not just prostate cancer. His e-mail address is:

edvo31@bellatlantic.net

47. Gavin Phillips web site.

Gavin is a dedicated crusader for alternative cancer cures. His non-profit web site: http://www.cancerinform.org has a wealth of background information for you on why we all need to co-doctor. First, you need to read the article he wrote which was published in "Clamor" magazine in 2001.

http://www.cancerinform.org/article.html

Browse Gavin's web site. You'll be impressed, as I was, at both his knowledge and his sincerity in fighting for your right to medical choice.

48. Alkalize for Health web site.

The web site "Alkalize for Health" is a comprehensive site. Among other things, it features a recipe for "Cancer Self-Treatment." You can find it at:

http://www.alkalizeforhealth.net/cancerselftreatment.htm

The eight-part program they outline for curing or preventing cancer includes information on: Cancer and Oxygen; The Importance of Exercise; Cancer and Ph; Acidity and Free Radicals; Purification Techniques; Enzymes to Dissolve Cancers; Vitamins to Fight Cancer; and Cancer and Meditation.

When you finish reading those 17 pages, you'll understand cancer a lot better. Check out their more in depth coverage of oxygen, alkalinity, meditation and hyperthermia. If you are more comfortable with another language, this site can be read in French, German, Italian, Portugese and Spanish.

49. CancerCured online forum.

If you are interested in joining the discussion forum on Yahoo Groups from which I get lots of my information, just send a blank e-mail to:

cancercured-subscribe@yahoogroups.com

You can just monitor the messages from well-informed people like Art Brown if you don't feel like contributing.

50. Direct Labs – do-it-yourself blood tests.

There is a new (at least new to me) service available now in the U.S. You can obtain your own blood tests, including some cancer tests, without going through your doctor for a "prescription" for the lab.

Take a look at this web site:

http://www.directlabs.com/

When you call them, they will direct you to a local blood lab in your area for getting a sample drawn. The lab will perform the tests and then mail the results in plain English directly to you. If you prefer, you can have the results sent to a doctor.

51. Aidan Clinic, Tempe, Arizona.

One of my readers is really enthused about the treatment – largely "alternative" – she got for her cancer at Aidan Clinic in Tempe, Arizona (near Phoenix). Their 3-week in-patient program costs about $13,000. Check them out at:

http://www.aidanclinic.com

52. The Foundation for the Advancement of Innovative Medicine (FAIM)

Monica Miller is a fine art painter turned political lobbyist and legal activist on behalf of doctors and "alternative" medical practice. She has been instrumental in getting "freedom of practice" legislation in place for MDs in her home state of New York.

She also has a website with information on what is happening with alternative medical politics in other states around the USA. She helps legal activists in these other states. You can check her web site to see if your state is progressive in these matters. Just go to:

http://www.healthlobby.com/

Twelve states have laws that protect patient access to alternative therapies from licensed physicians. They are: Alaska, Colorado, Florida, Georgia, Massachusetts, New York, North Carolina, Ohio, Oklahoma, Oregon, Texas and Washington.

Of these, Florida's laws are the most liberal. They protect your access to alternative therapies from ALL health care professionals. Two other states - Louisiana and Nevada - have regulations (not laws) that protect your rights of access to these treatments.

Monica and FAIM are trying to extend this freedom, state by state. We need to help her. Check out her web site and e-mail her with your offer of support. Her e-mail address is:

monica@healthlobby.com

Booklet #1 – Stop Your Aging With Diet

Someday we will sit down to a banquet of our own consequences.
Robert Louis Stevenson

A HEALTHY DIET

All of us have read about **diets**. Most of us have tried one or more. Most of them have been **unsuccessful** in terms of long-term benefit. Why?

Diets are seen as **temporary**. "I'll get on this diet and lose 20 pounds." Then what? To be **healthy forever**, you must simply adopt **eating habits** that are healthy. Nothing else works. If you don't believe me, ask your friends. Ask them to tell you about a diet where they **permanently** lost xx pounds. Do your own survey.

For now, let's assume that **no diet** is worth the paper it is written on. **Healthy eating habits** are what we're talking about.

SEVERAL OPTIONS

We want to eat healthy. **Forever**. What does that involve? I wish I could give you an easy answer. Let's look at two options.

Dr. Atkins' Diet Revolution

Talk about **controversy**. Ever since 1972, when he published his first Diet Revolution book, Robert C. Atkins, M.D. has been **ridiculed** by his peers. All the more reason, as we've seen, to explore his work.

As you'll find out when you visit his web site: http://www.atkinscenter.com/ Dr. Atkins is a practicing M.D. He has specialized in cardiology. He has treated 60,000 patients since he received his medical degree from Cornell University Medical School in 1955. His books have sold over 10 million copies worldwide.

Dr. Atkins believes that most fat people suffer from *hyperinsulinism*. That means their bodies are generating **too much insulin**, which turns sugar into fat. The trigger for the insulin generation in our bodies is **carbohydrates**.

He says you need to change your body's metabolism so it starts to **burn your stored fat**. You do this by **restricting** your consumption of **carbohydrates**. He obviously has a point.

In spite of all the fat labeling on foods and our society's obsession with "low fat" diets, **20 million more people in the U.S. are obese than 10 years ago**. Whatever we're counting — calories or fat content — it isn't **working**! Every man and woman is, on the average, **ten pounds heavier**. Look around you. Obesity is hard to hide. For **children**, the situation is **even worse**. Their obesity rates have **doubled** in the last ten years. Have you heard about the 120-pound three-year-old?

Dr. Atkins says our average **carbohydrate consumption** in those ten years has gone up by **50 grams a day**. He says that among the thousands of patients he has treated for obesity, **90 percent** have a **metabolic** disorder, not an **eating** disorder.

How often have you heard fat people say *"But I just eat small meals and I still gain weight!"*? I've heard at least **20 people** tell me that in the **last few years**. All were **grossly overweight**. They were not lying to me. They don't eat a lot. They just eat the **wrong things**.

Let me give you a personal example. When I first read Dr. Atkins book about 4 years ago, I weighed about **202 pounds**. I'm 6 feet, 1 inch tall. That was down from **229 pounds in 1992**, when I started working out with Dr. Joe Davis at Ultra Fit. I was still **too large**, by any standard. Today, I weigh **187 pounds** — the same as when I graduated from flying school in the Air Force in **1953**. I have been at that weight or **within 3 pounds** of it since **1997**. I plan to stay there for life.

What has changed? Mostly, **breakfast**. Counting the carbohydrates I ate for breakfast **astounded** me! I would typically have a bowl of cereal (usually Raisin Bran) with milk and a banana; two slices of toast with butter and jam; coffee with sugar; and a tall glass of orange juice. Healthy breakfast, no?

Was I shocked when I added up the carbos?!! For breakfast alone, I was eating **174 grams of carbohydrate**. The maximum anyone can eat and maintain their weight varies between 40 and 75 **per day**. Unbelievable? Here's the tally:

Raisin Bran cereal	41 grams
Milk (1% fat)	12 grams
Banana (1 medium)	26 grams
Bread (white-2 sl.)	28 grams
Butter (1 pat)	0.1 gram
Jam	26 grams
Sugar (in coffee)	12 grams
O.J. (8 oz.)	29 grams
Grand Total	**174 grams**

With all the other stuff — steaks, rice, pasta, pies, ice cream, etc. — I was eating, it's a wonder I didn't weigh 300 pounds.

What did I do? Well, the only drastic change I made was to change my breakfast to the following:

Turkey bacon (2 sl.)	0.2 grams
Eggs (2 large-scrambled)	0.2 grams
Coffee	0 grams
Stevia (1 pk)	1 gram
Grand Total	1.4 grams

Did I lose a lot of weight in a hurry? You better believe it!! About **15 pounds** in **three weeks**. Now, I eat a slice of bread (11 grams) with butter (0.1 gram) and put honey (18 grams) in my coffee. So, I'm up to **30 or so grams** for **breakfast**. But the rest of the day, I eat **mostly protein** (broiled chicken, fish, etc.), a vegetable and salad. At night, I eat a **very light snack**. My weight has stayed within 3 pounds of 187 ever since.

The important part about this set of "eating habits" is that I **never feel hungry**. Do I stray sometimes? You bet. **I'm human**. But as soon as I see myself start gaining a couple of pounds, I go right back to **watching my carbohydrate** intake closely.

My wife, Terry, is from Spain. She loves to make Spanish **paella** — a **rice dish** with lots of seafood. Occasionally, we celebrate some **special day** with cake, wine, etc. We have parties where we serve **all kinds of food**. We eat out about once a week.

I'm not talking about a **monastic, sterile life style**. All I feel I have done is **gained control** over my weight — and my life. Of course, part of this — the part I started in 1992 — is a **regular workout schedule**. We'll cover that in the booklet on Exercise.

Meanwhile, here are a few of the **common foods** in the typical American diet and their **grams** of carbohydrates:

Banana Split	91.0
Burrito, bean	48.0
Cheeseburger (1/4 pounder)	33.0
Corn bread stuffing (1/4 Cup)	69.0
Hot dog with bun	24.0
Onion rings (fast food order)	33.0
Shake (medium)	90.0
Mountain Dew (reg 12 oz. can)	46.0
Coca-Cola (reg 12 oz. can)	39.0
Diet Coca-Cola (reg 12 oz. can)	0.0
Diet 7-Up (reg 12 oz. can)	0.0

At Dr. Atkins' web site, you can get a ton of information. Included are convincing testimonials such as this one from Maura Blackburn in New York:

"Our success is almost too good to be true. People don't recognize us. Sometimes it is even hard to believe it myself. My husband lost 85 lbs. He went from a size 42 waist to a 30 waist. I lost 75 lbs. I went from a size 18 to a size 4. We both feel great. Most of all, I no longer suffer from bursitis and my asthma is much better. My husband's cholesterol and blood pressure are now within normal limits. We constantly recommend your diet and will live by it for the rest of our lives."

Also at the web site, you can order the latest book, *Dr. Atkins Age-Defying Diet Revolution*, by Robert C. Atkins, M.D., copyright 1999. Order it. You will be **very glad** you did.

Eat Right 4 Your Type

Another book on diet that we found fascinating is *Eat Right 4 Your Type by* Dr. Peter J. D'Adamo with Catherine Whitney, copyright 1996 published by G. P. Putnam's Sons of New York. This book has been on the NY Times bestseller list. It has sold over a million copies in hardback and been translated into 40 languages.

Dr. D'Adamo is a naturopathic physician, as was his father. In 1980, his father, Dr. James D'Adamo published his book *One Man's Food.* It was based on 23 years of research and experimentation with his patients. He had discovered that certain blood types — A, B, O and AB — correlated to better health with certain types of diets.

For example, Type A people, like me, thrived on vegetarian diets, including vegetable proteins like soy and tofu. They developed copious amounts of mucous discharge in the sinuses when they ate dairy products. Type O people, like my wife and daughter, did better on animal proteins.

Peter D'Adamo picked up his father's work and continued the study using more scientific methods starting in 1982. For example, he used blood samples from Type A, B, O and AB people. He challenged the samples with hundreds of different foods and recorded the reaction. His book is based on these studies.

What he discovered is that agglutination, the body's reaction to a foreign substance, occurred when certain foods met certain blood types. A food that may be beneficial to a certain blood type may be harmful to others.

He has taught his conclusions to many other doctors. All say their patients are getting good results with the guidelines.

Here is the essence of his theory:

- Your blood type — O, A, B, or AB — is a **powerful genetic fingerprint** that identifies you as surely as your **DNA**.
- When you use the individualized characteristics of your **blood type** as a **guidepost for eating and living**, you will be **healthier**, you will naturally reach your **ideal weight**, and you will **slow the process of aging**.
- Your blood type is a **more reliable** measure of your identity than race, culture or geography. It is a **genetic blueprint** for who you are, a guide to how you can live most **healthfully**.
- The key to the significance of blood type can be found in the story of human evolution: **Type O is the oldest**; **Type A** evolved with **agrarian society**; **Type B** emerged as humans **migrated** north into **colder, harsher territories**; and **Type AB** was a thoroughly **modern** adaptation, a result of the **intermingling** of disparate groups. This evolutionary story relates directly to the dietary needs of each blood type today.

Dr. D'Adamo summarizes it as follows:

"I realize that this is probably a completely new idea for you. Few people ever even think about the implications of their blood type, even though it is a powerful genetic force. You may be reluctant to wade into such unfamiliar territory, even if the scientific arguments seem convincing. I ask you to do only three things: Talk to your physician before you begin, find out your blood type if you don't already know it, and try your Blood Type Diet for at least two weeks. Most of my patients experience some results within that time period — increased energy, weight loss, a lessening of digestive complaints, and improvement of chronic problems such as asthma, headaches, and heartburn. Give your Blood Type Diet a chance to bring you the benefits I've seen it bring to the more than four

thousand people I've put on the diet. See for yourself that blood not only provides your body's most vital nourishment, but now proves itself a vehicle for your future well-being."

Blood Type Diet

In his book, Dr. D'Adamo lists **hundreds** of foods for each blood type. They are grouped into categories called **"Highly Beneficial"**, **"Neutral"** and **"Avoid."** For example, for me, a Type A, the Seafood category looks like this:

Highly Beneficial
Carp, Cod, Grouper, Mackerel, Monkfish, Pickerel, Red Snapper, Rainbow Trout, Salmon, Sardine, Sea Trout, Silver Perch, Snail, Whitefish, Yellow Perch

Neutral
Abalone, Albacore (Tuna), Mahi-mahi, Ocean perch, Pike, Porgy, Sailfish, Sea Bass, Shark, Smelt, Snapper, Sturgeon, Swordfish, Weakfish, White Perch, Yellowtail.

Avoid
Anchovy, Barracuda, Beluga, Bluefish, Bluegill Bass, Catfish, Caviar, Clam, Conch, Crab, Crayfish, Eel, Flounder, Frog, Gray Sole, Haddock, Hake, Halibut, Herring (fresh), Herring (pickled), Lobster, Lox (smoked salmon), Mussels, Octopus, Oysters, Scallop, Shad, Shrimp, Sole, Squid (calamari), Striped Bass, Tilefish, Turtle

Other categories of foods include Meats, Eggs and Dairy, Nuts and Seeds, Beans and Legumes, Cereals, Breads and Muffins, Grains and Pasta, Vegetables, Fruit, Juices and Fluids, Spices, Condiments, Herbal Teas, Miscellaneous Beverages and Vitamins and Supplements.

Does It Work?

Terry and I decided to give his ideas a try. We **carefully** avoided the foods in the "Avoid" category. We made a point of eating **as much** of the "Highly Beneficial" foods **as possible**. We kept it up **religiously** for three weeks.

The results were quite **dramatic**. Terry's chronic **gastritis disappeared**. She could not remember a period in her adult life when she had not suffered from this ailment. It caused her enough **pain**, we had talked to two doctors about it, and had her stomach examined with a **"swallowed camera"** device, all with **negative results**.

I, too, found the diet completely **freed me from gas**. More importantly, I felt a definite **increase in energy**.

We were so impressed that I went into this book and made up on the word processor a **one-page list** of the "Green Light" and "Red Light" foods for Type A (me) and Type O (Terry and our daughter). I picked from Dr. D'Adamo's list only those **foods we commonly ate**. I ignored the "Neutral" category. This was all done in an attempt to **summarize** so the list could be **posted** on our refrigerator door.

Some examples of changes we made: we have all **avoided Catfish**, which we ate frequently before; we **avoid** eating any kind of **white and wheat flour**; I eat **peanuts** ("Highly Beneficial" for Type A); Terry and Katie **avoid** them ("Avoid" for Type O); Terry avoids **coffee**; I avoid **beer**; I avoid **Beta Carotene** supplement; Terry avoids **Vitamin E** supplement.

We eat Ezekiel Bread, a **flourless bread**, which is high in protein. We get it at the health food store. But, be **careful**. It is high in protein, but also high in **carbohydrates.**

Having the list on the refrigerator has proven the **only practical way** to use these recommendations in our daily eating. There is **no way** to memorize the long lists from the book.

Dr. D'Adamo has a **very complete** web site. It is at: http://www.dadamo.com/ Included are a discussion forum, Dr D'Adamo's answers to critics, Frequently Asked Questions (FAQs), and a wide variety of other **useful information**. His clinic with address and phone number is also listed.

Blood Type and Cancer

The final chapter in this book deals with Dr. D'Adamo's research on how **Blood Types and cancer** interact. He has done extensive research on breast cancer. It shows that Blood Type **A and AB** are far **more susceptible** to this disease than Type O and Type B. There is information on other types of cancer. If I had cancer, I would **study this book** carefully. It seems that your eating and taking the proper supplements during the treatment can **substantially** increase your odds of conquering the cancer.

If you have any trouble with **gastritis**, bloating or whatever, you need this book. If you want to feel **more energetic**, you need this book. And, certainly, if you have cancer, you need this book. Don't knock it until you've tried it.

In Summary

Healthy eating habits are **essential** to good health. **Diet** definitely **causes** many degenerative **diseases**, such as diabetes, high blood pressure, heart disease, osteoporosis, gout and macular degeneration. Most **M.D.s** are **not qualified** to advise you on **healthy eating habits**…even if they had the time.

You must take control of your eating if you want to live a long and healthy life. It is **never too late**. Do it today!!

A HEALTHY MIND

Recent discoveries **prove** the thesis that there is a real **"mind-body connection."** We will discuss these below. **Deepak Chopra, M.D.** was the first author to make this connection clear to me.

Meet Dr. Chopra

Dr. Chopra has now written **25 books** that have been translated into **35 languages**. He has produced **over 100** audio and videotape series. In 1999, Time magazine selected Dr. Chopra as one of the **"Top 100 Icons and Heroes of the Century."**

I first encountered Dr. Chopra in his book called *Creating Health* in 1990 or so. Shortly after reading that book, my wife, Marge and I ordered a set of audiotapes he made called *Ageless Body, Timeless Mind.* I have found him to be an excellent source for wisdom on the **interconnections** between physical, mental, emotional and spiritual health.

I cannot improve on his words, so I will quote them from his book Creating Health:

"How to Be Perfectly Healthy and Feel Ever Youthful

HEALTH IS OUR NATURAL STATE. The World Health Organization has defined it as something more than the absence of disease or infirmity — health is the state of perfect physical, mental, and social well-being. To this may be added spiritual well-being, a zest for life, a sense of fulfillment, and an awareness of harmony with the universe around him. It is a state in which one feels ever youthful, ever buoyant, and ever happy. Such a state is not only desirable but also quite possible. And it is not only quite possible, it is easy to obtain."

As an experienced **medical doctor**, Chopra saw the limitations of "conventional" medicine. The **certainty** of the connection between emotions, attitudes, spiritual awareness and physical health arose from his **clinical practice**. This "epiphany" of the **"mind-body connection"** occurred to him about 17 years ago...in the mid '80s. He has devoted his life since then to bringing this message to people using all forms of media.

To understand and appreciate his message, you really need to **read one or more** of his early works. All available from amazon.com, they include:

Creating Health — How to Wake Up the Body's Intelligence, originally published in 1987, most recent revision in September 1995.

Quantum Healing — Exploring the Frontiers of Mind/Body Medicine, originally published in August 1991,

Perfect Health — The Complete Mind/Body Guide, originally published in August 1991.

Because his work covers a **complete view** of the universe and everything in it, it is **presumptuous** to quote **excerpts**. Let me instead quote a "blurb" from the jacket of *Creating Health.* Hopefully, this will **pique your interest** to get at least this one book and enjoy it.

"Creating Health was a breakthrough book — the first in which Deepak Chopra created a new understanding of health and illness and the healing power of the mind.

Dr. Chopra is considered the preeminent spokesman for the six-thousand-year-old tradition of health care from India — Ayurveda. In this book he blends Eastern and Western medical philosophy for a clearer, richer view of the road to perfect health, a balance between mind, body, and spirit.

An endocrinologist, Dr. Chopra has practiced in the Boston area since 1971 and is former chief of staff of New England Memorial Hospital in Stoneham, Massachusetts. He is now medical director of the Maharishi Ayurveda Health Center for Stress Management and Behavioral Medicine in Lancaster, Massachusetts."

Scientific Proof

In just the last few years, researchers in a **variety of fields** have concluded that the ideas expressed by Dr. Chopra do, in fact, conform to the **scientific evidence**. The best book I have seen on this subject is called *The Balance Within — The Science Connecting Health and Emotions*, by Esther M. Sternburg, M.D.

Published in 2000, this book states unequivocally that **stress does affect the immune system**. The medical "establishment" ridiculed this simple statement only a few years ago.

Dr. Sternburg describes her work as follows:

"The science of brain-immune system communications is by its very nature a field that does this [shows how one field of specialization can be applied to others to reweave the tapestry of the human body]. *It looks inward to the most detailed level of body chemistry and at the same time it looks outward to the larger concerns of health and emotion. It applies technologies that analyze molecules and genes with technologies that image the functioning of whole organs like the brain. It bridges specialized disciplines of basic science like immunology and neurobiology, and it bridges specialized fields of medicine such as psychiatry and rheumatology. It bridges the basic sciences with clinical medicine and both of these with the intangible but essential input of feeling and emotion. The end result is to make the body and mind whole again."*

Specifically, **immune system** molecules can and do cross the **"blood-brain barrier,"** previously thought to be impermeable, like the Great Wall of China. The result is that the **cytokines** (a particular kind of immune system molecule) do, in fact, **kill off neurons** in the brain and contribute to the slow loss of memory seen in dementia victims — e. g. Alzheimer's disease, AIDS, senility, etc.

This means that **weakened immune systems** lead directly to **degenerative brain disorders**. Possibly quite soon, this knowledge will lead to **breakthroughs** in the treatment of these diseases.

On the other hand, this science is finding that **"believing can make you well."** Examples that **all physicians** have seen, such as "I'll fight this cancer one more month until my grandchild is born," have a scientific basis. The body's nerve and hormone responses to stimuli, which are controlled by the brain, do, in fact, **directly affect** our immune system.

Work can be a positive or negative experience. Conditioning can occur in either direction. If the environment is nurturing, supportive and rewarding, the **stress** associated with work becomes a **positive stimulus**. If the workplace is hostile and unsupportive, it can literally make us **sick from the stress**. Studies in a variety of disciplines prove this — endocrinology, biochemistry, immunology, and psychology. Dr. Sternburg has documented them all in **very convincing fashion**. The bibliography at the end of her book documents hundreds of studies covering 14 pages.

We have all **experienced** this. It is **intuitive**. Any positive or negative emotion affects our immune system cells. Psychologists have proven again and again that **negative stress** leads directly to increased **vulnerability** to viral infections. **Grief**, for example, and the stress endured by caregivers of Alzheimer's and other terminal patients, correlate with **reduced** immune system function.

As Dr. Sternburg states, it was probably necessary to go through the period of **increasing specialization** from Descartes and Bacon until the **1960's** or so. Now, however, each scientific discipline is so **overwhelmed with detail** that focus on the parts has caused us to **lose sight of the whole**. In health, just now, the disciplines are beginning to come together to arrive at a **"unified theory,"** as sought in physics to explain the universe. We are not there yet, but this theory definitely includes an **interaction between the emotions and the immune system.**

Applying This Knowledge

So what, you say? What's in it for me? What should I do **differently**? Good questions, all.

There are at least **four major changes** you need to make in your life once you have acquired this knowledge:

> ➤ Change your **work environment**, if possible, to one that is **positive**. Easier said than done? Sure. But today there is infinitely more **flexibility** on when and where work gets done than **before the Internet**. Get **creative** about what you do and where you do it. Work at **home** as an **affiliate** to one or more web site promotions. **Telecommute**, if your work allows it. Change the **texture of your day** with breaks for workouts, meditation or just relaxing.

> ➤ If you are well, enhance your immune system with **positive interactions** with other people and the **joy of creation**. Join support groups. **Volunteer** at local hospice organizations or hospitals. Get started in **hobbies** that produce positive feedback — painting, writing, golf, tennis, singing, etc.

> ➤ If you are **sick**, boost your **immune system** with MGN-3, shark cartilage, Laetrile and a healthy dose of vitamin, mineral and amino acid **supplements**. Eat a healthy diet low in carbohydrates.

> ➤ Build up to 30 to 60 minutes of **exercise** at least **4 days a week**. It is proven that regular exercise produces a flood of positive feelings about yourself as well as building up your **stamina** and immune system. See the booklet on Exercise for some specific suggestions.

The Result

Once you have reached a positive mental and physical state, you'll know it. How? Well, here are some measurements for both your physical condition and your body that will help you tell when you're "there."

You will know that your body has reached its proper condition when:

> ➤ You can **walk two miles** in less than **twenty-four minutes**, and still maintain a conversation at the end of your walk.

> ➤ You **do not smoke**. You **limit your alcohol** to no more than one and a half ounces of whiskey or six ounces of wine per day.

> ➤ You **fall asleep readily** at night. You get an average of seven to seven and a half hours of sleep each night.

> ➤ Your weight falls within **5 percent** of your ideal body weight. These tables are available at any gym or health food store.

> ➤ Your **percent body fat** falls in the right range. If you are a man, your percent body fat is **8 to 12 percent**. If you are a woman, you have **15 to 18 percent** body fat. [Any gym can measure your body's fat percentage for you.]

You will know that your mental attitude is healthy when:

> ➤ You are doing exactly what you want to do in life and **feel generally happy**.

> You wake up each morning **feeling great**, not just good.

> You take **regular vacations**.

> You realize you are part of a large **mutual support system** and regularly **offer your support** to your family, friends and colleagues.

> You are committed to the basic **value of life** and see it as **worth living**.

> You believe you have a **mission in life**, that your mission fits into a purpose that connects with the family of man in a larger universe.

> You have a **sense of humor**. You can **laugh at yourself** when you find you take yourself too seriously.

Other clues that help you know you're healthy:

> You have **taken charge** of your health. You realize that, like illness, excellent health is a **composite**, made up of many different components. You recognize that **you are responsible** for those components.

> You have worked to make your **immune system** an ally. It is finely tuned, ready and able to battle infectious agents of all types, seeking out and **destroying** abnormal cells that could lead to allergies, arthritis, diabetes or even **cancer**.

> You not only meet the **average stresses** of daily life **head-on**, you seek out challenges of your own. Even your **vacations** become physical **challenges**.

255

➢ You have become an **informed consumer**. You carefully read the labels on all the food you eat and **understand** what those labels mean. You **co-doctor** intelligently, seeking knowledge on your own to help you get and stay healthy.

To Your Health!!

Booklet #2 – Stop Your Aging With Exercise

HEALTHY EXERCISE

What Ever Happened to Jim Fixx?

I'm sure there were lots of you who, as I did, wondered how a great runner and advocate of running for health purposes could **drop dead with a heart attack** as **Jim Fixx** did in 1984. Many of you are saying, "Who's Jim Fixx?"

I mention him only because he exemplifies the truism that **physical fitness** isn't everything. Jim Fixx was born in 1932, just like me. He published a book in 1977 called **"The Complete Book of Running."** He is credited with **starting** America's **fitness revolution**. Yet, he died in 1984 at age 52 practicing the sport he was an expert in. He had heart arteries **clogged with atherosclerosis**.

So what? Well, healthy exercise is **no guarantee** of either a long or a healthy life. So, can you couch potatoes **relax**? No way!!

Healthy exercise is an essential part of your **get and stay well lifestyle**. It is not just good for you. It is **essential**. However, it must be combined with **healthy eating habits**, which are also essential.

What is healthy exercise? That is the question I'm going to answer in this booklet. First, I **do not** recommend **running or jogging**. Why? It is hard to get someone to **gauge your progress**, particularly at first, and make sure you **don't overdo**

257

it. Also, it is notoriously **hard on knees, ankles and feet** … not just of us seniors, but of everyone.

A Step-by-Step Approach

STEP ONE: Get a membership in a gymnasium. Two reasons. Every good gym has people to **supervise** your initial attempts to **regain your fitness**. And second, once you begin paying for something like a gym membership, it's a **powerful incentive** to continue to use it. The typical price is $35 - $40 a month.

This is **not** your father's gym. In fact, the "politically correct" name for a gym nowadays is "health club" or "fitness center." I'll continue to use "gym", thank you.

If you haven't been in a gym for a while, go take a look. You will be pleasantly surprised. A good gym is **attractive, airy and air-conditioned.** You do not feel like it's just a sweatshop for muscle builders. The facilities are modern, quiet and **computerized**. There are TVs available to watch while you're doing your treadmill or bicycle aerobics. Some rent headsets to listen to the TV. Or, you can take your own earphone radio, as I do.

Most gym memberships involve a **contract** for some period of time. Typical is **two years.** These people aren't dummies. They know, as **Dr. Joe Davis** told me when I first joined his Ultra Fit gym, that once you exercise regularly for **three months**, you're **hooked**. You feel and look so good that you will continue it and **give it priority.**

The gym Terry and I exercise in has members of **all ages**. Many of the people we see there are older than I am. A few of these **seniors** are in **better shape than me**. We have made **friends** there. It is a social experience we share. When someone hasn't been there for a week or two, we **get concerned** about them and vice versa.

Ideally, you join with a **friend or loved one**. You keep each other honest. But **don't** count on that. Your friend or loved one may not be as motivated as you are. Plan to **do it yourself**. Take your friend or loved one, if you can, but don't wait for that. We're talking about **your life** here.

STEP TWO: Line up a **trainer** at the gym. If they don't have qualified trainers, look for a gym that does. Check this on the phone. Gyms are **competitive**, just like other businesses. Make them **prove the value** of their membership to you.

The gym may **provide you a trainer** for your first couple of workouts as part of the sign-up agreement. If not, the trainer will typically charge **$20 per hour**. You will need one for only the **first two weeks**. Plan on spending **$100** on the trainer.

During that time, the trainer will do an **assessment** of your fitness level, muscle **measurements** and fat percentage. They will outline a program for you to start a **comprehensive** exercise routine. They will check you out on the weight machines — another **prerequisite.** They will calculate for you a **maximum heart rate** to use as you begin using the **aerobic** machines. And, most important, they will **monitor** your first few workouts to make sure you are doing them **correctly**.

I will give you some **general guidelines** here. But there is **no substitute** for a trainer to get you familiar with all the **exercise options** to improve your fitness level. The trainer will show you how to **start slowly** enough so there is **no muscle pain**. No pain, no gain...**NOT!!** Your routine should include a mixture of **weight exercises** (circuit weights), **aerobics** (treadmill, bicycle, step climber, etc.) and **stretching**.

The gym should offer **periodic assessments** — fitness level, muscle measurements, fat percentage measurement and recommended exercises — **free**. Another **prerequisite**. Don't sign up without it.

STEP THREE: Join an aerobics class. This **jump-starts** the social aspect of going to the gym, which is **very important**. You need this to be a **pleasant experience.** You need the support of a group.

Any gym you join should have a **wide variety** of aerobics, Tae Kwan Do, jazzercise, yoga, etc. classes for you to choose from. One popular option involves using a large rubber ball to lie on in various positions to **stretch** your muscles. This absolutely needs to be done **with supervision** when you're starting.

STEP FOUR: Just do it!!

Can't I Do It At Home?

Sure you can. But **you won't**. Those fancy exercise machines you see on TV are useful only if you want **another "white elephant."** We have one in the storage closet. Take it from a **champion procrastinator**. Without the social and financial pressure of a **gym membership**, you will **not** exercise systematically and regularly.

In **1961**, the U. S. Air Force adopted a **British system of aerobic exercise** as its official fitness routine for all members. We were to do it **on our own, at home**. Did we do it? Sure. **Some of us. Some of the time**.

In **1967**, I heard a lecture at Randolph Air Force Base in San Antonio by **Dr. Kenneth Cooper**. At that time, he was a Captain in the Air Force. He has since become **famous** for his fitness clinic in Dallas, where he works with seriously ill people, particularly those with **heart problems**.

The Air Force adopted Dr. Cooper's program as its **official exercise routine** for all members. We were to do it **on our**

own, at home. Did we do it? Sure. **Some of us. Some of the time.**

Believe me, this is one rut that I've fallen in enough times that you can **use my experience to avoid it**. Isn't that what we all hope **our kids** will do? Do they do it? **Some of them. Some of the time....**

Well, you get the idea. Get started on a **supervised routine** of exercise **now**. Whatever **age** you are. However much **money** or time you have or don't have. It's the only way that works long-term.

What Specifically Does a Good Workout Routine Look Like?

Let me describe mine for you. I do this 3 or 4 times a week. Remember, I built up to this level over a period of about **two years**. At first, I did a **very modest** version of this. I was **60** at the time, in 1992.

My experience before this with regular gym workouts was limited to my Air Force days and **a few months** when I was in my mid-50s. At that time, I did not have any **social support** and the gym environment **wasn't friendly** and I quit.

My workout takes **about an hour** and breaks down into **four parts**:

1.   **Warm-up**. I ride the stationary bike for five minutes. It has various levels of pedal resistance. I use #4. This gets my pulse up to about 120 beats per minute and loosens up my muscles.

2.   **Circuit Weights**. These are **computerized** weight machines — 12 of them. When I come in, I punch in my **member number** at the central computer. Then,

when I get to each machine, I punch the number in again and it **"remembers"** how much weight I used in my **last workout**.

This is the major advantage of computerized circuit weight machines. You don't have to **remember** where you were last time. It also **automatically** adds a certain percentage (varies by machine) to your weight for the negative (back to GO) stroke. The first three and last three repetitions are at a lower weight, to get you started and ease you back to normal at the end (nice, but not essential).

Also, at anytime, you can get **a printout** of your history of workouts — first workout, best workout, most recent workout, etc. with the **weights for each**. I do **2 sets** of **12 repetitions each** on each of the 12 circuit weight machines. Here is my latest workout:

Leg Press 132 lbs positive/152 lbs negative
Leg Curl 84 lbs positive/117 lbs negative
Leg Extension 70 lbs positive/98 lbs negative
Chest Press 119 lbs positive/166 negative
Lat Pulldown 82 lbs positive/103 lbs negative
Fly 69 lbs positive/86 lbs negative
Seated Row 109 lbs positive/152 lbs negative
Shoulder Press 50 lbs positive/63 lbs negative
Arm Curl 30 lbs positive/42 lbs negative
Tricep Extension 37 lbs positive/46 lbs negative
Abdominal 96 lbs positive/120 lbs negative
Back Extension 130 lbs positive/163 lbs negative

Does that make you tired just looking at it? **You can do it, too**. I have added some muscle mass, but not a lot. Obviously, ladies, you would need **less weight** to maintain your muscle strength.... but you, too, **need** this. It's not just a guy thing.

Mostly what this does is build up your **muscle tone**, and strengthen your tendons, ligaments and everything else that will help keep you **free** of joint problems, arthritis, diabetes (see the separate booklet on diabetes) and all sorts of other degenerative disease problems.

3.   **Abdominal/Back Exercises.** Next, I do a group of exercises designed to strengthen my **abdominal** and **lower back muscles**. These have cured a **chronic back pain** I suffered from in my 50s. By 1992 when I started regularly exercising, the pain included **extreme shooting pain** down my right sciatic nerve. The sciatic nerve runs from your hip area down the back of each leg.

There are **five types** of exercise. Each helps in a different way. I have had only occasional **mild twinges** in my lower back since 1992. These usually occur after I have **missed a week or so** at the gym due to a heavy slate of commitments. I now do these exercises **almost every day**, wherever I am. They can be done on the carpeted floor anywhere **in the house or a hotel room**. They require no equipment. Try them; you'll like them!

   Partial Sit-ups ("crunches"). Lie on the floor (mat) on your back with your feet flat on the floor (knees raised). With your hands on opposite shoulders (right on left, left on right), raise your head and shoulders a few inches off the mat. Return to the start position. I do 30 - 35 of these. You should start with **no more than 10**. Increase at the rate of **5 more per week**. In time, you can begin lifting your shoulders higher off the mat, but **never to a full sit-up position**.

Oblique Sit-ups. The oblique muscles are very important in toning up your abdominal muscles (which **erase back pain**). They run vertically down the outside of your abdomen, on both sides.

First, from the same start position as for the Partial Sit-ups above, place your right ankle on your left knee. Place your left hand behind your head. Keep your right hand flat on the mat. Raise your **left elbow** to touch your **right knee**. Again, start with 10 repetitions. Reverse positions and raise your **right elbow** to touch your **left knee.** Add no more than 5 repetitions per week. As you gain muscle tone, you can make the exercise a little harder by placing your calf and finally your knee on the other knee instead of your ankle. I do 30-35 of these with my knee on my other knee.

Leg Lifts. From the same start position as the Sit-ups, **raise your legs** (with knees bent) toward your chest. At the highest position, be sure your **butt is off the mat** and your feet are together. Slowly **lower your legs** until they are **10 inches or so** off the mat and then **raise them again**. Do only 3 or 4 of these to start. Add one per week. I do 20 of these.

Legs to Chest. Finally, an exercise that a Physical Therapist showed me 15 years ago. She said that if I did **25 of these every day**, I would **never again** have back problems. **She was right**.

Begin in the same position as for the Sit-ups. Raise **both legs together** (with knees bent) until they are as **close to your chest** as possible. Grasp them with both arms and hold for a **six second count**. Lower them to the floor and repeat the exercise. Do **no more than 8** of these to begin. Add 1 or 2 per week. I do 35 of these.

When you get up from the mat, **be cautious**. It is common to **be dizzy** at first as your circulation readjusts to the vertical position. Sit down with your **head between your knees** for a couple of minutes until the dizziness goes away.

4.   **Aerobic Exercise.** So far, except for the warm-up, the exercises have been designed to **strengthen and-or stretch** your muscles. Essential to your fitness routine is a session of **aerobic** exercise. Most experts say that for optimum gain, you need to **elevate your heart rate to 80 percent** of your maximum and keep it there for **at least 20 minutes**. Do this at least 3 times a week.

What is your maximum heart rate? You and your **trainer** will figure that out at the **first session**. There is a standardized table based on your age. But, like the standardized weight tables, there is a **lot of variation** based on blood pressure, heart condition, level of fitness and **other variables**. Don't try this at home!!

For the aerobic part of my workout, which if you **insist** on ranking them, is **probably the most important**, I use the treadmill. It is the most popular of the aerobic machines at the gym I go to. Probably, that is because of the **wide variation** of routines available (and the convenience of their location in front of the bank of TV screens).

I use a **heart rate option** on the computerized machines at my gym. That means you can **set the maximum heart rate** you and your trainer have figured out. You also enter your body weight, the speed you want and the number of minutes for your workout. The machine then **figures out the elevation** of the treadmill necessary to produce that heart rate for you.

It **continually monitors** your heart rate through a set of handles that you grasp during the workout. When your heart rate has reached your desired maximum, the machine **automatically** adjusts the elevation to keep it there. If it has lowered it to level (zero degrees of elevation) and your actual heart rate is **too high**, it will tell you to **reduce your speed** (from 4.0 to 3.5 miles per hour, for example) so the maximum heart rate can be maintained.

Also included on the treadmill (and the bicycle and stair climber) is a **"fitness test."** This will put you through a five minute drill using varying elevations and give you a **readout** on how you did (poor, average, good or excellent) based on your heart rate.

At the end of your workout, the machine will go through a one-minute "cool down" period at reduced speed and elevation designed to **gradually** get your heart rate back to normal.

I do **22 minutes 3 or 4 times a week** with the maximum heart rate set at **125 beats per minute**. That is the "standard" maximum for a person 47 years old. One of the trainers recommended that level after a fitness test.

Summary

The routine I have described above takes me **almost exactly one hour**. I try to do it in the morning, but you can do it **anytime**. Most modern gyms are open 24/7. The level I've reached **required about two years** of gradual buildup. Since then (1994), I have remained at a **"maintenance"** level of fitness.

You can certainly do as well or better than I did. **Challenge yourself**. But, above all, don't **get in a hurry** to reach some particular level of fitness. This is a **lifelong highway.** There will be signposts along the way, but you will continue traveling down it **as long as you live**.

Because of it, you will live longer. Dr. Roizen's book, *Real Age*, estimates that my level of exercise adds three years to my life or reduces my "Real Age", in his terms, by three years. More important than that, **I feel great**.

I play **golf twice a week**. When the temperature is below 90 degrees (about 7 months of the year here in San Antonio, I **walk** the 18 holes). When it is hotter than that, I play, but I ride a cart. I have **no muscle or joint pain**.

I feel full of energy and stamina every morning. At least once, sometimes twice, a week I stand on the "risers" and **sing with a men's chorus for 2 1/2 to 3 hours**. I play bridge on the computer with people from all over the world.

I enjoy **vacations** with my family about three times a year, plus weekend excursions. I am happier than ever before in my life (thanks largely to Terry, my beautiful wife) and I feel much **younger than I did 40 years ago.**

GENERAL GUIDELINES ABOUT EXERCISE

Here are several general guidelines for you to keep in mind when you exercise. Your **trainer** may give you more.

1.   **Breathe out** during the **positive** stroke of each exercise. That is, take a breath just before you start. For the weight machines, it is **obvious** what the positive stroke is. It's the **first thing you do** during each repetition, whether it's the Fly, the Seated Row or whatever. **Do not hold your breath.** This will avoid herniating a muscle in your abdomen. Breathing in will occur normally on the negative stroke. To **avoid hyperventilation**, purse your lips as you breathe out. This will slow it down.

     On the floor exercises (partial sit-ups, etc.), the positive stroke is also the first thing you do during each repetition. As you lift your head and shoulders, for example, you should be **breathing out**.

     During the aerobics portion of your routine, it is a good idea to adopt a **rhythmic breathing pattern**. For example, breathe in for four steps on the treadmill, and breathe out for six steps. This will help build up the **oxygen carrying capacity** of your lungs.

2.   Perform the exercises **slowly**. **Don't** try to show off as the "macho man/Superwoman" and do each repetition as fast as you can. You get **much more effect** from the same number of repetitions if you do them slowly.

3.   **Accent the Negative**. Experts say the negative stroke in each exercise contributes 80% of the value of that exercise. This is not intuitive. This is why the computerized weight machines add a **percentage**

more weight during the negative stroke. In addition, you should consciously take longer to do this negative stroke than the positive stroke. If you do the **positive** in a **count of two**, do the **negative** in a **count of four**.

4.   Increase the weight until you feel you can **just barely complete** the last repetition on that machine. Exception: if you feel pain, stop! It's quite simple to increase the weight on the computerized circuit weight machines. The idea is to **continue stressing** your muscles as they develop strength and stamina.

   For the floor exercises, the same principle applies. At the end of each set, you should feel like you could not possibly do another repetition.

5.   Keep your muscles **stressed** all the time during your exercises. In other words, **don't relax between repetitions**. The idea is to tone up your muscles as quickly as possible **without pain**. That occurs when you **maintain the stress** on your muscle between repetitions.

6.   If you miss **a week or so** (because of illness or whatever), assume that your progress has been set back **three weeks**. When you start again, try to go back to where you were **three weeks before**. If you miss three weeks or more, assume you are starting over from scratch.

   NOTE: As you pursue the routines of diet and exercise in this book, you will be pleasantly surprised that the colds, flu and other common maladies you have been used to **quietly disappear** from your life.

7.   Anytime you feel pain of any kind, **STOP**. No well-planned and executed exercise routine should be

painful. The pain is warning you that you are **overdoing** whatever you are doing. Stop. Take a rest and try it again at a lower stress/weight level. If the pain persists, **bypass** that exercise completely for a few days until you can perform it without pain.

NOTE: It is a good idea to **weigh yourself** every time you go to the gym. Just remember, **muscle weighs more** than fat. If you are not losing weight as fast as you like, it could be because your muscles are **"bulking up."** This is also a great excuse when you don't lose a pound or so a week!

Best of luck, and remember…Just do it!

Booklet #3 – Beating Diabetes

DIABETES

Do you **know someone** who suffers from **diabetes**? Do **you** suffer from it? For most of us, it's **one or the other**.

A recent article by Erin McClam, distributed by Associated Press and published in the San Antonio Express-News pointed out that diabetes increased at an **alarming rate** in the United States during the **past decade**. It has risen **70 percent** among people **in their 30s**. Nationally, the share of the population diagnosed with diabetes jumped **33 percent** between 1990 and 1998.

What's even more frightening is that a recent study published by the UK Prospective Diabetes Study suggests that before most patients are actually diagnosed with Type II diabetes (also called "adult-onset diabetes"), the pancreas has lost its ability to properly control post-meal blood sugar levels **for over 8 years** and insulin resistance has been present for **up to 12 years**.

Until recently, the earliest Type II diabetes was seen in those in their 40s or older. That has changed **dramatically**. In the last few years, an alarming number of children have been diagnosed with Type II diabetes. Type II is appearing more frequently in pre-pubescent children, and has even been documented in children as young as **four years old** (American Diabetes Foundation).

The cause? Very simple. **Obesity**. The nation's weight problem is well documented. The number of Americans considered obese **soared** from about one in eight in 1991 to nearly **one in five** in 1998.

Some **16 million** Americans have the disease, and the number is expected to rise to **22 million** by 2025. And remember, this is counting only those who have been **diagnosed** with diabetes…not the millions who have it but are **unaware** of it.

According to the American Diabetic Association, almost **25 percent** of Mexican-Americans between the ages of 45 and 74 have diabetes. In San Antonio, where I live, local health officials say **120,000 residents** either have diabetes or are at risk of developing the disease. From 35 years of personal observation of San Antonians, it is increasingly **hard for me to find** an adult Mexican-American (62% of our population in San Antonio) who is **not obese**.

The Cause — Details

Let's take a **more detailed look** at why you or your loved one has diabetes. I cannot improve on the explanation published by Dr. David Williams (remember him?) in his newsletter *Alternatives* in August 2000. This newsletter with a **long article** titled *"Sugar is Slow Suicide"* is available at his web site: http://DrDavidWilliams.com

*"For decades 'health nuts,' including yours truly, have been warning about the **dangers** of increased **sugars** and/or **refined carbohydrates** in the diet.*

> What are "refined carbohydrates?" Any "packaged" food containing carbohydrates — canned soup; packaged spaghetti, noodle, rice dishes; canned fruit; snack food (all kinds), and so on and on.

*Let me tell you, it has been a **real uphill battle** trying to convince the public that consuming **too much sugar** could eventually lead to diabetes — especially when **conventional** medicine kept asserting that sugar is **totally harmless**. Even today, as diabetes reaches epidemic proportions in this country, most doctors continue to preach that dietary sugar has **no connection** to behavior problems, mood swings, depression, or the **increased incidence of adult onset diabetes***.

> Remember what I said up there about biases? Why do you think our medical system doesn't tell us the truth about sugar? Could we be seeing the results of the big money of the food industry in our political system again? Just wondering...

*Our **FDA** says that the **only problem** sugar causes is **dental caries**. And with the support of the American Dietetic Association, the **Sugar Association** has stuck to the position that at only 15 calories per teaspoon, sugar is a **healthy, low-calorie sweetener** that is no different than any other carbohydrate. Nothing could be **further from the truth**. In fact, **decades of research** support the fact that a 'sweet tooth' will **invariably** lead to a lifetime of poor health and a **premature death**.*

My brother died in July 2000. He was 70 — two years older than I. He loved sweets, ate lots of packaged "dinners" and had a huge "bay window." He never exercised, as far as I know. He had health problems his entire adult life and died of a brain aneurysm (dilation of a blood vessel). I am quite sure he had undiagnosed diabetes. Our mother is alive and kicking at 98. Could it be that my brother overcame our good genes with his eating habits? I loved him and wish he was still here. His death spurred me on to finish this book.

*The carbohydrates we eat are converted by the body into a simple sugar called **glucose**. This glucose, or 'blood sugar,' enters the **blood stream** to be transported throughout the body. **Blood sugar** is the **primary energy source** used by the brain, the nervous system, and the muscles. To be utilized, the blood sugar must get from the bloodstream **into the nerve and muscle cells**. This is where **insulin** comes into the picture. As I'm sure many of you recall from high school biology, insulin is the **pancreatic hormone** that opens up the cell walls so blood sugar can enter. It is the **key** to the whole energy process.*

> I don't know about you, but if I heard this in high school biology, I've long since forgotten it. Until I read this article, diabetes and its cause were both mysteries to me. In hope that they were to you and that you appreciate this enlightening discussion, I will continue. If this is old news to you, skip this section.

*Insulin is **secreted** in **two phases**. A surge of insulin is initially released **immediately following a meal**, or when sugar or sweetness is detected in the mouth and digestive system. A **second round** of insulin is released shortly after a meal and **continues to be released gradually** for several hours.*

*For insulin to work properly, it must be present in **sufficient quantities**, and the **cells** in your body must be 'sensitive' to its effects. When cells don't react to the effects of insulin by allowing sugar to enter through their cell walls, a condition called __insulin resistance__ exists. Insulin resistance **isn't fully understood** at this point. However, we **do know** that __insulin resistance is often directly related to obesity.__ This is especially true when a person has a fat build-up in the **waist or abdominal area.***

> I read the above about two weeks after I returned from my brother's funeral in California. It felt eerily like he was talking to me.

*Studies have shown that obese, non-diabetic individuals can reduce their levels of circulating insulin **simply by losing weight**. This reduction in the amount of insulin occurs **without any changes** in blood sugar levels. In other words, by **losing weight**, one can often **overcome** insulin resistance. This is true because, with **less fat** to complicate the picture, existing insulin levels become **more effective** at lowering blood sugar levels.*

Remember earlier in this book where Dr. Atkins associated fat buildup with a combination of too many carbohydrates and **"hyperinsulinism."** He and Dr. Williams are saying the same thing. The excess insulin that cannot be taken up by the blood cells turns glucose into fat cells. **Vicious circle?** You bet! Does your doctor understand this connection? Should you discuss it with him/her?

*On the flip side of this coin, excess abdominal fat and fat that has been accumulated **around the liver** increase the amount of circulating free fatty acids in the blood. As these fatty acids break down, they **increase toxicity levels**. In turn, increased toxicity has been shown to do two things: First, it **inhibits** the **production** of insulin; and second, it makes muscle cells **less sensitive** to the insulin that is available. Muscle tissue is **crucial** in helping to balance blood sugar levels. Under normal circumstances, over **80 percent** of the blood sugar released immediately following a meal is taken up by **muscle cells**.*

I did not begin to pay serious condition to building muscle and losing weight until I was 60 — in 1992. You say you can't do it. Why not?

A Wrench in the Works

It should be obvious from this simple biology review that the **regulation of insulin** is a **very** important part of staying healthy and alive. Unfortunately, an **increasing percentage** of the American population cannot maintain this balance. And when their insulin and blood sugar regulation capabilities get **seriously out of whack**, their condition is referred to as **diabetes**."

Well, so much for the cause of this insidious, silent killer. Let's take a look at how you treat it once you or your loved one have been diagnosed with it.

Treating Diabetes

Dr. Williams gives us some **priceless** advice about what to do about it.

*"Most doctors fail to tell their patients that, even if they use the **best** conventional therapies available, type II diabetes will only get **progressively worse**. If your doctor has led you to believe that taking your prescription medication will either **fix your diabetes** or keep it from getting worse, you've been **terribly misinformed**. When you look at the current treatment programs, this shouldn't come as any surprise.*

> Type II diabetes, which we're talking about here, is the most common form of diabetes, affecting 90 percent to 95 percent of all diabetics. As we said above, it usually takes 8 to 12 years after the onset of insulin resistance before the diabetes is diagnosed.

*The whole idea in treating diabetes is to bring fluctuating blood sugar levels back to normal **as quickly as possible**. This must be done immediately after eating and then **gradually continue** for several hours, as food is being digested. In non-diabetic individuals, this process occurs **very smoothly** because the body constantly **adjusts** its secretion of insulin depending on the levels of blood sugar....*

*...Using either of these **drug** types [stimulating insulin production; and various newer drug types] is a **shotgun approach** at best. When **too little insulin** is released, blood sugar levels rise, causing the formation of **triglycerides and***

fat storage. *When there's **too much insulin**, blood sugar levels begin to fall (hypoglycemia), triggering a **feeling of hunger** and the constant need to eat, which also **causes weight gain and fat storage.***

Doesn't this sound like drug treatment of diabetes is futile, or even counterproductive. Do you think the drug companies are informing your doctor of this yo-yo effect and the futility of treating it with drugs? Yeah, sure....

*...These problems explain why diabetics treated with **oral medications** ... have a **weight gain** of anywhere from **6 to 12 pounds or more**. And, as I explained earlier, this weight gain and the extra deposits of fat become part of the vicious cycle that causes diabetes to **progressively worsen.***

*Additionally, the **roller-coaster effect** from constantly fluctuating blood sugar levels contributes to increased blood fats, high blood pressure, increased stickiness of the blood and clot formation, heart failure, poly-cystic ovary disease, nerve pain and degeneration, and damage to the small blood vessels, especially those in the eyes, the kidneys, and the lower limbs.*

My brother was being treated for kidney problems, edema (swelling) in his feet and ankles and he died of the bursting of a blood vessel. See why I think he had an undiagnosed case of diabetes? But even with better diagnosis, his doctor(s) would have only offered him more prescription drugs.

*Before you place **complete trust** in your medication to take care of your diabetes problem, take a look at this list of **complications** linked directly to progressing diabetes. It comes from the **American Diabetes Foundation**.*

Diabetes is now:

278

➤ the **leading cause of blindness** in people age 20 to 74
➤ the **leading cause of kidney failure**
➤ the **leading cause of amputation of the lower limbs**
➤ responsible for 50 to 60 percent of the **impotence** problems in males over the age of 50
➤ responsible for **severe nerve damage** in 60 to 70 percent of all diabetics
➤ the **major cause of stroke** in the United States
➤ known to increase the **risk of heart disease** by 2 to 4 times over normal. (In the UKPDS study I mentioned earlier, researchers found that even when intensive efforts were made to control blood sugar levels in diabetics, the risk of developing heart problems was not affected. **Diabetics without any previous history of heart attack had the same high heart attack risk as non-diabetics with a previous heart attack.**)

Diabetes is one of those diseases that can make the treating doctor look **like an absolute genius.** After placing a patient on diabetic medication, the doctor can predict with **uncanny accuracy** the chain of health problems that will begin to develop **like clockwork** in the upcoming years. Keep in mind, the chain of events will happen **even if you comply** perfectly with the therapy. In essence, the doctors can predict the **progressive decline** — but do nothing to prevent it.

> If you or anyone you know has diabetes, this should **shock** you! Their treatment is not going to help. Expensive brand name prescription drugs like Glucophage and Glyburide do no good.
>
> Many doctors understand this paradox. However, frustrated with their patients unwillingness to change their lifestyle (diet and exercise), they continue to give them the expensive drugs they request.

An Epidemic in the Making

*The increasing incidence of diabetes creates a **perfect marketing target** for pharmaceutical companies. Just look at the facts — and the trends.*

*Diabetes is a **growing epidemic** in this country, with **no end in sight**. Adult-onset diabetes has increased between **600 percent** and **1,000 percent** in the last 60 years. It is currently increasing at a rate of **6 percent a year**, and that rate is **expected to accelerate**.*

*Currently, **one in every five** American kids is obese. And since obesity is directly linked to diabetes, the **target population** for diabetic pharmaceuticals now extends clear down to **four-year olds**. Yes, diabetes is a pharmaceutical company's **dream come true**.*

What a sad commentary on the American lifestyle! A disease that is purely associated with improper diet and lack of exercise is growing alarmingly. And our answer is **more and better drugs**, which do nothing to treat the causes and do not even change the progress of the disease and its horrible consequences.

As I said before, pharmaceutical companies are the **best marketers** in the world — but don't get caught up in believing that they have the magic bullet for diabetes. That would be a **fatal mistake.** Diabetes is a disease in which you have to address several **underlying factors**.

Muscle Up to Help Control Blood Sugar

First and foremost, the most important factor is to get your weight down. In **almost every case** of type II diabetes, the body can control blood sugar fluctuations **naturally** when the **obesity problem** is taken care of. Obviously, this will require both **changes in the diet** and at least **moderate amounts of exercise**.

Exercise provides you with four important benefits. It

> ➢ increases lean body tissue
> ➢ burns fat
> ➢ increases the sensitivity of insulin, enabling the pancreas to produce less,
> ➢ and raises the metabolic rate."

> Dr. Williams has given you the REAL magic bullet. Healthy eating habits (not a "crash diet") and healthy exercise habits are the answer. **Please,** go back to my booklet on exercise and reread my recommendations. For healthy eating, which is low in carbohydrates and thereby **reduces the need for insulin**, get Dr. Atkins' book (see the booklet on diet). For the diabetic, it is never too late to try to get your body functioning normally again.

Artificial Sweeteners

One final comment before we leave the subject of diabetes. Don't be fooled into thinking that the use of **Sweet and Low, Equal**, etc. sweeteners "help" control your blood sugar. If you are a diabetic, the only artificial sweetener you should use is **stevia.** It is now **widely available** in health food stores. Here's an e-mail from the wife of a diabetic to Dr. Williams:

*"My husband is diabetic. He drinks 4 or 5 cups of blueberry tea every day. We sweeten it with **stevia.** It keeps his sugar controlled. He started taking the tea steadily about a year ago, and gradually the doctor saw the **good numbers** that my husband recorded for his **sugar reading** each day. His medicine was **decreased by half**, then a few months later, **all**. Stevia does not have the same effect on the pancreas as does sugar, Sweet and Low, or Equal.*

Dorothy D."

From Today's Newspaper

Remember my describing the high rates of diabetes among the Mexican-American population of my hometown, San

Antonio? Following is an article by Paul Elizondo, County Commissioner for Precinct 2 in Bexar County (the county that includes San Antonio). He titled it *"Do yourself a favor: Get a diabetes test."*

"I scheduled a doctor's appointment because I had this terrible rash that was really ugly. After the doctor ran a blood test, he came in and said, 'Congratulations, you have diabetes. At last, you'll have to do what I tell you or there will be consequences!'

That was about four years ago, and the disease has taken its toll on me, particularly on my eyesight.

*I have Type 2 diabetes; years ago, it was called adult onset diabetes. In many instances, it can be controlled with the proper diet and exercise, but **my busy schedule makes it difficult.***

I know there are thousands of San Antonians like me who have demanding jobs. My days run long into the night, like when we were working on the contract for the new arena, which required 16- to 18-hour days.

*Plus, I have my own band, meaning I work two jobs. I try to walk three miles every other day and eat planned meals, but many days **I just can't do it**.*

These are some of the excuses we conjure up for not changing our lifestyles. But when we look at the potential consequences of diabetes – blindness, stroke, heart and kidney failure and limb amputation – it's a no-brainer: Change lifestyle or perish!

The first step is awareness. San Antonio has a diabetes epidemic, and I urge everybody to take advantage of free screenings today and Saturday.

The screenings are hosted by the Diabetes Alliance of Bexar County. The collaborative is hoping to screen 25,000 people all around town this week. In this city, there are approximately 80,000 people who have diabetes – and they don't even know it!

The alliance includes the Texas Diabetes Institute, American Diabetes Association and the Juvenile Diabetes Foundation and is dedicated to awareness, education, prevention and treatment of diabetes.

By marshalling their forces and convincing residents to take control of their health, perhaps we can help stem the tide of this deadly disease.

My best advice is to look at the risk factors. Do you have family members with diabetes? Are you Hispanic, Native American, Asian or African-American? Are you overweight? Do you have a bad diet? Do you love sweets and drink too many sodas? Do you drink too much and exercise too little?

Then, my friend, you are a prime candidate for diabetes.

If you love your family and if you love yourself, you need to be screened as soon as possible. There is nothing more insidious to our families than diabetes.

Look at the odds. Are you among the 80,000 walking around who don't know they have diabetes? Get screened today. Call xxx-xxxx for times and locations."

Commissioner Elizondo has given you good advice. Remember, it is never too late to begin treating your diabetes with proper diet and exercise. Your miracle immune system will restore your God-given body to normal functioning, if you'll just give it the support it needs.

God Bless You!!

Booklet #4 – Cure Your Back Pain

BACK PROBLEMS

TMS — An Interesting Mind-Body Connection

Back pain and, to a lesser extent, shoulder and neck pain, are common complaints. Around **80%** of the U.S. population has some history of one or the other. It is the first cause of **worker absenteeism** in this country. It ranks second behind respiratory infections as a reason for a **doctor visit**. An article in Forbes magazine in August 1986 reported that **$56 billion** are spent annually to deal with the consequences of back and neck pain. It's **much higher now**, you can be sure.

Doctors **cannot** see pain. Thus, theories about what **causes** back and neck pain are just that — **theories**. At best, an operation to "fix" a **"slipped disc"** in your spine is a **guess** that it is causing your pain. There is a great deal of evidence that many of the **operations** done on the spine **are unnecessary**.

Back in **1985,** Dr. Hubert Rosomoff, a well known neurosurgeon and chairman of his department at the University of Miami School of Medicine, published an article titled *"Do Herniated Discs Produce Pain?"* Dr. Rosomoff did **back operations** for many years. His conclusions were **based on logic** as well as his experience. He said that **continued compression** on a nerve would cause it to **stop** transmitting pain messages after a **short time**. The result is **numbness**. How could the herniated disc then cause **continuing pain**? His answer. **It couldn't**.

Chiropractors do **"adjustments"** on your back. They can't see pain, either. In most cases, in my experience, back pain

285

sufferers who go to chiropractors achieve only **temporary relief**. The same can be said for massage therapists, Reiki practitioners, Rolfing, Voodoo and….well, **you name it**.

For me, **exercise** has been the "magic bullet" which **permanently** cured my back pain. Possibly, the **reduced stress** of my present life style **contributed** to the "cure." I don't know.

My former wife, Marge, had **chronic muscle spasms** in her shoulders and neck that caused **almost unbearable pain**. No doctor was able to fix it. A physical therapist gave her some **relief**, but only **temporary**. She was under **constant stress** over the shenanigans of her irresponsible daughter and grandchildren. Her daughter (my stepdaughter) died in September 2000 — **six years** after her mother's death. She was 56, a neurotic with a lifelong history of alcoholism, smoking and obesity.

My experience tells me that the following study of the **cause and cure** for back pain (and neck and shoulder pain) is pretty close to the **real truth**. "Tension Myositis Syndrome (TMS)" is the name given to most of these pains by John E. Sarno, M.D. in his book *Healing Back Pain — The Mind-Body Connection*. Published in 1991, this book **preceded** most of the research on the interaction of the mind and body documented by **Dr. Sternberg** and covered in Booklet #1 on Diet. The first edition of Dr. Sarno's book, in 1984, also preceded **Dr. Chopra's** inspired insights about the **mind-body connection**.

What Causes Back and Neck Pain?

Dr. Sarno says the cause is **repressed emotions**. Further, that the pain acts as **camouflage** so that you and I don't have to deal with the **psychological pain** of making these repressed emotions conscious. I can't just dismiss this theory, and I hope you don't either. It is the result of **26 years** of treatment of **thousands** of patients suffering from back and neck pain. Dr.

Sarno's experience began as **director** of outpatient services at the Howard A. Rusk **Institute of Rehabilitation Medicine** at New York University Medical Center. He says:

*"**Conventional** medical training had taught me that these pains were primarily due to a variety of **structural abnormalities** of the spine, most commonly arthritic and disc disorders, or to a vague group of **muscle conditions** attributed to poor posture, underexercise, overexertion and the like.*

*...The experience of treating these patients was **frustrating** and depressing; one could **never** predict the outcome. Further, it was troubling to realize that the **pattern** of pain and physical examination findings often **did not correlate** with the presumed reason for the pain. For example, pain might be attributed to degenerative arthritic changes at the lower end of the spine but the patient might have pain in places that had **nothing to do** with the bones in that area. Or someone might have a lumbar disc that was herniated to the left and have pain in the right leg.*

*Along with the **doubt** about the accuracy of conventional diagnoses there came the realization that the **primary tissue** involved was muscle, specifically the muscles of the neck, shoulders, back and buttocks. But even more important was the observation that **88 percent** of the people seen had histories of such things as tension or migraine headache, heartburn, hiatus hernia, stomach ulcer, colitis, spastic colon, irritable bowel syndrome, hay fever, asthma, eczema and a variety of other disorders, all of which were **strongly suspected** of being related to **tension**. It seemed logical to conclude that their painful muscle condition might **also** be induced by tension. Hence the Tension Myositis Syndrome (TMS). (Myo means 'muscle;' Tension Myositis Syndrome is defined here as a change of state in the muscle that is painful.)*

> Dr. Sarno points out the **difficulty** he's had "selling" this theory to his medical contemporaries. Here's how he puts it:

Gentle, non-toxic treatments

*What do doctors think of this diagnosis? It is **unlikely** that most physicians are **aware of it**. I have written a number of medical papers and chapters for textbooks on the subject but they have **reached a limited medical audience**, primarily physicians working in the field of physical medicine and rehabilitation. In recent years it has become **impossible** to have medical papers on TMS accepted for publication, undoubtedly because these concepts **fly in the face** of **contemporary medical dogma**. For those physicians who might see this book, I would point out that it is **more complete** than any of the papers I have published and will be useful to them despite the fact it is written for a general audience.*

Does **lack of general acceptance** by the medical "establishment" mean he is **wrong? Hardly!** No medical pioneer in my limited knowledge has **ever** been warmly embraced by his/her colleagues.

*The primary purpose of this book is to **raise the consciousness** both inside and outside the field of medicine, because these common pain syndromes represent a **major public health problem** that will not be solved until there is a change in the **medical perception** of their cause.*

*Having stated the purpose of the book, I would be less than candid if I did not report that many readers of its predecessor, Mind Over Back Pain, reported amelioration or **complete resolution** of symptoms. This substantiates the idea that it is*

Dr. Sarno's prose sounds like he's written too many medical journal articles. What he is saying is that **it works!** People, probably many of whom were **skeptical** when they first read or heard about it, have been **cured.** Why not you or your loved one or friend?

Here is just one example of one of Dr. Sarno's **many thousands** of patients:

288

identification with and *knowledge of the disorder which are the **critical** therapeutic factors.*

*The patient was a middle-aged woman with a grown-up family; she had been essentially **bedridden** for about **two years** when she came to my attention. She had suffered from low back and leg pain **for years**, had been **operated on twice**, and had gradually deteriorated to the point where her life was **restricted** almost entirely to her upstairs bedroom.*

*She was admitted to the hospital where we found **no evidence** of a continuing structural problem but **severe manifestations of TMS**. And no wonder, for the psychological evaluation revealed that she had endured terrible **sexual and psychological abuse** as a child and that she was in a **rage**, to put it mildly, and had **no awareness of it**. She was a pleasant, motherly sort of woman, the kind that would automatically **repress anger**. And so it **festered** in her for years, always **kept in check** by the severe pain syndrome.*

*Her recovery was stormy, for as the details of her life came out and she began to acknowledge her **fury**, she experienced a **variety of physical symptoms** — cardiocirculatory, gastrointestinal, allergic — but the pain **began to recede**. Group and individual psychotherapy was intense. Fortunately, she was **very intelligent** and grasped the concepts of TMS quickly. As the pain reduced, the staff helped to get her mobile again. Fourteen weeks after admission she went home essentially **free of pain** and ready to resume her life again."*

It's NOT All In Your Mind

Dr. Sarno is **not** saying, "It's all in your mind." Far from it. He points out that pain can be a **strong warning sign** of real **physical problems**. Your doctor should rule all these out before you begin to suspect that it is TMS.

In the last chapter of his book, Dr. Sarno reprints 10 long letters from his patients. They are **emotionally charged** and very convincing. I do not have room here to quote all 10. I've selected **one** that is quite **typical**. Remember, Dr. Sarno was doing this work in the **early 1980's**. None of the **scientific data** that today is confirming the mind-body **physical connection** was available. Here's the letter:

"Dear Dr. Sarno:

I want to thank you for how much you have helped my health and therefore the quality of my life....

*I had been suffering from severe back pain (both upper and lower, including sciatic) for **seven years** at the time I called you. I also had regular severe intestinal cramps, intense sharp pains in my chest; pain in my knees, ankles, elbows, wrists, knuckles and one shoulder.*

*All this pain, especially the back pain, **severely limited** my ability to work and play. I could not sweep the floor, do dishes, pick up babies (or anything over about three pounds, for that matter), join in sports, etc. Even brushing my hair hurt.*

*I had been a very strong, active person with a great need to exert myself physically — which I (and everyone else) **blamed** as the **cause** of my back problems.*

*On the first visit to my doctor, I was told to **back off** as much activity as possible, to **do nothing** that hurt, and that probably a lot of things would hurt.*

*I followed that advice. Over the next seven years, I became an 'expert' on the supposed causes and cures of back pain, but **to no avail**. I had fourteen sessions of acupuncture, seventeen chiropractic sessions, seventeen 'body balancing' sessions, thirteen rolfing sessions, several physical therapy sessions,* *used a 'neuro-block TENS unit,' attended 'bad-back exercise class,' joined a health spa — went swimming and used a Jacuzzi and sauna, received many massages, etc. One doctor thought it might be 'primary fibromyalgia syndrome' and tried putting me on L-Tryptophan and B6.*

All these treatments seemed to help a little at the time, but I still continued to suffer incredible pain.

*After my conversation with you, I considered seeing a psychotherapist, but I decided to try it without one first. I came to realize that it was not one big underlying problem causing my tension, but instead **any little thing** in my daily life that I had **learned to fear and/or that caused tension**, would begin my cycle of pain, more tension, more pain, etc. If the cause was an unresolved psychological conflict, I noticed that most of the time I didn't actually have to **resolve it** for the pain to go away but instead just be **aware** that this was the source of my pain. But I do find that now I tend to resolve things more quickly than I did before.*

*I was so mind-blown and happy over the ability to turn a **wrenching spasm** into a signal that something must be bothering me (emotionally or mentally) and then **dissolve the pain** completely within a matter of a minute or less.*

*It took me four months to get the process under good control, and within **less than a year,** I was able to say to friends and family, 'Yes, my back is finally **cured.** I am free of pain!'*

*At the same time that my back became free of pain, so did **every single other body part** that I mentioned earlier. Finally I could work and play again like I had not done for seven years. **What a relief!***

I will always be grateful to you, Dr. Sarno, for having the courage and kindness to do what you've been doing for over twenty years — *helping people become* **permanently** *free of disabling pain.*

Thank you."

Ancient History

Most of us reading the above for the first time will consider this a new idea. **Wrong!** Dr. Sarno points out that **Hippocrates** himself, **2,500 years ago**, advised his **asthmatic patients** to be wary of **anger.**

*"In the late nineteenth century the famous French neurologist Jean-Martin Charcot gave new life to the principle of the interacting mind and body when he shared with the medical world his experiences with a group of intriguing patients. Called hysterics, they had dramatic neurological symptoms, like paralysis of an arm or leg, with **no evidence of neurological disease**. Imagine the effect on his medical audience, however, when he demonstrated that the paralysis could be **made to disappear** when the patient was **hypnotized!** One could not ask for a more convincing demonstration of the mind-body connection."*

Dr. Sarno describes the current medical "establishment" as under the thrall of **Rene Descartes (1596-1650).** Descartes' theories about the **separateness** of mind and body still drive most medical thought **today**. The body is the **purview of physicians** and all their technology. The mind is the **purview of psychologists and psychiatrists.** A significant number of doctors in the U. S. and most of them in Europe and other countries have **grown beyond** this view since 1991, when Dr. Sarno wrote it.

This mindset still persists in many doctors. It has led to reliance on **chemical "cures"** for mind and body illness. This, of course, **delights** the pharmaceutical companies. Many doctors still **treat symptoms** rather than **seeking out the causes**.

As for **"mind-body interaction,"** most doctors even today consider it folklore or **voodoo.**

Confirmation is Here

As far as acceptance by the medical "establishment", **little has changed** in the twelve years since Dr. Sarno's observation above. You and I are indeed **fortunate**, however. We have available to us **confirmation** of Dr. Sarno's theories in the form of **physical evidence**. Esther Sternberg, M.D. (Booklet #1 above) has documented it in her beautifully written book, *The Balance Within.* Just listen to her *bona fides.* She is Director of the Molecular, Cellular, and Behavioral Integrative Neuroscience Program and Chief of the Section on Neuroendocrine Immunology and Behavior at the National Institute of Mental Health and National Institutes of Health. Despite Dr. Sternberg's difficulty in printing her title on her business card, we **owe her a careful listen**. Take another look at the section on her book in Booklet #1 on Diet.

If you have been diagnosed with **any** of the following, this information on **TMS** is relevant to you: back, neck or shoulder pain; slipped disc; heartburn; hiatus hernia; ulcers; peptic ulcers; irritable bowel syndrome; spastic colon; constipation; gas; fibromyalgia; allergic rhinitis (hay fever); shingles; rheumatoid arthritis; bursitis; diabetes; lupus erythematosus; multiple sclerosis; heart palpitations; mitral valve prolapse; and arteriosclerosis.

Take Dr. Sarno's book to bed with you. **Read it with an open mind**. Get up determined to do all you can to overcome the **mental/emotional** component of your "disease." I'm not belittling the seriousness of your condition. I'm only urging you to try the technique that has worked for **so many other**

patients without the need for chemicals, with all their **expense and side effects**.

Be well and God Bless You!

ABOUT THE AUTHOR

When his former wife, Marjorie, died on November 1st, 1994 after a four-year bout with ovarian cancer, Bill vowed that "there must be a better way" to treat cancer. Six years later, he published the first edition of his book "Cure Your Cancer." Since early 2001, he has spent full time helping cancer patients by counseling them by phone and e-mail and publishing a bi-weekly newsletter with the latest developments in cancer therapy.

Bill retired as an Air Force Colonel in 1977 after 25 years service, including a combat tour in Vietnam. He founded a successful software publishing company in 1978, which he sold in 1995 to devote his life to helping cancer patients and their loved ones.

Printed in the United States
48388LVS00003B/136-138

9 781410 735928